Mindful Leadership for Schools

Also Available from Bloomsbury

Decolonizing University Teaching and Learning, *D. Tran*
The Roma in European Higher Education, *Louise Morley, Andrzej Mirga and Nadir Redzepi*
Learning to Lead for Transformation, *Emmanuel Ngara*
Leading Educational Networks, *Toby Greany and Annelies Kamp*
Strengthening Anti-Racist Educational Leaders, *edited by Anjalé D. Welton and Sarah Diem*
Leading Disadvantaged Learners, *David Middlewood and Ian Abbott with Roberto A. Pamas*
A New Theory of Organizational Ecology, and its Implications for Educational Leadership, *Christopher M. Branson and Maureen Marra*
Exploring Consensual Leadership in Higher Education, *edited by Lynne Gornall, Brychan Thomas and Lucy Sweetman*
Preparation and Development of School Leaders in Africa, *edited by Pontso Moorosi and Tony Bush*
Sustainable School Leadership, *Mike Bottery, Wong Ping-Man and George Ngai*

Mindful Leadership for Schools

Wisdom from Confucius

Charlene Tan

BLOOMSBURY ACADEMIC
LONDON • NEW YORK • OXFORD • NEW DELHI • SYDNEY

BLOOMSBURY ACADEMIC
Bloomsbury Publishing Plc
50 Bedford Square, London, WC1B 3DP, UK
1385 Broadway, New York, NY 10018, USA
29 Earlsfort Terrace, Dublin 2, Ireland

BLOOMSBURY, BLOOMSBURY ACADEMIC and the Diana logo are trademarks of
Bloomsbury Publishing Plc

First published in Great Britain 2023
Paperback edition published 2024

Copyright © Charlene Tan, 2023

Charlene Tan has asserted her right under the Copyright, Designs and Patents Act, 1988,
to be identified as Author of this work.

For legal purposes the Acknowledgements on p. xix constitute an
extension of this copyright page.

Cover design: Grace Ridge
Cover image: © molotovcoketail/ Getty Images

All rights reserved. No part of this publication may be reproduced or transmitted
in any form or by any means, electronic or mechanical, including photocopying,
recording, or any information storage or retrieval system, without prior
permission in writing from the publishers.

Bloomsbury Publishing Plc does not have any control over, or responsibility for,
any third-party websites referred to or in this book. All internet addresses given in this
book were correct at the time of going to press. The author and publisher regret any
inconvenience caused if addresses have changed or sites have ceased to exist,
but can accept no responsibility for any such changes.

A catalogue record for this book is available from the British Library.

A catalog record for this book is available from the Library of Congress.

ISBN: HB: 978-1-3502-9199-7
PB: 978-1-3502-9203-1
ePDF: 978-1-3502-9200-0
eBook: 978-1-3502-9201-7

Typeset by Newgen KnowledgeWorks Pvt. Ltd., Chennai, India

To find out more about our authors and books visit www.bloomsbury.com
and sign up for our newsletters.

To Lim Pin (twb)

Contents

List of Illustrations		viii
List of Tables		ix
Preface		x
Acknowledgements		xix
1	Mindfulness and Mindful Leadership	1
2	Confucius, Mindlessness and Mindfulness	33
3	Respectful Mindfulness	53
4	Exemplary Living	79
5	Serving Others	97
6	Transforming Society	123
7	Conclusions	143
Notes		161
References		217
Index		237

Illustrations

Photos

1.1	A sign in a nature park that reads 'Slow down'	2
2.1	A statue of Confucius	34
3.1	Officials attending an important ceremony in ancient China	60
4.1	Calligraphy in a classroom that reads 'Be a teacher through study, be a role model through correct behaviour' (*xue gao wei shi, shen zheng wei fan*)	85
5.1	A community of learners in ancient China	107
6.1	A sign on a building that reads 'The hall of respecting the Way' (*zun dao ting*)	125
7.1	A sign in a Chinese garden that reads 'Keep silence' (*zhi yu*)	144
7.2	The entrance to Robert Black College of the University of Hong Kong	159

Figures

0.1	An overview of the chapters	xviii
1.1	Collective mindfulness, mindful organizing and organizational mindfulness	14
2.1	R|E|S|T	52
3.1	Respectful mindfulness	54
3.2	Salient features of respectful mindfulness	56
3.3	A Confucian worldview of respectful mindfulness	67
4.1	Exemplary living	80
5.1	Serving others	98
6.1	Transforming society	124
7.1	Confucian Mindful Leadership (CML) through R|E|S|T	148

Tables

1.1	A Literature Review of Mindfulness Initiatives in Schools	16
2.1	Main Differences between a Frame of Mind and an Intentional State	47
7.1	An Example of a Lesson Plan for a Mindful Classroom	152

Preface

The cover photo of this book depicts bamboo, still water, majestic mountains and birds against a Chinese landscape. It evokes quietness, restfulness, peace and harmony – characteristics of mindfulness. The flock of birds on the right side of the photo are guided by a leader as they soar freely in the vast sky. The photo aptly illustrates the three broad themes of this book: mindfulness, leadership and the Chinese context. The topic of this study is *mindful leadership for schools*, based on the insights and example of Confucius, who is arguably the greatest educational leader in China.

Before we discuss Confucius, we need to answer this question: Why do we need another book on mindfulness and mindful leadership?

Why mindfulness and mindful leadership?

Many of us live mind-*full* lives. Our minds are constantly preoccupied with information and to-do-lists, and we often multi-task.[1] The word 'preoccupied' describes how our minds are like a box that is 'pre-' or already cluttered with a multitude of things. It is as if we are hoarders inside our brains! The Covid-19 pandemic has been an attention-grabber, bombarding us with never-ending updates on the latest virus mutation, infection numbers, vaccines, lockdowns, social distancing measures, school closures and arrangements for working/studying from home. The pressure – from within and without – to check and respond to every message on multiple social media apps and services, has aggravated the chronic fatigue, anxiety, burnout and other socio-emotional and health problems experienced by many.

Students, teachers and school leaders are not spared from the relentless stresses engendered by modern living. Young people, as digital natives, are particularly susceptible to *telepressure* – the obsession to reply to an avalanche of electronic messages as soon as possible.[2] In the hope of helping their students (and staff) de-stress, schools have increasingly turned to *mindfulness*.

Mindfulness, paradoxically, is not about having a mind that is full, but about freeing the mind from the clutches of fleeting, distracting and even disturbing thoughts. It is about replacing a reactive, auto-pilot and information-overloaded mind with present-centred calmness, clarity and alertness.

Closely associated with mindfulness is *mindful leadership*. The coupling of mindfulness and mindful leadership in education is not suprising. After all, schools that promote mindfulness should ideally be spearheaded by leaders who know something about mindfulness, or, better still, are mindfulness practitioners themselves. Expectedly, there has been a proliferation of books, magazines, websites, training programmes, conferences and retreats on mindful leadership in recent years.[3]

> Schools that promote mindfulness should ideally be spearheaded by leaders who know something about mindfulness.

Despite the burgeoning number of publications and activities surrounding mindful leadership, there remains two research gaps on this topic: (1) a lack of clear definition of mindful leadership and (2) insufficient focus on mindful leadership for schools. These two points will be explained in the next section.

Current research gaps on mindful leadership

A lack of clear definition of mindful leadership

Despite the growing volume of writings on mindful leadership, it remains unclear what this concept refers to and consists of.[4] A literature review points to three broad, overlapping understandings of mindful leadership that highlight the cognitive, social-emotional and organizational aspects, respectively:[5]

Cognitive aspects

Examples:

- a sense of focus, awareness and living in the moment (Sethi, 2009).
- the training of one's mind to gain greater attention and clarity (Hougaard et al., 2016).

Social-emotional aspects

Examples:

- the exploration of self-compassion (Silverthorne, 2010).
- adaptability, perspective-taking, empathy and emotion regulation (Chaskalson et al., 2021).

Organizational aspects

Examples:

- intentional practices that include and empower followers (Cissna & Schockman, 2021).
- a form of shared mindfulness that produces organizational resilience (Levey & Levey, 2019).

> Is mindful leadership synonymous with good leadership?
> What makes mindful leadership distinctive?

The above qualities are often considered important for leadership. After all, who doesn't want a leader who is focused, empathic, present, self-aware and empowering? However, what makes such a leader a *mindful* leader, and what is *mindful* leadership really about? An initial response may be that a mindful leader is one who is 'mindful' or conscious of being a good leader, and tries hard to be one. But shouldn't all leaders be mindful in this sense? What makes mindful leadership distinctive, as the aforementioned attributes are traits that describe good leadership in general?

A case in point is this approach to mindful leadership: 'giv[ing] people the ability to bring one's whole self to work without fear of rejection (sense of belonging) and by confidence (self-esteem), which is built on trust, physiological and psychological safety'.[6] A main issue with this formulation is that it is unclear what 'bringing one's whole self to work' means. Also, should not all leaders, not just mindful leaders, build trust as well as physiological and psychological safety in their organizations? What then is unique about mindful leadership? Is there more to mindful leadership than the conscious effort to be a good, effective and successful leader? In other words, what distinguishes mindful leadership from other leadership concepts such as charismatic, servant and transformational leadership? The extant literature on mindful leadership, in short, lacks a cogent theoretical foundation – an explanation of key ideas and assumptions to support and justify this leadership construct.[7]

A good start to provide a persuasive grounding of mindful leadership is to make clear the terms used to describe this form of leadership. For example, returning to the representative interpretations of mindful leadership listed above, what does 'living in the moment' mean? Is it drawn from the Stoic philosophy of living a life of virtue, in view of the brevity of life? Or is it based on the Buddhist doctrine of karma, where one needs to live one's life intentionally, because of the future consequences of one's actions? What motivates a leader to develop 'a sense of focus, awareness', 'greater attention and clarity' or 'intentional practices that include and empower followers'? The last question depends on broader epistemological, ontological and ethical considerations, such as the leader's life goals, personal philosophy and management style. Overall, there is insufficient attention to and rigorous research on the definitions and significance of mindful leadership, beyond the presupposition that it is recommended for leaders.

There has also been limited exploration on the *moral underpinnings* of mindful leadership. It is widely assumed that mindful leadership is good, but who or what is it good for? Is good for the leader, followers, organization and/or society? Is it for the larger good or the pursuit of the good life, among other reasons? These questions should not be taken lightly because (mindful) leadership can be easily (ab)used for immoral purposes, causing harm and misery to people, society and the natural environment.

> It is widely assumed that mindful leadership is good, but who or what is it good for?

The absence of a coherent, ethical basis for mindful leadership does not mean that values are totally absent in the current writings on mindful leadership. With respect to the characteristics of mindful leadership listed earlier, such as having a sense of focus and cultivating perspective-taking, most have pragmatic value in that they contribute to effective management. Nevertheless, they are not virtues that attest to the character of the leader or the ethos of the organization. Take the example of perspective-taking, which presupposes attributes such as awareness and objectivity. Leaders certainly need to listen to their followers with an open mind and put themselves in the shoes of others. Even so, qualities such as awareness and objectivity are not *moral* values, in the sense of being character traits to guide a leader to know what is right or wrong, or good or bad. Even when devoid of a moral conscience, a leader can still be 'mindful' in the sense of being aware of and adept at manipulating followers and circumstances to achieve their nefarious agendas.

Clearly, the concept of mindful leadership needs to be rooted in moral principles and motivations. To begin defining these, we could ask a leader why they want to be a mindful leader. A typical response might be, 'Because I want to be a good leader.' This raises another question about why they want to be a good leader.[8] Here we can expect a variety of replies, such as 'I want my organization to be successful', 'I want my followers to look up to me', 'It is the right thing to do as a leader', 'This is what God expects me to do' and 'Doing so is who I am.' These answers, all justified in their own right, reflect and depend on the leader's prior ethical commitments, such as prioritizing consequences, the larger good, self-interest, moral duty, religious adherence and moral character. Regardless of the response one gives, it is critical to spell out the normative basis of mindful leadership – an area of inquiry that is currently under-explored in the current literature.

Insufficient focus on mindful leadership for schools

The second research gap concerns the application of mindful leadership to schools. Most of the writings pertain to leading companies and businesses such as Google and Goldman Sachs Group Inc.[9] Relatively limited attention has been devoted to mindful leadership in and for schools. This is not to say that the ideas and strategies developed for mindful leadership in the corporate world, such as 'organizational mindfulness' and 'mindful organizing', are not relevant to educational institutions. There are certainly convergent goals between commercial and educational set-ups, such as fostering a culture of mindfulness and empathic listening among the staff. Nevertheless, there are also crucial differences between schools as learning sites for children and youth, and profit-making companies such as Google. In particular, there are two main reasons why the current mindful leadership theories and techniques devised specifically for companies and businesses are not totally appropriate for schools.

> School leaders are not – and should not be – CEOs who are mindful only of company profits or the demands of shareholders. Rather, school leaders are called to ensure the holistic well-being of all their students.

First, the existing notions of mindful leadership and mindfulness that are intended for non-educational institutions tend to be instrumentalist, with a de-emphasis on moral purpose. A major shortcoming of a skills-based conception of mindful leadership is that it points to behaviourist and generic theories on competence, where a person's abilities are measured by a set of externally determined performance standards. As a result, mindful leadership is largely reduced to technical rationality, which centres on technological and scientific know-how for routines and specifications. Mindfulness is simply a tool to help leaders to be more effective and enable employees be less stressed and more productive.

Researchers have even coined the word *McMindfulness* – a reference to McDonald's fast-food concept – to capture the quick-fix approach of organizations to achieve its bottom-line through mindfulness practices.[10] Such a functionalist and amoral reading of mindfulness and mindful leadership is obviously unsuitable for schools, which have a core mission to care for and nurture young learners.[11]

Related to the previous point is that school leaders are not – and should not be – CEOs who are mindful only of company profits or the demands of shareholders. Rather, school leaders are called to ensure the holistic well-being of all their students. This responsibility requires school leaders to go beyond a narrow focus on test scores and school league tables to 'draw out' (*educere*) and 'cultivate' (*educare*) each child's potential, talents and moral character.[12]

Evidently, more research is needed on how school leaders can cater to the individual needs of their students and collaborate with other educational stakeholders through mindful leadership frameworks. School principals need to be mindful leaders who locate student development within social practices, roles and relationships, teaching students to attain personal autonomy by synthesizing their knowledge, values, dispositions and actions. Unfortunately, the prevailing literature on mindful leadership has not adequately articulated the ethical issues, decisions and ramifications of this leadership concept.[13]

In all, there has been a dearth of in-depth examination of the nature, theoretical foundation and ethical justification of mindful leadership, particularly in the school setting. This book, therefore, is a response to fill the above research gaps. This study aims to offer a well-reasoned account of mindful leadership for schools that is built upon and informed by the educational thought of Confucius.

Why Confucius?

Mindfulness has a long history in Eastern religious, philosophical and sociocultural worldviews and practices.[14] In contrast, mindfulness as a scholarly endeavour and research topic is relatively new in the West, emerging only around the 1970s.[15] The Asian tradition on mindfulness that people in the West are most familiar with is Buddhism.[16] Mindfulness and mindful leadership in Anglo-American societies originate from Buddhism. This does not mean that Buddhist teachings have been incorporated into the current conceptions of mindful leadership. On the contrary, the prevalent notions of and approaches to mindful leadership in the contemporary world are, for the most part, free of Buddhism and other religious undertones. Such an orientation is understandable, given that organizations, especially schools in the West, are predominantly secular in nature.

> Although Confucius did not use the terms 'mindfulness' and 'mindful leadership', he had much to say about them.

That said, Buddhism is not the only Asian system that teaches and advocates mindfulness. Other Eastern philosophies, such as Daoism and Confucianism, have rich discourses and resources on mindfulness and the corresponding leadership construct too. Aware of the need to expand the extant understandings of mindfulness and mindful leadership beyond Buddhism, researchers have called for more studies into East Asian cultures and ideologies.[17]

This book seeks to provide an extensive analysis of mindful leadership from a Confucian viewpoint, which is lacking in current research.[18] Although Confucius (孔子 *Kongzi*) (551 BCE–479 BCE) did not use the terms 'mindfulness' and 'mindful leadership', he had much to say about them, as I shall explain in this book. Pertinently, Confucian scholars have used the word 'mindfulness' to translate the Confucian concept of *jing* 敬 since the 1980s.[19] I have also published articles and a book on Confucian perspectives on mindfulness and mindful education.[20]

The various chapters of this book shall show how the ideas and example of Confucius question some existing assumptions and provide new insights on mindfulness and mindful leadership. This study proposes the idea of Confucian Mindful Leadership (CML) that synthesizes Confucius's teachings and the available research on mindful leadership. I shall delineate how CML is about influencing others towards the achievement of a common goal through R|E|S|T, an acronym that stands for **R**espectful mindfulness, **E**xemplary living, **S**erving others and **T**ransforming society.

The primary source for the educational thought of Confucius is a Chinese classic known as the *Analects* (論語 *Lunyu*). The *Analects* (literally 'compiled sayings') is a collection of the sayings, ideas and conduct of Confucius and his disciples.[21] The *Analects* first came into being when Confucius's teachings were put together, shortly after his death, in the form of little books; these books were subsequently systematized into a single collection, which is known today as the *Analects*.[22] A word on the English translation of the *Analects*: All the passages of the *Analects* cited in this book are taken or adapted from Lau (1997), unless otherwise stated. A significant amendment I have made to Lau's translation is to change all male pronouns to gender-neutral ones. My decision is guided by accuracy – the classical script, which is the traditional style of written Chinese used in the *Analects*, does not use gender-specific pronouns for the passages cited in this book. Non-English words are italicized, and the *pinyin* (拼音) system of transliteration is used for Chinese characters throughout the chapters.

This book is intended primarily for those with little or no background knowledge of Confucius's teachings and the Chinese language. To make this book accessible to everyone, I have removed the more academic and esoteric discussions, research findings and references from the main text, and placed them in the endnotes for interested readers.

Outline of the book

To help readers to understand the thesis of each chapter and how the chapters are connected, Figure 0.1 provides a quick overview of the essential questions each chapter aims to answer.

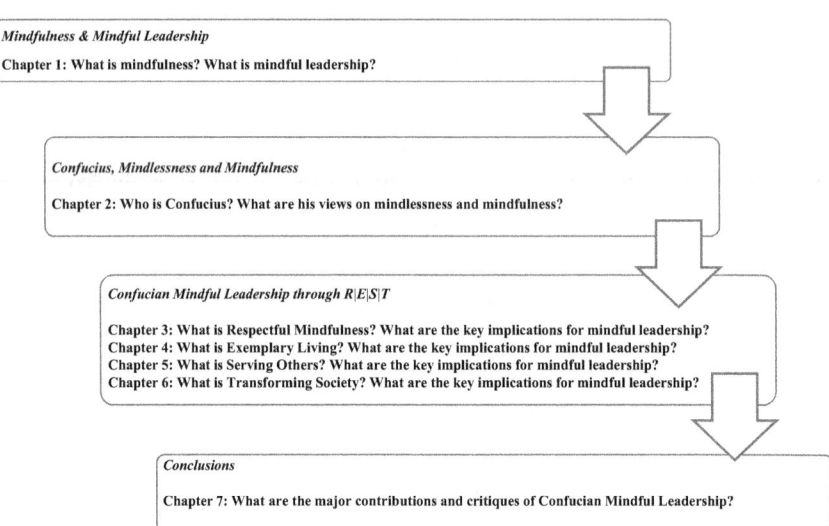

Figure 0.1 An overview of the chapters.

Acknowledgements

I thank Professor Lin A. Goodwin for her kind support and exemplary leadership, the school leaders and teachers in Hong Kong for their generous sharing on the mindfulness programmes in their schools, Ms Alison Baker and Ms Anna Elliss of Bloomsbury for their wonderful assistance, Mr Shyam Sunder and Ms Zeba Talkhani for their professional copyediting, Ms Tan Bee Leng for her expert research assistance and Ms Elizabeth Tan for her excellent proofreading. This book is dedicated to my husband Lim Pin, my valley of Achor. *Soli Deo Gloria.*

1

Mindfulness and Mindful Leadership

>Ironically, our attempts to multitask have made us less, not more, productive.

Photo 1.1 shows a sign in a nature park to remind motorists to decelerate when driving up the hill. This message of slowing down is also timely for people in the modern world. Many of us live in a fast-paced, digital era that demands our constant attention and expects us to be efficient by doing many things at once.[1] Ironically, our attempts to multi-task have made us less, not more, productive. In the United States, for example, more than one trillion dollars in productivity is lost each year as a result of work interruptions and reduced concentration of employees; a study of Microsoft employees reported that they were interrupted, on average, ten to thirty times per hour, and typically needed ten to twenty-five minutes to get back on task.[2]

Leaders themselves do not fare much better as they also experience increasing stress in a post-pandemic, uncertain and complex world. Busyness not only induces irritability and rigidity in leaders, but also reduces their ability to empathize with their colleagues and reduces the time they have to self-reflect and focus.[3] People in positions of power have to juggle multiple demands in a new normal, where previous leadership practices and the old ways of thinking and doing may no longer be relevant.[4]

In light of the unyielding pressures and burdens of modern life, mindfulness is perceived to be a remedy and valuable solution for individuals and organizations.[5] Mindfulness has become a fixture in many workplaces through an array of mindfulness initiatives, courses, retreats and seminars.[6] Schools have also joined in by running a host of mindfulness programmes for their students; two notable service-providers are the *Mindfulness in Schools Project* (MiSP) in the UK and *Mindful Schools* in the United States.[7]

Photo 1.1 A sign in a nature park that reads 'Slow down'.

This chapter introduces the concepts of mindfulness and mindful leadership based on a review of the existing literature. The discussion begins by expounding on mindfulness in terms of its genesis, definitions and salient characteristics. This is followed by a description of mindful leadership with regards to its conceptions and essential features. The last segment evaluates the prevailing approaches to mindfulness and mindful leadership by highlighting their benefits and shortcomings.

Mindfulness

Genesis

The word 'mindfulness' was first used by T. W. Rhys Davids in 1910, when he translated the Pali word *sati* (*smrti* in Sanskrit) into English. Rhys Davids explained that although the etymological meaning of *sati* is 'memory', *sati* is not just about recollection – the word connotes the awareness that all things in life are impermanent.[8] This metaphysical slant reveals the Buddhist roots of mindfulness. Indeed, the term 'mindfulness', as used in the West, is traced back to Buddhism, which has existed for over 2,500 years.[9] Buddhist mindfulness emphasizes the spiritual and moral teaching for all to do no harm to ourselves and others, through moment-by-moment consciousness.[10]

Nevertheless, the notion and practice of mindfulness are not synonymous with or restricted to Buddhism. Mindfulness, which encompasses a wide range of histories, schools of thought, proponents and forms of meditation, contemplation and concentration, predates Buddhism.[11] In Asia, mindfulness is featured prominently in various cultural and religious systems, such as Confucianism, Hinduism and Daoism.[12] At the same time, mindfulness is observable in Western traditions through the works of thinkers such as Socrates and Foucault, who presented philosophy as a way of life and spiritual exercise.[13] It is also salient to note that the existing mindfulness theories in the West are largely secular without Buddhist teachings.[14]

> Mindfulness is about the moment-by-moment attention to and engagement with, oneself, people, things and events.

Definitions

Rhys Davids's formulation of mindfulness in the early twentieth century has since evolved, resulting in multiple and even competing interpretations, orientations and presuppositions of the term. One definition that deserves special mention is the one forwarded by Jon Kabat-Zinn. Widely acknowledged as the 'father of mindfulness', Kabat-Zinn made mindfulness popular in the West through his Mindfulness-Based Stress Reduction (MBSR) course. Kabat-Zinn viewed mindfulness as 'the awareness that emerges through paying attention on purpose *in the present moment*, and *nonjudgmentally* to the unfolding of experience moment by moment'.[15] This conception is one of the most widely used definitions in the current discourses on mindfulness.[16] Kabat-Zinn's construal of mindfulness as non-judgemental, moment-by-moment awareness contrasts with Rhys Davids's more spiritual reading of mindfulness.[17] We see here a discernible shift from a religious and normative conceptualization of mindfulness at the beginning, to one that is comparatively secular and values-neutral.

Another widely cited definition of mindfulness – one that is also non-religious and nonmoral, but relatively more evaluative – was formulated by Ellen Langer, a professor of psychology at Harvard University.[18] She described mindfulness as 'a flexible state of mind in which we are actively engaged in the present, noticing new things and sensitive to context'.[19] A mindful person, according to her, is the antithesis of a *mindless* person who operates on an auto-pilot mode and lets others do the thinking for them. Mindless learning takes place when information is transmitted as indubitable truths, devoid of competing viewpoints and contexts. A mindless person is trapped by routines, patterns and associations learned in the past, and consequently performs like a robot in their thinking, feelings and conduct.[20]

Langer maintained that mindlessness is the result of two phenomena: recurring actions and unitary exposure. *Recurring actions* occur when a person relies on the same pattern to accomplish a goal, such as driving on a familiar road. *Unitary exposure* takes place when a person accepts the information that one is given unquestioningly. Mindless identification narrows one's thinking and favours the status quo, whereas mindfulness welcomes multiple points of view and focuses on both the processes and outcomes.[21] Langer has developed the Langer Mindfulness Scale that measures psychological, physical, and social and organizational well-being. Examples of psychological well-being are life satisfaction and humour; aspects of physical well-being are strength and flexibility; and domains of social and organizational well-being include job satisfaction and creativity.

The works of Kabat-Zinn and Langer constitute the two leading schools of thought in mindfulness research in the West, which began in the 1970s.[22] These, however, are not the only two approaches to mindfulness that are in circulation in the West. There is an assemblage of concepts and theories on mindfulness proposed by different scholars and practitioners, with substantial variations and even contestations, on what mindfulness means, consists of and implies, among other issues.[23] Nevertheless, a survey of the literature reveals a common understanding: mindfulness is mainly about *moment-by-moment attention and engagement*. Returning to the interpretations of mindfulness by Kabat-Zinn and Langer, they share a focal point on the present, be it through purposeful attention (Kabat-Zinn) or active engagement (Langer). Mindfulness may thus be generally understood as the present moment attention to and engagement with, oneself, people, things and events.

Salient characteristics

This section gives a brief overview of mindfulness in terms of its main categories, forms, approaches, traditions and programmes.

Categories

> Employees high in trait mindfulness experience more positive work attitudes, greater work engagement, less burnout, lower stress levels and lower rates of absenteeism.

Mindfulness has been classified in diverse ways. Two main categories are highlighted here. First, mindfulness can be *individual* or *collective*, depending on whether the focus is on personal experience or group practice.[24] Second, mindfulness can be *instrumental* or *substantial*; the former sees mindfulness as a means to enhance the wellness and capabilities of individuals or groups, whereas the latter situates mindfulness within the context of what is good and meaningful for individuals and organizations.[25]

Forms

Mindfulness can take the form of a trait, state or practice. *Trait mindfulness*, also known as 'distal sources of mindfulness', is the tendency or disposition to be mindful, and is generally stable.[26] Employees high in trait mindfulness experience more positive work attitudes, greater work engagement, less burnout, lower stress levels and lower rates of absenteeism.[27] *State mindfulness*, also known as 'proximal sources of mindfulness', is the degree to which one is aware of the present moment, which can vary over time.[28] A major difference between trait mindfulness and state mindfulness is that the former is manifested between persons, whereas the latter is felt within a person.[29] An example of trait mindfulness is a person who is an active listener, with a habit of paying attention to what another person is saying regardless of who one is with. In contrast, state mindfulness, as a within-person experience, is influenced by external conditions. For instance, a person's level of mindfulness will likely go up upon seeing a snake in the park, as compared to seeing the usual flora and fauna in a park.

Finally, *mindfulness practice* sees mindfulness as a skill to be acquired and mastered, with the help of exercises such as meditation and controlled breathing. Through mindfulness-based interventions, a person gradually improves their state mindfulness and ultimately internalizes mindfulness as a character trait.[30]

Approaches

There are two well-known approaches to mindfulness: the common multicomponent approach that is more abstract, and the metacognitive practice approach that is more concrete.[31] The *common multicomponent* approach consists of the following dimensions:

1. being aware of one's surroundings,
2. responding with present-centred focus,
3. accepting oneself,
4. being conscious of one's thinking and being,
5. being open-minded,
6. being non-judgemental and non-reactive,
7. not identifying oneself with one's thoughts or emotions and
8. being able to share how one thinks and feels.

The *metacognitive practice* approach, on the other hand, interprets mindfulness as nestled within specific activities and social interactions. Emphasizing both the system in which mindfulness is learned and the system in which it is enacted, metacognitive practice comprises the following three beliefs:

1. *attentional sufficiency*: one's focus is not depleted over time;
2. *the virtue of monitoring*: the advantages of being conscious of one's thinking and feelings, including unpleasant ones and
3. *map-terrain differentiation*: one's thinking and feelings about a state of affairs do not always mirror objective truth.

In distinguishing Eastern and Western traditions of mindfulness, scholars point to two key criteria: meditation and cognitive development.

Traditions

Researchers also distinguish between Eastern and Western traditions of mindfulness. The former is associated with meditation, contemplation and a non-judgmental awareness of one's moment-to-moment experience, as exemplified by Buddhism. Western traditions, on the other hand, underline cognitive aspects such as an openness to new ideas and creation of categories.[32]

In distinguishing Eastern and Western traditions of mindfulness, scholars point to two basic criteria: meditation and cognitive development. Some scholars see *meditation* as a necessary feature of Eastern traditions of mindfulness, evidenced through activities such as yoga or quiet sitting. This orientation turns inward to the experiences of the participant and involves non-evaluative observation rather than information processing and assessment.[33] In contrast, Western traditions of mindfulness, according to these scholars, are more interested in *cognitive development* such as knowledge acquisition and problem solving.[34] Following the Western traditions, a mindful person exhibits mental flexibility, as seen in the extent to which one pursues new standpoints, partakes in creative activity, and cultivates one's intellectual faculties.[35]

In my view, the above dichotomy of Eastern and Western traditions of mindfulness is too simplistic, as it does not apply to Confucian mindfulness. First, Confucius's conception of mindfulness does not require any meditation, in the sense of relying on a set of techniques to achieve a heightened state of consciousness. Second, his approach to mindfulness involves the exercise of one's cognitive development, such as examining and critiquing ideas. I shall return to and elaborate on these two features of Confucian mindfulness in the rest of the book.

It is also a moot point that the meditative aspect of mindfulness is absent in Western histories and cultures. A case in point is St Ignatius Loyola's *Spiritual Exercises*, written in the sixteenth century, that compiles meditations on Scripture, prayers and visualising exercises. Another example, mentioned at the start of this chapter, is the contemplative philosophy of Socrates and Foucault, which is consistent with the thoughtful direction of Eastern mindfulness. It is also noteworthy that educators such as Montessori and Waldorf-Steiner, as well as a number of modern Christian schools in the West, privilege reflection and introspection in their school curriculum.[36]

> Confucius's conception of mindfulness does not require any meditation, in the sense of relying on a set of techniques to achieve a heightened state of consciousness.

Programmes

As for mindfulness-based programmes, there is a buffet spread of courses that differ in terms of their contents, duration, frequency and impact. Most mindfulness courses involve one or more of the following three activities: (1) meditation through present-moment, non-judgmental attention to one's experience, (2) breathing exercises and (3) body scans.[37] In the school context, popular mindfulness training programmes include MindUP, Holistic Life Foundation's Stress Reduction & Mindfulness Curriculum, and courses designed by the *Mindfulness in Schools Project* (MiSP).[38] These initiatives are either offered as a stand-alone initiative or integrated into the existing school curriculum.

In general, mindfulness programmes can be identified on the basis of two conditions: whether they involve meditation, and whether they are structured:[39]

1. *Meditation-based, structured*: Examples are Mindfulness-Based Stress Reduction (MBSR) initiated by Kabat-Zinn, and Mindfulness-Based Cognitive Therapy (MBCT).
2. *Meditation-free, structured*: Examples are Acceptance and Commitment Therapy (ACT) and Dialectical Behaviour Therapy (DBT).
3. *Meditation-free, non-structured*: An example is Langer's mindfulness theory that approaches mindfulness from cognitive and social

psychological perspectives, and emphasizes making distinctions and creating new categories.

Mindfulness programmes can also be categorized into first-generation and second-generation mindfulness-based initiatives.[40] *First-generation mindfulness-based* initiatives bring to the fore the individual and instrumental aspects of mindfulness so as to enhance personal performance, health and well-being. Examples are programmes such as MBSR and MBCT, which are mentioned earlier. *Second-generation mindfulness-based* initiatives, on the other hand, are more collective and substantive. An example is Mindfulness-Based Business Ethics Education that aims to combine mindful practices and business ethics.[41] Some second-generation mindfulness-based initiatives are also more spiritual or religious in nature, such as Buddhist-Derived Interventions (BDI).

> Mindfulness-Based Stress Reduction (MBSR) represents the awakening view by presupposing that the qualities of healing are inherent in each individual. The role of the mindfulness instructor is to help the participants recognize and exercise their natural ability to obtain personal well-being.

Another way to differentiate the varied mindfulness programmes is to understand their views and presuppositions on the nature of the mind. There are two major standpoints: *the awakening view* that assumes that wellness is innate and *the enlightenment view* that assumes that wellness is not innate and needs to be developed.[42]

Accordingly, MBSR represents the awakening view by presupposing that the qualities of healing are inherent in each individual. The role of the mindfulness instructor is to help the participants recognize and exercise their natural ability to obtain personal well-being. Cognitively Based Compassion Training (CBCT), on the other hand, represents the enlightenment view. This approach is more prescriptive, where the mindfulness instructor directs the participants towards healing. Finally, Sustainable Compassion Training (SCT) integrates both views by positing that the qualities of awakening are inborn, but individuals still need to be guided through constructivist practices by the instructor.

Related to the content is the evaluation of mindfulness-based programmes. There are currently five key assessments for mindfulness, as follows:[43]

1. Mindful Attention Awareness Scale (MAAS): examines a person's disposition to be present in everyday life.

2. Freiburg Mindfulness Inventory (FMI): assesses a person's present-moment consciousness and non-judgemental attitude, especially towards negative encounters.
3. Kentucky Inventory of Mindfulness Skills (KIMS): appraises a person's skills in observing, describing, responding with awareness, and being non-judgemental.
4. Cognitive and Affective Mindfulness Scale (CAMS): determines a person's concentration, observation, recognition and openness in daily life.
5. Mindfulness Questionnaire (MQ): analyses the extent to which a person reacts to distressing stimuli mindfully.

Having briefly introduced the concepts, characteristics and practices of mindfulness, the next segment turns our attention to the topic of mindful leadership.

Mindful leadership

> Mindful leadership is about influencing others towards the achievement of a common goal through moment-by-moment attention to and engagement with oneself, people, things and events.

In uncertain times, effective leadership is needed to rally the people around inspiring visions, ideas and ways of life.[44] More important than positional leadership, as indicated in job titles, is the ability to influence others to reach a common goal.[45] In a post-pandemic educational landscape, transformational leadership is needed for successful and continual school improvements. Unfortunately, school leaders themselves are often besieged by exhausting demands, resulting in them reacting to external circumstances in an auto-pilot manner. Tellingly, a survey of a group of school leaders, conducted at the Harvard Graduate School of Education, reported that 89 per cent felt overwhelmed, 84 per cent neglected to take care of themselves in the midst of stress, and 80 per cent scolded themselves when they performed less than perfectly.[46]

A silver lining is that leaders are turning to leadership training and support that go beyond the standard management strategies to the cultivation of the leader's internal awareness. This shift of training contents explains why mindful leadership is in the spotlight for leaders and their organizations.[47] Institutions such as Google and the US Army, and prominent leaders such as Bill George who was the CEO of Medtronic, have advocated mindfulness approaches for leaders and employees.[48] The next section gives details on what mindful leadership is about.

Definitions and salient characteristics

As with mindfulness, there are many definitions, theories and applications of mindful leadership. Following our understanding of mindfulness as stated earlier in this chapter, mindful leadership is essentially about *influencing others towards the achievement of a common goal through moment-by-moment attention to and engagement with oneself, people, things and events*. Researchers have shed light on this form of leadership by drawing upon a variety of disciplines and domains, such as management studies, neuroscience, metacognition and social-emotional intelligence.[49]

A number of mindful leadership constructs have been derived from Langer's socio-cognitive approaches to mindfulness which focus on new information, myriad viewpoints and novelty.[50] Another discernible trend is to link mindful leadership to two related concepts: resonant leadership and authentic leadership. Briefly, a *resonant leader* is one who is fully conscious of their whole self, other people and the environment. A mindful resonant leader channels their emotional intelligence to connect with others, empathize with them and inspire them.[51] An *authentic leader*, as signified by the name, is genuine and transparent, establishing trust and ethical behaviours in others. A chief proponent of authentic leadership is Bill George who integrated Eastern meditation and Western thinking in his formulation of mindful leadership.[52]

We can sum up the existing literature on mindful leadership by noting three principal characteristics: (1) ways of being, (2) emotional intelligence and (3) mindful engagement.

> A chief proponent of authentic leadership is Bill George who integrated Eastern meditation and Western thinking in his formulation of mindful leadership.

Ways of being

First, a mindful leader transcends acts of doing to *ways of being*.[53] Mindfulness practice helps leaders to be present-centred, in touch with their own feelings and sensitive to the impact of their behaviour on other people. Being present enables leaders to be less reactive, deal with stressful circumstances and let go of inconsequential worries.[54] Mindful leaders are distinguished by their possession of *trait mindfulness* which predisposes them to be mindful, and empowers them to make better decisions by considering alternatives and be more accepting of others.[55] Leaders with higher trait mindfulness also demonstrate greater leadership quality by remaining calm and alert regardless of contextual demands, and showing the capacity to make sense, select and utilize information in their decision-making.[56]

Emotional intelligence

Besides exercising power and exerting influence, mindful leaders also need to engender trust by building and sustaining strong transpersonal, caring relationships. This requires leaders who are *emotionally intelligent*. Emotionally intelligent leaders are in touch with their own feelings and manage them well; they are also sensitive to the emotions and responses of people around them. Mindful leaders are strong in self-awareness, regulation of their emotions, self-motivation, empathy and management of human relationships.[57] The emotional intelligence of a mindful leader is seen in the following six areas:[58]

1. *Spirit* – is aware of one's destination which serves as a compass;
2. *Emotion* – is in tune with but not controlled by one's emotions;
3. *Mind* – focuses on one's thoughts so as to inform decision-making;
4. *Body* – prioritizes one's physical well-being through self-care;
5. *Connecting* – pays attention to others through active listening and establishing trust and
6. *Inspiring* – motivates others through one's vision and passion.

> Leaders can bring about a culture of mindful engagement in their organizations through collective mindfulness, mindful organizing and organizational mindfulness.

A mindful leader is empathic by practising deep listening, focusing their attention on others without being bound by one's agenda or pre-judgements about the other person.[59] Such a person adopts a range of non-judgemental perspectives, actively self-evaluates and reframes the issues, and is sensitive to language use, such as avoiding excessively prescriptive and absolute language.[60]

Mindful engagement

Finally, mindful leaders demonstrate *mindful engagement*, which refers to being aware of and reflecting on their lived experiences so as to advance personal growth and learning.[61] Leaders can bring about a culture of mindful engagement in their organizations through (1) collective mindfulness, (2) mindful organizing and (3) organizational mindfulness.[62]

First, *collective mindfulness* is about having arrangements and habits of practice that encourage employees to channel their energies and respond to specific situations in a timely manner.[63] Collective mindfulness is not just about one's actions, but also includes one's feelings, thoughts and will; it is the inclination to act with focus, whole-heartedness and concern.[64] Collective mindfulness is achieved by infusing it into the organization's day-to-day routines, rules, operations and interactions among staff in small groups.[65] Leaders can implement these five processes that promote collective mindfulness:[66]

1. *Paying attention to day-to-day operations*: checking that the team is cognizant of contingent changes that occur in daily operations and surroundings;
2. *Anticipating obstacles and mistakes*: attending to information that points to problems, and responding swiftly before these problems escalate;
3. *Facilitating decision-making by real-time experts*: acknowledging the existence of many experts rather than assuming that the experts are necessarily or only those who are most senior or respected by peers;
4. *Prizing resource flexibility*: setting aside time and energy to help team members to be familiar with one another's responsibilities, so as to enable more agile staff deployment and
5. *Resistance to simplify issues*: constantly inquiring into whether the existing solutions are the best and how they can be improved.

Complementing collective mindfulness is *mindful organizing*. The main difference between them is that collective mindfulness is about the *patterns* of organizing whereas mindful organizing focuses on the *processes* of organizing. Specifically, mindful organizing refers to the activity of a collective, such as a sub-unit or work group, to deal with situations based on shared understandings and interactions.[67] Mindful organizing is comprised of five interrelated processes:

1. a focus on failure,
2. resistance to simplify interpretations,
3. careful attention to operations,

4. devotion to resilience and
5. enactment of malleable decision structures.[68]

The last related concept is *organizational mindfulness*. Mindful organizing and organizational mindfulness, although overlapping in practice, are differentiated as follows: the former is implemented at the operational level, whereas the latter occurs at the strategic level through the decisions made by the institution's top administrators.[69] Leaders who embrace organizational mindfulness work towards a culture of openness, preserve employees' attentional resources, develop a flexible state of mind in all staff, and facilitate a better allocation of attentional resources and stronger information processing.[70]

Figure 1.1 summarizes the relationship between collective mindfulness, mindful organizing and organizational mindfulness. The figure depicts organizational mindfulness at the centre as it is initiated by the leader and senior management team. The circle of organizational mindfulness is surrounded by the

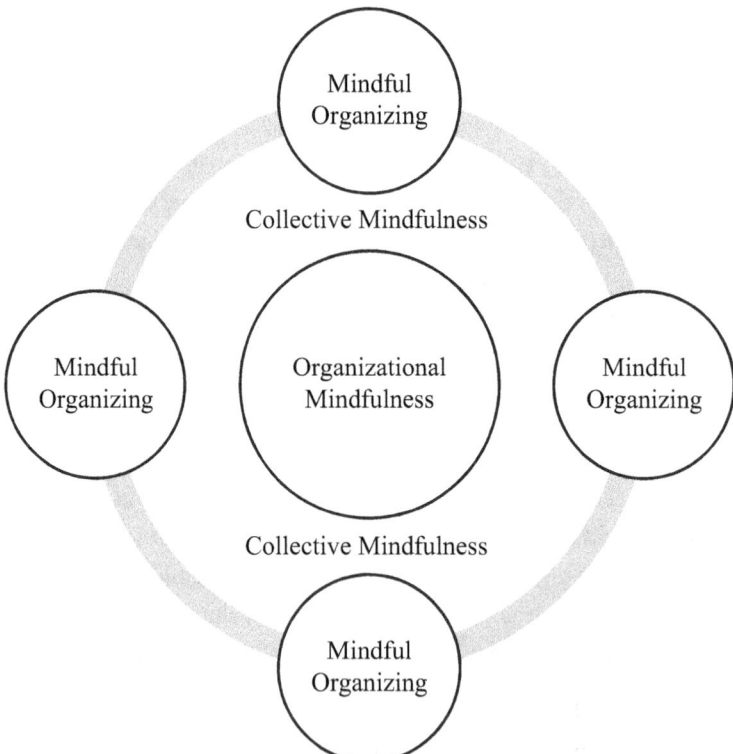

Figure 1.1 Collective mindfulness, mindful organizing and organizational mindfulness.

smaller circles of mindful organizing, which is comprised of multiple subunits or workgroups. All the staff are engaged and immersed in an environment of collective mindfulness, which are patterns of mindfulness.

A final point concerns 'how mindfulness is introduced in a workplace. Leaders should ensure that mindfulness is the building block of organizational practice and culture, and not just something that is piecemeal or impromptu. There are two main approaches to promoting mindfulness for staff: the ad hoc approach and the integrated approach.[71] The *ad hoc* approach comes in the form of mindfulness training programmes, where attendees receive a short training course and are largely left to practise mindfulness in their personal lives. This approach is not ideal as it treats mindfulness as an optional and private practice. The other arrangement, the *integrated* approach, is more sustainable and inclusive, where mindfulness permeates the organizational system, operations, interactions and cultures.[72]

> Leaders should ensure that mindfulness is the building block of organizational practice and culture, and not just something that is piecemeal or impromptu.

Mindfulness and mindful leadership in schools

Table 1.1 provides an overview of the initiatives, programmes and activities related to mindfulness and mindful leadership, which are implemented in schools around the world. They are classified into the following categories: curriculum, pedagogy, leadership and management, teacher training and other programmes.

An evaluation of mindfulness and mindful leadership

Benefits

There is an extensive body of literature that reports on the benefits of mindfulness. As the advantages are well-documented and widely publicized in the academic and popular media, I shall not go into the details here. Instead, I shall only discuss briefly the overall findings.

Table 1.1 A Literature Review of Mindfulness Initiatives in Schools (Prepared by Tan Bee Leng)

a) Curriculum

1. Mindfulness practices have been widely introduced into the Australian schools, but there has been insufficient appraisal of its impact on primary- and high-school students' learning experiences. This study examined a South Australian primary school's pilot *Mindfulness at School* teaching programme, which consists of components of the Mind-up curriculum, the Australian Smiling Mind Education Program and Meditation Capsules Mindfulness Program. The research findings raised a number of issues related to the incorporation of mindful practices in the school curriculum, for example, the uncertainties concerning the requirements of mindfulness practices and instructional methods, the ethical considerations for mindfulness-practice implementation in a middle-school setting, the question of safety and well-being of students, particularly the sensitivity of those who have had past traumatic experiences, as well as the feasibility of such programmes in a school population that is diverse in socio-economic and cultural backgrounds. As such, the author proposed that the merits of incorporating mindfulness practices in schools should be further analysed (Arthurso, 2017, pp. 55–75).

2. Research findings on a mindfulness course offered by the University of Amsterdam in the Netherlands, which studied the origins and applications of mindfulness in (child) psychiatry, revealed some differences in responses to the course from the international and domestic students, as well as the 'meditator' and 'novice' students. All students demonstrated a diminished mindful awareness before the course. Although the mindful awareness of the international students and moderators increased during the course, domestic and novice students only showed a heightened mindful awareness at the follow-up. The research concluded that a low-intensity mindfulness curriculum could be beneficial in enhancing students' performance and quality of life as they deploy mindfulness techniques to help them manage stress (De Bruin et al., 2015, pp. 1137–42).

3. This qualitative study examined a fifteen-week experiential meditation course that offered an experience in Buddhist and mindfulness practices for college students. It aimed to analyse the influence of the mindfulness practices on college students' life attitude and social relationships. The study found that the course had positive effects on the students as they demonstrated heightened mindfulness, empathy and happiness, thus enhancing their sense of self-fulfilment and emotional well-being. However, the authors suggested that further research on the college level meditation course is necessary to validate its benefits for the students (Crowley & Munk, 2017, pp. 91–8).

4. The authors argued that Langerian Mindfulness is useful in promoting Social-Emotional Learning (SEL) in an inclusive classroom. This was based on the successful implementation of mindful teaching and learning strategies in the New School San Francisco, an inquiry-based learning charter school catering to students from diverse social-economic and racial backgrounds. They proposed that Langerian Mindfulness strategies are relevant in developing the twenty-first century skills and SEL in primary classrooms. Thus, the feasibility of mindfulness practices in primary and secondary schools is worthy of further investigation (Davenport & Pagnini, 2016, p. 1372).

Table 1.1 (continued)

5. Students from a middle school gifted language arts class were taught mindfulness techniques to help them cope with their overachieving tendencies and anxieties, which caused them undue stress and frustration. The thirty-day unit of study on mindfulness allowed students to practice daily meditation with guidance from their instructors. The mindfulness programme yielded different outcomes for students. Some were successful in using the mindfulness practices to manage their negative emotions; others saw the practices as lacking purpose and having little positive impact on their mental or emotional competency (Doss & Bloom, 2018, pp. 181–92).

6. This research study examined the effects of the implementation of a Christian meditation programme in Catholic primary schools in Australia. Teachers underwent a training workshop to learn how to apply the meditation technique. Students practised meditation through the recitation of ancient prayers for eight minutes. The researchers did a qualitative analysis of the feedback and viewpoints collected from the students' and teachers' focus groups regarding the practice of regular meditation in a classroom setting, to examine its impact on their emotional and social well-being. The findings suggested that the meditation program was beneficial to the emotional state of mind and the social relationships for both teachers and students in school. Further research is required to examine how the meditation techniques offer mutual benefits for both teachers and students in a classroom, and whether the same process and benefits can be replicated in other primary school systems (Graham & Truscott, 2020, pp. 807–19).

7. This study investigated how students' well-being was impacted by the introduction of mindfulness into the curriculum of an elementary school characterized by high poverty and linguistic and cultural diversity. It also aimed to study the perceptions of the school's teaching and administrative staff, as well as the community members, on the programme's impact on the school. The findings revealed that through the mindfulness practices, students were able to achieve better self-understanding, verbalize their emotional needs, choose appropriate strategies to manage emotions and extend mindfulness outside of the school context (Haines et al., 2017, pp. 189–205).

8. This study explored how students' learning was impacted by the introduction of a mindfulness programme in an undergraduate class. The research findings indicated that students had varying degrees of acceptance of the six mindfulness-based techniques that they learnt, which included mindfulness meditation, walking meditation, body scan meditation, mindful eating, loving-kindness and Tonglen meditation (a meditation practice rooted in Tibetan Buddhism). The benefits of practising these mindfulness actions were perceived favourably by majority of the students, although some saw little impact on their well-being. Most students gained an enhanced level of self-awareness and calmness through these mindfulness-based practices (MBPs). The mindfulness techniques also helped to promote a higher standard of classroom communication and improve students' learning when introduced at the beginning of class. Direct teaching of the mindfulness-based techniques was proposed to help students acquire strategies to support personal care (Ingram et al., 2019, pp. 814–25).

(continued)

Table 1.1 (continued)

9. The author examined the trend of MBPs in the context of local and international schools in Singapore. MBPs were more prevalent among the international schools than the local schools, although there was an increasing interest to incorporate mindfulness in the local elementary, secondary and post-secondary school programmes. However, a wider implementation of the MBPs within the local schools was hindered by some obstacles, for example, a lack of qualified teachers to conduct the mindfulness programmes, as well as resistance from staff, parents and students to fully embrace MBPs because of its associated religious undertones. The author suggested that further research should look into school-based mindfulness programmes that are customized to the local environment, and explore existing mindfulness practices already adopted by some local schools (Khng, 2018, pp. 52–65).

10. The author described students' learning experiences in a college contemplative education course that integrated the practice of mindfulness. In the course, students developed the capacity to gain insights into their 'performance of self' through guided mindfulness meditation and reflective writing, which enhanced their self-awareness and possibly helped mould their personal and professional lives. Thus, the practical application of the theory of contemplative practice is evidenced through the novel and imaginative use of this instructional method during the course (Klatt, 2017, pp. 122–36).

11. This research study examined a sixteen-week mindfulness course offered as an elective academic subject to students in a Moroccan University. It aimed to explore the possibility of instilling the spirit of 'transformative and lifelong learning' in students via the adoption of a contemplative pedagogy and the integration of mindfulness strategies into the core curriculum of a university. In the course, students explored several mindfulness practices such as meditation, mindful breathing and art activities to deepen the understanding of 'self' to support a fuller learning experience. The study concluded that the course yielded positive outcomes for students in terms of their emotional and intellectual well-being and preparedness for 'transformative learning' as they were able to relate the mindfulness practices to their own religious and cultural experiences (Kumar, 2021, pp. 241–60).

12. A range of mindfulness programmes such as the *Inner Explorer*, *Master Mind* and *Mindful Schools* have been introduced into the curriculum of the K-12 schools in the United States, but the efficacy of these programmes has yet to be established with research. To bridge this research gap, this study identified ten school-based mindfulness programmes to review their strengths and limitations, and provided ideas for further research into the practicality of these programmes. The authors commented that the evaluation of the effectiveness of these programmes should involve the joint efforts of researchers, educators and mindfulness practitioners (Semple et al., 2017, pp. 29–52).

b) Pedagogy

1. This study analysed the mindset and perceptions of experienced teachers with regards to the role they play in imparting mindfulness to their students. Eight teachers from the United States and Australia were interviewed using the methodology of Interpretative Analysis. The findings revealed that the teachers' well-being, the ability to practise what they preached, their feelings of connectedness and a sense of devotion were among several components crucial to defining a teacher's mindful pedagogy (Albrecht, 2016, pp. 133–48).

Table 1.1 (continued)

2. This study probed into the effects of a short mindful breathing exercise on writing performance. It also aimed to investigate the effectiveness of mindful breathing as an intervention strategy for community college students who are generally most disadvantaged in tertiary institutions in the United States. Data from the Daly Miller Writing Apprehension surveys and narrative writing samples of students from a southeastern US college were analysed. The findings showed that students who practised mindful breathing at the beginning of the class sessions were relatively less anxious and committed fewer mechanical errors in their writing performance as compared with those from the control group, thus validating the efficacy of mindful breathing as an intervention measure (Britt et al., 2018, pp. 693–707).

3. The author argued that the successful introduction of mindfulness in a classroom is dependent on the teachers' willing acceptance and application of mindful practices in their personal and professional lives. Interviews were conducted with two experienced teachers who participated in the Mindfulness-Based Stress Reduction (MBSR) programme several years ago and have since been practising mindfulness. Both were able to translate their personal mindfulness experiences into their teaching practice. They demonstrated qualities of mindfulness such as high emotional and social competencies, and were rational and impartial, which helped to construct a conducive classroom environment that enhanced students' positive behaviour and performance (Grant, 2017, pp. 147–52).

4. The authors of this article, two university educators, discussed their experiences of forming a self-study partnership as one of them attempted to incorporate mindfulness, which encompasses loving-kindness, empathy and deep listening when teaching a multicultural course in the college. The authors argued that this is particularly essential for new teachers when dealing with the predicaments of addressing the issue of White privilege, which inevitably surfaced in a classroom comprising students with diverse experiences. One of the authors reflected on how his personal life experience in mindfulness, for example, the practice of contemplative meditation, had influenced him to adopt a mindful teaching practice. The other author considered her role as a critical friend providing an alternative voice in the study. The study contended that the educator's pursuit of a mindful teaching practice had yielded beneficial outcomes in his professional work, for example, creating a classroom environment that is conducive to students' learning (Griggs & Tidwell, 2015, pp. 87–104).

5. Using the teaching of mindfulness practices in tertiary education as a case study, the authors considered the use of technology as a countermeasure to address the issue of people losing connection with the 'other' as they develop an increasing reliance on technology. The cell phone is suggested as a viable instrument. It represents, to some degree, an extension of one's body, and contributes to one's appreciation of the existence of 'self'; this enables a better appreciation of interconnectedness. The authors concluded that the use of cell phones fosters mindful attention, which is a prerequisite and attribute of 'I-thou' relationship (Hadar & Ergas, 2018, pp. 99–107).

(continued)

Table 1.1 (continued)

6. This study looked into how teachers in a Canadian rural elementary school exercised mindfulness in their teaching practice with the support of the school principal. It examined the personal and professional stories shared by two teachers, one who was experienced in contemplative meditation practice and the other, a novice teacher, with no prior experience in mindful practices. The findings concluded that mindfulness practice experiences have an impact on teachers' identification and awareness, as well as the quality of their interactions with their students, for example, the ability to be more attentive and receptive, and to show greater care and love (Kavia & Murphy, 2021, pp. 189–202).

7. The authors proposed the Mindful Self in School Relationships (MSSR) model as a theoretical framework to draw attention to the teacher's role in influencing mindfulness in school. Mindfulness research in other disciplines, particularly psychology and neuroscience, and the central role of teachers in influencing how students work and grow in social situations, form the basis of the MSSR model. The MSSR model shows that teachers' positive influence is dependent on the key mechanism of reduced egocentrism, which results in the manifestation of their caring capacities such as emotional control, benevolence and sensitivity towards others. This enhances teachers' aptitude in connecting positively with students and enables them to promote their own welfare and efficacy, thus contributing to students' well-being, as well as interpersonal and academic progress (Lavy & Berkovich-Ohana, 2020, pp. 2258–73).

8. This research study examined the experiences of four southern Ontario primary school teachers in employing mindfulness techniques in their classes. They implemented mindfulness practices in their teaching profession to address work-related stress and difficulties in their personal life, and also to help their young students cope with stress or other negative emotions within the classroom setting. Although the findings demonstrated that the teachers perceived mindfulness practices such as mindful breathing, awareness of self, the exercise of loving-kindness and meditation to have positive effects on the young students' classroom behaviour and performance, they faced practical constraints such as the issues of big class size and physical exhaustion. Such constraints dented the beneficial effects of the mindfulness practices. The authors advocated that teachers need to consider the potential negative effects of mindfulness practices on young children and highlighted the necessity of customizing their mindfulness instruction to suit the needs of their students (Piotrowski et al., 2017, pp. 225–40).

9. The authors discussed how the language and writing skills of students from a Spanish public rural school improved through a mindful teaching strategy. These students were from a community that placed low priority on education. The authors stated that adopting a pedagogy which combines mindfulness and metacognitive strategies with the knowledge of the language system and language topic background, allows students to be more focused in their learning, be more in control of their emotions and have a better comprehension of the errors made in the Spanish language. This is achievable in a language classroom through the organizing of individual or group activities that help to re-create students' prior knowledge. The authors further proposed that students' perception of their communicative and social skills in the larger society could potentially be positively altered if their sense of achievement increases and language skills are improved through mindful practices (Santucho & Arce-Trigatti, 2021, pp. 23–9).

Table 1.1 (continued)

10. The authors explored the probable beneficial effects of introducing mindfulness training for teachers. They proposed that mindfulness practices are useful in three ways for teachers. Practising mindfulness helps teachers to become more aware of personal care, be a mindful and reflective educator and develop the capacity to apply a mindful teaching approach in school. The authors reviewed the current curricula, resources and recommendations that teachers could explore if they intend to integrate mindfulness training and practices into their teaching. The author concluded with a list of seven main criteria required for advancing future research (Shapiro et al., 2016, pp. 83–98).

11. Online courses are becoming more widespread in the field of higher education, and there are indications that the likelihood of students being overwhelmed by information overload and obstacles experienced with remote learning is real, particularly with group work. The authors conducted this study to investigate whether meditation would have positive outcomes for students involved in teamwork. The research showed that in an online environment, the meditation practice contributed to a lower level of group cooperation behaviour and mindfulness from the students when compared with the outcomes of those who did not meditate (Tan & Molinari, 2017).

c) Assessment

1. The authors suggested that instead of using assessments as a mere measurement tool to gauge students' achievement levels at the end of a learning unit, mindful approaches should be considered for assessment to help students boost their performance. They argued that mindful assessment encourages deployment of more individualized and humanistic evaluation strategies that acknowledge students' achievement in their entire learning experience. The authors illustrated how students were better supported in their learning through dialectical evaluative practices that allowed them to be mentored in a manner that respected their agency as whole persons (Camfield & Bayers, 2019, pp. 121–44).

2. The author presented a case study of how she introduced mindfulness in the assessment of her students' learning in a contemplative course at the university. Evaluation and feedback on students' writing were based on the concepts of mindfulness, for example, acknowledging strengths, paying attention to specific views, providing constructive suggestions for incremental improvements, celebrating attempts at novelty in terms of insights and ideas and encouraging inquisitiveness for further probing of ideas. These mindful responsive strategies complemented the author's effort to focus on cultivating self-awareness in students' learning (Watts, 2016, pp. 98–122).

d) School leadership/School Management

1. The author examined the development of school leadership mindfulness in three aspects. The effects of mindfulness practices in education and the latest developments of mindful school leadership were first explored. Next, the merits, concepts and significance of mindful school leadership were analysed. Finally, several practical applications of mindfulness to enhance school leadership effectiveness were recommended, for example, principals should pay full attention to circumstances, cultivate self-awareness, establish positive relationships, observe moral standards and ensure the emotional well-being of teachers and students (Hsieh, 2018, pp. 69–86).

(continued)

Table 1.1 (continued)

2. The authors argued that feedback is a useful evaluation tool to enhance educators' and school leaders' professional growth and learning. However, the effective use of feedback is dependent on educators' mindfulness, ego and a mindset that appreciates feedback. The author proposed that a mindful school leader is open-minded, has the ability to shape a school climate that is receptive to various types of feedback and promotes a learning attitude that is open to risk-taking. Mindfulness, which fosters the awareness of the present moment without any prejudices, is thus necessary to ensure optimal delivery and application of feedback to enhance the professional development of a school leader (Day & Gregory, 2017, pp. 363–75).

3. The author proposed that the model of high-reliability organizations (HROs), which draws inspiration from the premises of Western and Eastern concepts of mindfulness, provides effective strategies for school leadership to adopt a mindfulness approach in managing a school community. Understanding the process of HROs will enable school leaders to focus more on developing resilience, and rely on expert knowledge that encourages collaborative learning to improve instructional practices. This would be preferable to the existing focus on accountability, which limits the ability to reflect on existing practices to avoid mistakes. Mindful leadership, therefore, is a prerequisite to mobilize all stakeholders in the work of reforming schools. Developing training programmes to prepare school leaders for the work requires sufficient time and resource commitments from the public administration and tertiary institutions (Gilbert, 2019, pp. 136–61).

4. This study analysed the relationship between school leadership's mindfulness with students' academic competency using quantitative and qualitative data collected from public school teachers and principals in Texas. The findings showed that a mindful principal contributes positively to the school climate, which enhances students' potential for success. A mindful school leader will intentionally assign time to reflect on and work collaboratively with teachers to explore effective pedagogy. The formation of relationships based on trust and effective communication and the encouragement of continuous effort to acquire new knowledge also characterized a mindful school leadership (Kearney et al., 2013, pp. 316–35).

5. This study investigated how school leaders deployed mindfulness strategies to help them manage stress when they faced the uphill task of transiting schools to remote learning during the Covid-19 pandemic. The findings confirmed the efficacy of mindful practices in maintaining the school leaders' mental and emotional well-being. Breathing practices and the concept of 'being the thermostat, and not the thermometer' were the two mindfulness strategies commonly used by school leaders to enhance self-care and well-being. The study concluded that the successful implementation of mindful practices requires long-term commitment, adequate support, as well as an investment of time and space (Liu, 2020, pp. 15–20).

Table 1.1 (continued)

6. The effectiveness of the Cultivating Awareness and Resilience in Education (CARE), a mindfulness-based professional development programme, on the leadership and well-being of thirteen school leaders was studied in this pioneer research on the programme. The research data revealed desirable results in terms of improvement in the leadership qualities, for example, an enhanced capacity to examine and care for oneself and the ability to build stronger relationships. The participants also displayed greater sensitivity to their emotional state, which allowed them to have a greater appreciation of their role in determining the school climate as a school leader. This study expounded on how mindfulness could be vital to the personal and professional lives of school leaders, and how they could gain specific positive outcomes from mindfulness-based training (Mahfouz, 2018, pp. 602–19).

7. The study examined how organizational trust, that is, trust in the professionalism and expertise of the principals and teachers, affected mindfulness in an educational setting. The participants of this research study were from the Istanbul public schools. The data analysis findings confirmed that there was a co-relationship between organizational trust and mindfulness in school, which contributes to the general school performance. School mindfulness is enhanced when there is trust in the school leadership and colleagues. This is evident in the positive work relationship between principal and teachers, as well as between teacher and students. The study concluded that consolidating organizational trust is an important factor to consider if principals intend to improve mindfulness in school (Tabancalı & Öngel, 2020, pp. 14–25).

8. This research paper discussed how spiritual-based mindfulness meditation was practised by twelve Jamaican secondary school principals, who worked in rural, urban and inner-city schools, to help them manage stress and anxieties caused by an increased workload. The findings indicated that personal religious faith and mindfulness meditation or prayer provided the key source of comfort for the principals and contributed positively to their well-being. The findings served to advise future education and health policies relating to educators' welfare and formed the basis for further studies on the well-being of Jamaican and Caribbean principals (Walker, 2020, pp. 467–80).

e) Teacher Training

1. This study explored how mindfulness training produced positive outcomes for elementary school teachers from a rural school district. It also examined how school leadership provided support for their teachers through mindfulness training to help them alleviate stress and occupational burnout. The teachers implemented mindfulness teaching strategies in their classes for two weeks after attending two mindfulness training sessions. The findings indicated that mindfulness training helped teachers to effectively use intrapersonal mindfulness practices to have more successful communication with students and also improved their stress management (Akhavan et al., 2021, pp. 24–42).

(continued)

Table 1.1 (continued)

2. This research paper aimed to find out how pre-service elementary teachers responded to mindfulness training, which formed an element of a literary education course at a northeastern US university. Findings based on the quantitative data showed that the inclusion of mindfulness instruction in the literary education course over a semester had no significant impact on the pre-service teachers' mindfulness and stress levels. However, qualitative data based on oral and written responses indicated some beneficial outcomes: the pre-service teachers recognized preferred practices and perceived reduced stress during teaching. Conflicts with religious beliefs, time constraints and an overloaded course were some of the reasons cited for not committing fully to the mindfulness practice (Brown, 2017, pp. 136–46).

3. This study aimed to address the lack of integration of mindfulness practices to supplement logical thinking in the undergraduate teacher education programmes, despite meditation exercises evidently fostering introspective thinking ability. Analysis of the contemplative practices used by twenty-two teachers and educational leaders of varied backgrounds from New Zealand and Australia revealed different motivations, types of application and effects of meditation on them. Most participants perceived that the contemplative practices not only effected changes for themselves, but also influenced them to serve the interest of others, particularly their students. The author recommended the incorporation of contemplative practices, for example, mindfulness meditation, into mainstream teacher education and professional development, in consideration of the benefits of these practices (Denford-Wood, 2017, pp. 125–48).

4. The authors presented two different perceptions that focused on understanding oneself to decipher the function of mindfulness in teacher education, denoting a shift from the path of stress management and well-being. The first perception of mindfulness defines 'self' as a continuous emotional and spiritual experience that gears us towards human connections. These experiences form the new basis of the teachers' values perceived as essential to their teaching vocation. The other perception is the 'socio-political self' that leads to one's higher commitment in critical pedagogy calling for teachers' 'fluid self' based on non-prejudice, thus becoming a social justice practice acknowledging the disadvantaged and marginalised. The authors proposed that besides well-being, the contemplation of teacher identity is to be considered when exploring the role of mindfulness practice in teacher education (Ergas & Ragoonaden, 2020, pp. 179–96).

5. Recent research has shown that mindfulness-based programmes aid in stress reduction and promote the well-being of teachers, which may have a positive influence on their turn-over rate. This study aimed to analyse the effectiveness of a six-week mindfulness-based programme in addressing stress and symptoms of depression, and promoting mindfulness and well-being for pre-service teachers in Hong Kong. The research findings showed that the mindfulness programme was useful and beneficial as the pre-service teachers' mindfulness and well-being were notably improved. The author concluded that the mindfulness programme should be recommended for teachers to enhance their well-being and stress management, as well as to prevent professional burn-out (Hue & Lau, 2015, pp. 381–401).

Table 1.1 (continued)

6. This study examined the inclusion of mindfulness practice in the professional development of teachers to strengthen their stress management capacity, and also to apply mindfulness in their pedagogical practice to promote a conducive classroom environment for students. Twenty-six K-12 Hawaii teachers and counsellors participated in the three-day mindfulness course that required them to practise various mindfulness techniques daily and reflect on their experiences, as well as conduct mindfulness lessons with their students. The research findings revealed that the mindfulness practice benefitted the educators as it helped to improve their ability to manage stress; they became more conscious of their negative thoughts and feelings. Teachers also experienced greater success in improving their students' lives when introducing mindfulness into their classroom teaching practices (Le & Alefaio, 2019, pp. 627–41).

7. This study examined the merit of incorporating mindfulness practices in teacher education. The research subject was the Mindfulness-based Wellness Education (MBWE) programme, offered as an elective in the teacher education course at Ontario University. Teacher candidates experienced different aspects of well-being using a myriad of formal and informal mindfulness practices, for example, mindful sitting, yoga, being mindful in social interactions and others, during the nine-week course. Five main themes emerged from the research – reflective practice, teacher identity, social and emotional competence and well-being during their practicum, learning to fail and teacher engagement. The study concluded that teacher candidates acquired traits and skills from the mindfulness training that prepared them adequately for their teaching profession (Soloway, 2016, pp. 191–205).

8. The author described the promotion of mindfulness practices in a pre-service teacher training programme administered by a faculty member at a state university in midwestern United States. The goal was to remould the teacher candidates through peer mentoring and mindful engagement. The professor introduced mindfulness strategies such as deep breathing through daily sitting, heightened awareness of one's own thoughts, and mindful intention practice to improve teacher candidates' mental and physical well-being. Throughout the programme, teacher candidates were encouraged to be contemplative and to actively participate in the mindfulness practices and feedback-reflection sessions for clinical-field experiences and professional internships (Trube, 2017, pp. 159–67).

9. The authors proposed that most studies on the mindfulness practice to promote teachers' health and well-being were based on Western industrialized democracies (WEIRD societies). This study thus aimed to examine the impact of mindfulness training for teachers in Hong Kong, a non-Western society. A random sample of elementary and secondary school teachers went through an eight-week mindfulness training. The analysis findings from the teachers' returned surveys showed that the intervention group experienced an improvement in their quality of life, for example, experiencing greater contentment, less stress and better sleep quality. The positive benefits of mindfulness practices enabled teachers to implement a higher level of mindfulness-based teaching practice in their profession. The study concluded that the benefits of mindfulness training for teacher can be replicated outside of WEIRD societies (Tsang et al., 2021, pp. 2820–31).

(continued)

Table 1.1 (continued)

10.	The authors examined the application of mindfulness-based reflective practice to improve the pre-service teachers' understanding of the course content and their capacity to self-scrutinize for change. Their research focused on how to enhance thoughtful reflection and implement reflective journals effectively and meaningfully in a college classroom. The evaluation of the twenty-seven students' journal entries allowed the instructors to assess whether the course content was comprehended. They also gained a better appreciation of students' cultural beliefs. The authors concluded that journals were useful and effective for comprehension and assessments in this particular pre-service teacher course (Zimmerman & Musilli, 2016).

f) Others

1.	The authors gave details on the work of the 'Mindful Campus', a joint student and staff study group from the California State University-Chico campus. The Mindful Campus primarily supports mindfulness and contemplative pedagogy at the university and within the Chico community. Some of the mindfulness activities that the study group conducted were meditation sessions, short business meetings and book discussions. The authors argued that mindful living and contemplative pedagogy can have positive impacts on student learning and performance, and also offer them a more fulfilling learning experience. It also enhances teaching staff's satisfaction through the creation of an innovative and nurturing environment in the university and community (DuFon & Christian, 2013, pp. 65–72).
2.	The author argued that a more mindful and pragmatic approach should be adopted towards education, which will eventually lead to the cultivation of a genuine passion for life-long learning. The Covid-19 pandemic has provided the right opportunity for educators to re-assess the shortcomings of the existing model of schooling, for instance, the heavy emphasis on overloaded curricula and assessment scores to determine students' level of learning (Hughes, 2020, pp. 69–72).
3.	This study investigated the possibility of applying mindful learning in geography education based on the hypothesis that an open-minded and non-biased outlook towards regions could be formed through mindful learning. Three experiments were conducted at the classroom level to test the hypothesis. Analysis of the study outcomes supported the proposition that mindful learning or mindful teaching methods are useful in re-modelling students' perceptions towards the idea of regions in geography education (Lee & Ryu, 2015, pp. 197–210).

On the whole, research shows that mindfulness practice helps individuals by reducing absenteeism, burnout, stress, depression and anxiety, and enhancing self-efficacy, creativity, resilience, optimism, collaboration and job satisfaction.[73] Mindfulness also enables leaders to be more influential, efficient, innovative, attentive, positive and healthy.[74] Significant effects of mindful leadership are as follows: it supports the physiological platform that enables intelligence, promotes social relationships, harnesses the power of emotion, expedites the construction of knowledge, builds a culture of reflection and cultivates productive dispositions.[75] Other outcomes include advancing organizational safety climates, organizational attention, IT security, creativity, innovation and learning, adaptation and performance.[76] Corporations (including Fortune 500 companies) that have introduced mindfulness practices to their employees have reported the salutary effects of mindfulness on the physical, mental, emotional and social wellbeing of their staff.[77]

In the school context, mindfulness has positively affected the mental functions of students, such as attention, close observation, drawing novel distinctions, information-processing and working memory.[78] Mindfulness has also improved the students' performance in mathematics – good news for educators and parents who are concerned with exam results and academic performance.[79]

Shortcomings

Inconsistent research findings

Despite the glowing accounts on the benefits of mindfulness, there are also studies that caution against accepting mindfulness unreservedly. By way of illustration, some adults reportedly experienced heightened psychological distress while participating in mindfulness-based interventions.[80] Researchers have also cast doubts on some findings by noting the possibility of positive reporting bias.[81] A recent study known as the My Resilience in Adolescence (MYRIAD) trials, carried out by experts from Oxford University, Cambridge University and other institutions in the UK, reported that mindfulness did not benefit all pupils.[82] Furthermore, the report noted that the mindfulness training provided to pupils was not more effective than other ways of teaching them to manage their mental health. The broad conclusion is that the impact of mindfulness on students, although promising, is still incipient, tentative and inconsistent at the moment.[83]

Self-therapy and McMindfulness

> There is an overemphasis on self-therapy in mindfulness, with relatively less regard for social and moral considerations.

Another major deficiency of the existing approaches to mindfulness and, by extension, mindful leadership, is an overemphasis on self-therapy, with relatively less regard for social and moral considerations. Mindfulness meditation has become increasingly psychologized – a coping mechanism for individuals to overcome their persistent and lingering feelings of incompleteness.[84] At the same time, mindfulness has become individualistic and consumer-orientated; it is valued primarily for personal benefit at the expense of collective and organizational interest.[85] This quick-fix approach to school-based mindfulness reflects McMindfulness – the instrumentalization of mindfulness as a technique to deliver fast results.[86] The problem with McMindfulness is that mindfulness has been reduced to a programmatic practice that treats the symptoms, rather than the causes, of human problems.[87]

It is worth pointing out that even though mindfulness programmes do not espouse any explicit moral values, it does not mean that they are values-neutral. A strong case can be made that these programmes presuppose and transmit the worldviews of the mindfulness designers, instructors and practitioners.[88] A particular concern is the *neoliberal* values, assumptions and influences of mindfulness in an era of digital capitalism.[89] Believing that knowledge is the new capital in the twenty-first century, many countries are competing to equip their graduates with 'new economy competencies'. Supporting educational policies across the globe are neoliberal criteria and values that define and measure 'progress' within performative regimes.

In schools, neoliberal education means the entry of the market into schools, and the ensuing utilization of technologies such as competition, decentralization, school autonomy, accountability measures and performance goals. The mission of schools, accordingly, is to churn out enterprising and economic agents in an increasingly market-driven society. Schools are expected to respond to market and state demands by submitting themselves to specifications by management over workloads and course content. In a nutshell, the value of education is transformed into a production function that is determined by the rules of economics. It is especially worrying if mindfulness and mindful leadership endorse, or worse, perpetuate a functionalist view of education that focuses on test scores at the expense of the students' holistic education. Other, and arguably better, motivations for learning, such as the love for and joy of learning, and achieving human flourishing – what Aristotle calls *eudemonia* or living well – would then be side-lined.

Ethical concerns

> A point of contention is whether empathy for mindful leaders is a moral or nonmoral virtue. Empathy, if it is limited to perspective taking, is not necessarily moral.

Stripped of its ethical foundation, mindfulness and mindful leadership may contribute to or reinforce self-centred values. This is seen in individuals – whether leaders or followers – privileging their personal wellbeing over care and love for others.[90] What is overlooked are the value systems, normative frameworks and cultural worldviews that buttress, shape and accompany mindfulness in practice. Not only do mindfulness and mindful leadership neglect ethical and communal responsibility, they may inadvertently foster egoism and blind conformity to neoliberal norms and behaviours.[91]

To drive home the primacy of ethics for mindfulness and mindful leadership, let us take the example of empathy. On the one hand, researchers have highlighted the close relationship between mindfulness/mindful leadership and empathy.[92] On the other hand, it is not clear how empathy functions as a virtue, which is an admirable character trait. There are two types of virtues: moral and nonmoral.[93] Virtues are *moral* when they are tethered to moral principles, which are guidelines on what is right or wrong. Examples of moral virtues are kindness, integrity and benevolence. *Nonmoral* virtues such as courage, rationality and patience, on the other hand, are not tied to moral principles. A person who desires to cook well, for example, needs nonmoral virtues such as diligence and focus to achieve this goal.

Nonmoral virtues, although necessary and useful, can be employed for immoral purposes: think of a scammer who cheats others through resourcefulness and persistence. Although nonmoral virtues are essential for leaders to function well, they are insufficient without the concomitant presence of moral virtues.[94] As with the case of the scammer, a leader who possesses nonmoral virtues without moral virtues is prone to exploiting others and abusing one's power to serve one's selfish agendas.[95]

A point of contention is whether empathy, which is often mentioned alongside mindful leadership, is a moral or nonmoral virtue.[96] Empathy, if it is limited to perspective-taking, is not necessarily moral. Perspective-taking, also known as *cognitive* empathy, is when a person observes another person in a situation, believes that another person is in a certain situation, or imagines oneself to be in another person's situation.[97] These experiences in themselves do not ensure that the person will act morally by doing good to another person. The same reasoning applies to *affective* empathy, where a person experiences personal distress that generates self-oriented feelings, such as anxiety, discomfort and shock. This form of empathy does not guarantee that the person will act to alleviate the sufferings of others. In fact, personal distress may even hinder pro-social behaviour, by prompting the person to protect oneself and remove the source of one's distress.[98] To identify empathy as a moral virtue, researchers have introduced the term *empathic concern*, which encompasses the desire to care for the welfare of others based on shared feelings.[99]

The same critique of an inadequate attention to moral considerations for mindful leadership applies to the concepts of 'collective mindfulness', 'mindful organizing' and 'organizational mindfulness', which were discussed earlier. These three approaches are largely instrumental and de-emphasized the moral aspects of organizations. A leader who fosters collective mindfulness and organizational mindfulness directs one's focus towards the day-to-day operations, anticipates obstacles and mistakes, develops a flexible state of mind in all staff and so on. Likewise, staff who model mindful organizing are expectedly skilful in analysing failure, devoting to resilience and resisting a simplification to interpretations, among others. But these qualities, although critical for organizational success, are not moral virtues in themselves.

> These three concepts – collective mindfulness, mindful organizing and organizational mindfulness – are largely instrumental and de-emphasize the moral aspects of organizations.

The strategies of collective mindfulness, mindful organizing and organizational mindfulness serve, first and foremost, to enhance workplace efficiency and productivity, the facilitation of technical expertise and organizational success. On balance, more needs to be said about the relationship between mindful leadership and ethics, especially moral virtues.

To be sure, some writers have spotlighted the moral dimension of mindful leadership, for instance, the notion of '*caritas*-focused leadership'.[100] This refers to a concern for others that is premised on a spirit of dignity, respect and compassion. Rooted in love and compassion (the Latin meaning of *caritas*), mindful leaders rely on self-awareness obtained through reflective practices to achieve courage, purpose and joy.[101] To attain this desired outcome, a leader needs to know oneself and one's source(s) of purpose, inspiration, loving-kindness and equanimity. Questions to guide a leader in exploring one's source include the following:[102]

- How do I feel cared for?
- How do I express my care for others?
- What are the triggers that I am not feeling nurtured?
- How do I replenish myself?
- How does self-replenishment relate to the leadership service of others?
- What brings me strength?
- What/who inspires me?
- Where do I find joy and meaning?
- What legacy do I hope to leave with my leadership influence?
- What rituals can I build into my daily routine that will help me remember my connection with self and source?
- What makes me happy?
- What are my personal rituals for letting go of work/obligations at the end of the day?
- Am I growing?
- Am I helping others to grow professionally?

The above questions are certainly pertinent for mindful leaders. However, it is unclear what love and compassion – the Latin meaning of *caritas* – mean and consist of, which traditions they are derived from, and how they reflect the moral character of the leader. For example, do the above questions draw upon religious traditions such as Catholicism, a secular ethics of care, or the philosophical idea of *eudamonia* (happiness)?[103] Furthermore, the list of questions does not elaborate on the moral virtues that propel leaders to be other-regarding and altruistic. Without moral virtues that benefit others, leaders may use mindful leadership strategies purely for self-serving motives and even deleterious agendas.

Overall, what is lacking in the extant literature is a more in-depth and cogent discussion of the ethical basis of mindful leadership. This necessitates more research into the definitions, characteristics and ethical underpinnings of mindfulness. In particular, we need a conception of mindfulness and mindful leadership that underscores the interpersonal, moral, social and long-term characteristics and benefits of mindfulness.

Conclusion

The English word 'mindfulness' initially connoted a Buddhist awareness of the impermanence of all things. This term has since evolved to include multiple and even competing definitions, types, approaches, assessment methods, programmes and traditions. Against a backdrop of modern-day multitasking and stresses, mindfulness and mindful leadership have become increasingly popular for individuals and in organizations. This chapter has introduced the concepts of mindfulness and mindful leadership based on a review of the existing literature. This chapter has expounded on mindfulness and mindful leadership in terms of its genesis, definitions and salient characteristics. Empirical research has mainly attested to the benefits of mindfulness and mindful leadership, such as improving one's well-being, strengthening personal qualities such as self-efficacy and resilience, as well as contributing to employee productivity, collaboration and job satisfaction.

A major critique, however, is that mindfulness and mindful leadership are largely treated as 'competencies' – knowledge, skills and abilities for knowledge workers to meet the demands of the fourth industrial revolution by mobilising psychological resources. Mindfulness and mindful leadership are consequently regarded as 'doing' and technical 'how to', which disregards the moral virtues, character traits, attitudes and dispositions associated with being a mindful person and leader. What is still deficient is a more comprehensive justification of the ethical basis of mindful leadership. Addressing this lacuna, this book draws inspiration from the educational thought of Confucius, who is the subject of the next chapter.

2

Confucius, Mindlessness and Mindfulness

Photo 2.1 shows a statue of Confucius in a Confucius temple. The name Confucius, coined by Jesuit missionaries in the sixteenth century, is a Latinized version of Kong Master (孔夫子Kong Fuzi or 孔子Kongzi) (551 BCE–479 BCE). Confucius's real name was Kong Qiu (孔丘) where 'Kong' was his family name and 'Qiu' was his given name.[1] In the *Analects* (論語*Lunyu*), which is a Chinese classic that collates Confucius's teachings and conduct, he is simply known as 'the Master' (夫子Fuzi).

Confucius's aphorisms are well-known, but the same cannot be said about his life. After all, he lived more than two millennia ago, which makes it challenging for us to separate fact from fiction regarding accounts of his life. Confucius has been variously portrayed as a perfect sage, a progressive teacher, an antiquated philosopher, a sexist moralist and a supporter of authoritarian government, among others.[2] Instead of joining in the debate on who the historical Confucius really was, this book treats Confucius as a cultural symbol. In other words, the focus is on Confucius as a philosopher and educator, whose sayings and actions were preserved in the Chinese classics and other historical records.

> This book treats Confucius as a cultural symbol. The focus is on Confucius as a philosopher and educator, whose sayings and actions were preserved in the Chinese classics and other historical records.

As it is helpful to have some background information about Confucius before we examine his thought, this chapter draws upon the *Analects* and other sources to give the readers a picture of his life and personality.[3] The first segment of this chapter provides a brief biography of Confucius; this is followed by a discussion that relates his thought to mindlessness and mindfulness.

Photo 2.1 A statue of Confucius.

Biography of Confucius

Confucius was originally from the Lu state, which is near Qufu of Shandong province in China today. He was a member of the *shi* (士) – learned people and experts on the rites who sought to be employed as court officials and tutors.

His father was a military officer in the Lu state. However, he did not live long to see Confucius grow up, as he died when Confucius was about three years old. Confucius was brought up single-handedly by his mother, who struggled to make ends meet. Confucius was not the only child; he had a brother who was crippled and was fortunately cared for by Confucius for the rest of his life. Growing up in poverty, Confucius contributed financially by learning menial skills from a young age. When his mother passed away and Confucius had to arrange for her funeral, he made a special effort to locate his father's burial site so that he could bury them next to each other in a new gravesite.[4]

Confucius was married, but little is known about his wife; we do know from the *Analects* that he had at least one son and a daughter. Confucius was interested in rituals from a young age, often playing games using various religious vessels. That hobby laid the foundation for him to master the rites later on in life. Significantly, Confucius taught profound truths about the transformational powers of rites, which he expanded to include moral character, habits of mind and conduct. On top of his scholarly achievements, Confucius was well-versed in military skills; this was evidenced in him guiding his disciple Ranyou to lead the army of Lu to defeat the forces from the state of Qi.

Confucius attempted to put his talents to good use by offering his service to the feudal lords of his day. The Spring and Autumn Period (722 BCE–468 BCE), which Confucius lived in, was a time of political and social upheaval. Appalled by the lawlessness in a society where 'might makes right', Confucius tried to influence the political rulers with his ideas on governance and morality. His solution was for China to return to the 'golden age' of the Zhou dynasty (1046 BCE–256 BCE) where sage-kings reigned. That period was glorified for its ideal political, social and ethical order, and harmony.[5] Confucius aspired to bring comfort to the old, inspire trust in his friends and cherish the young. He expressed his confidence in improving the sociopolitical conditions in a state within one year and delivering tangible results within three years, if given an opportunity to do so. His desire for an official appointment was granted when he was appointed the Minister of Public Works first, and then Minister of Crime, in the state of Lu. True to his word, he succeeded in reforming the state by inculcating the virtues of integrity, modesty, frugality and kindness in the masses. The officials stopped taking bribes and rampant corruption ceased. The people were so honest that an item that was dropped in the street would be left exactly where it was, making it easy for the owner to find it.[6]

Sadly, Confucius's success was short-lived. He left the state of Lu a few years later when the Duke lost interest in governance and stopped paying heed to

Confucius. Confucius travelled to the state of Wei and was employed by the Duke in that state. History repeated itself, however, and Confucius left after ten months when the Duke neglected state affairs and ignored Confucius's advice. Confucius then tried in vain to assume an official position in neighbouring states such as Chen and Qi.[7] That said, Confucius's main challenge was not in obtaining an official appointment in a state. He could have carved out a more illustrious political career had he been more willing to compromise on his ideals and convictions. Nevertheless, he persisted in holding on to his integrity and sociopolitical vision for China, and chose to leave the state when the rulers rejected his counsel.

> Confucius succeeded in reforming the state by inculcating the virtues of integrity, modesty, frugality and kindness in the masses. The people were so honest that an item that was dropped in the street would be left exactly where it was, making it easy for the owner to find it.

A case in point was his conversation with Wang Sunjia. The latter was a military commander of Wei who sought to persuade Confucius to join his camp. The dialogue was recorded in the *Analects* (all citations are from this text and translated by Lau (1997), unless otherwise stated).[8]

3.13 王孫賈問曰：與其媚於奧，寧媚於(灶)，何謂也？

子曰：不然；獲罪於天，吾所禱也。

Wang Sunjia said: 'Better to be obsequious to the kitchen stove than to the south-west corner of the house. What does that mean?'

The Master [Confucius] said: 'The saying has got it wrong. When you have offended against Heaven, there is nowhere you can turn to in your prayers.'

At that time, there was a power struggle in the state of Wei, particularly between Wang Sunjia and Nanzi, who was the concubine of Lord Ling. Wang's mention of 'south-west corner' was an allusion to Nanzi who lived in the private, inner palace with other concubines. The 'kitchen stove' – an open, cooking area – was an indirect reference to Wang himself, who was seen publicly as the military commander. Wang's proposition to Confucius was understood by the latter, who responded that his allegiance was to Heaven rather than to him or Nanzi. To offend Heaven was to violate the Way (*dao*) of Heaven by doing what was immoral.[9] Confucius was effectively telling Wang that support would be given only if Wang was committed to do what was moral and good for the people. This message naturally did not go down well with Wang and many of his contemporaries, as their agenda was self-aggrandizement during a chaotic period.

When not holding on to an official position in a state, Confucius visited various places with his disciples. In his sojourn, he met and conversed with people from all walks of life, and also had some harrowing encounters. For example, he was captured by the people of Kuang while travelling from the state of Wei to the state of Chen (9.5). His life was again in jeopardy in the state of Song when Huanzhui, the military minister of Song, sought to kill him (7.23). After fourteen years of moving from state to state, he returned to Lu at around 484 BCE, when he was in his late sixties. He spent his remaining years teaching and editing some Chinese classics, such as the *Book of* Songs, *Book of History* and *Spring and Autumn Annals*. He passed away at the age of seventy-two, leaving behind a group of disciples who would go on to propagate his teachings in China and beyond.

> Confucius persisted in holding on to his integrity and sociopolitical vision for China, and chose to leave the state when the rulers rejected his counsel.

His personality

The *Analects* portrays Confucius as amiable, kind, modest and obliging (1.10). He struck a balance between being gracious yet serious, awe-inspiring yet not severe, respectful yet at ease (7.38). Far from being stoic and reserved, Confucius was a sociable man who was unafraid of showing his emotions. A case in point was his immense sorrow over the death of his favourite disciple Yanhui, declaring: 'Alas! Heaven has bereft me!' (11.9, 11.10, also see 6.10).[10] Confucius also enjoyed simple pleasures and joys in life; he found delight in applying what he had learned (1.1), being with his friends and disciples (1.1, 11.26) and relishing in music (7.14, 7.32).

Confucius did not boast about how much he knew. He chose instead to make known his passion for learning from the age of fifteen (2.4, also see 7.2, 7.20) and his love for lifelong learning (5.28). His zeal for learning is illustrated in his enthusiastic reception of a dignitary from a distant kingdom in 525 BCE; Confucius stayed long after the welcoming banquet to ask the latter about rites and worship.¹¹ His relationship with his disciples was not distant, alienating and strictly hierarchical but was instead marked by warmth, affection and light-hearted moments (e.g. 5.7, 17.4). Neither dogmatic nor self-centred (9.4), Confucius also displayed a self-effacing sense of humour, as evident in the following incident documented in the *Records of the Grand Historian* (史記 *Shiji*):

> Somehow, in their hasty flight to Zheng, Kongzi [Confucius] got separated from his disciples. 'Have you seen our master?' The locals described a man they had seen standing alone at the East Gate of the city: While he had something of the air of the sages of old about him, he also reminded them of a forlorn dog worn out and addled by neglect 'in the house of mourning.' Modestly declining the comparison with the sage-kings, Kongzi roared with laughter at the townsfolk's depiction of him as a dog unwanted and underfoot. 'That is just what I really am!'.¹²

Confucius practised what he preached about exemplary leadership. His character was attested to in the following dialogue between a disciple of Confucius and a political leader who was considering employing Confucius:¹³

Jikangzi asked:	'What sort of person is Confucius?'
Ran Qiu replied:	'He is someone who will use force only when there are good reasons to do so; and someone who has no regrets if his plan is broadcast to the people and made plain to the gods and spirits. And if by following his way, I were to gain a territory of one thousand *she*-units of household, my teacher would not want any part of it.'
Jikangzi said:	'If I want to send for him, would that be all right?'
Ran Qiu answered:	'If you want to send for him, then [once he is here] do not use the means of a petty man to make him feel constricted. If you can manage that, then it will be all right.'

Ran Qiu's comment about Confucius highlighted the latter's good sense of judgement ('will use force only when there are good reasons to do so'), integrity ('no regrets if his plan is broadcast to the people and made plain to the gods and spirits'), lack of covetousness ('if by following his way, I were to gain a territory of one thousand *she*-units of household, my teacher would not want any part of it') and uprightness ('do not use the means of a petty man to make him feel constricted'). Ran Qiu's mention of 'petty man' (*xiaoren*), in Confucian parlance, signifies an immoral person who is the direct opposite of a virtuous person.

To use the means of a petty person to make Confucius feel constricted is to influence him to do what is unethical, such as lying or stealing.

> Confucius was the first person in China to provide education to the masses. This was ground-breaking as private education was hitherto available only to aristocrats.

His teachings

Confucius was most famous for his role as a teacher. He was the first person in China to provide education to the masses. This was ground-breaking as private education was hitherto available only to aristocrats. His teaching approach was dialogic, where he conversed with his disciples and people around him about everyday life and current affairs (e.g. 3.1, 3.2, 3.6, 3.10, 5.18, 12.18). Espousing the principles of equality and meritocracy, Confucius declared his desire to teach everyone without exception (15.39); his only condition was for his student to be motivated and teachable (7.7, 7.8). The following episode reveals Confucius's belief in the utmost importance of education:[14]

> One of the first to join Confucius was a brash teenager called Zilu, who boasted to Confucius that his most treasured possession was his long, sharp sword. Confucius replied: 'That, and an education would make you smart.' Zilu retorted that he could cut down a strip of bamboo and sharpen it, turning it into a weapon that would penetrate the hide of a rhino – he demanded to know how education would improve his ability. Confucius pointed out that an intelligent man would have tipped the bamboo with metal and turned it into an arrow, implying that education would hone Zilu in a similar fashion.

The above conversation sheds light on the teaching approach of Confucius: he persuaded Zilu of the relevance of education by deliberately referencing something Zilu could identify with – turning his bamboo into a stronger weapon. Confucius's pedagogical method, where the teacher tailors one's teaching to suit the specific needs of one's students, is preserved in the Chinese tradition through a well-known proverb, *yincai shijiao* (因材施教 'customized teaching').

> Confucius was also ahead of his time by not judging people based on their social status or family background, but by their moral character instead.

Content-wise, Confucius taught his students culture (文 *wen*), conduct (行 *xing*), the virtues of giving one's best (忠 *zhong*) and trustworthiness (信 *xin*) (7.25). The domains of 'culture' consist of the 'six arts' in ancient China (7.6), namely, rites (禮 *li*)[15], music (樂 *yue*), archery (射 *she*), charioteering (禦 *yu*), calligraphy (書 *shu*) and mathematics (數 *shu*). Apart from imparting traditional knowledge, Confucius also alerted his students to fallacious judgements and objectionable practices of his day. He pointed out the wrong ideas about filial piety among the masses and highlighted the egregious abuses of rituals by the rulers, among others.

Furthermore, Confucius offered new interpretations to established ideas and even introduced novel concepts and theories. For example, he changed *li* (禮) from a narrow meaning of ceremonial rites to 'normative behaviours', *ren* (仁) from a descriptive term associated with nobility to the supreme virtue of humanity[16] and *junzi* (君子) from 'son of a lord' to an exemplary person.[17] Confucius was also ahead of his time by not judging people based on their social status or family background, but by their moral character instead. The ideal human being, according to him, was a *junzi* – a paradigmatic figure whom all could aspire to become (1.16). That is why Confucius was so keen to provide education for all and exhorted everyone to cultivate themselves to become a *junzi*.

A disputable issue regarding Confucius's ideal of a *junzi* is whether women can be one. On the one hand, the etymology of *junzi* ('son of a lord') has a masculine connotation. It is also probable that Confucius, as a man of his time, had men rather than women in mind when he discussed *junzi*. Historically, the overwhelming majority of Chinese women in antiquity did not – and could not receive an education or hold political office.[18] The exception were daughters of aristocrats who were tutored at home. Naturally, Confucius did not have any female students and had little interaction with women, apart from his female family members.[19] On the other hand, there is no evidence in the *Analects* and other Confucian classics that Confucius's teachings were only meant for males, as the language used in the texts is gender-neutral. It is for this reason that I object to using male pronouns in interpreting the *Analects*. Take, for instance, this passage from the *Analects*, which is translated into English by Lau (1997):

4.5 君子去仁，惡乎成名？

If the gentleman forsakes benevolence, in what way can he make a name for himself?

By rendering the *junzi* (君子) as 'gentleman' and using the male pronouns ('he', 'himself'), Lau had assumed that the *junzi* is male. However, the original passage, which was written in classical Chinese, is actually gender neutral. A more literal and accurate translation is as follows, with words added for the sake of clarity in brackets:

4.5 君子去仁，惡乎成名？

[If a] *junzi* forsakes benevolence, in what way can [such a person] make a name [for oneself]?

To sum up, Confucius's teachings, especially his willingness to teach anyone and his call for everyone to be *junzi*, are applicable to all human beings regardless of gender.[20] Having introduced the person of Confucius, the next segment elucidates his views on mindlessness and mindfulness.

Confucius, mindlessness and mindfulness

A detailed exposition of Confucius's idea of mindfulness will be given in the next few chapters. It is helpful, though, to point out at the outset that the concepts and practices of mindlessness and mindfulness are not new in the Confucian traditions.[21] It is instructive to set the stage for our exploration of Confucian mindfulness by examining how Confucius viewed mindlessness.[22]

> Confucius's teachings, especially his willingness to teach anyone and his call for everyone to be *junzi*, are applicable to all human beings regardless of gender.

Mindlessness

Confucius rejected mindlessness, which is basically a simplistic and rigid mindset. Mindlessness, as discussed in the previous chapter, is observable through two main ways: (1) an overreliance on categories drawn in the past and (2) a failure to consider alternative perspectives and contexts.[23] I shall explain Confucius's views on mindlessness by referring to the above two ways.

An overreliance on categories drawn in the past

First, Confucius objected to mindlessness, where one leans excessively on one's prior knowledge and mental models. He gave his reasons for rejecting rote-memorization:[24]

> 13.5 誦詩三百；授之以政，不達；使於四方，不能專對；雖多，亦奚以為？
>
> If a person who knows the three hundred Odes by heart fails when given administrative responsibilities and proves incapable of exercising one's initiative when sent to foreign states, then what use are the Odes to that person, however, many one may have learned?

During Confucius's time, it was common for learners to commit the classics to memory and regurgitate them. The ancient Chinese exalted the classics as the repository of the authoritative and praiseworthy teachings of the worthies.[25] Confucius was not against learning the Odes from the *Book of Odes* (also translated as the *Book of Songs*). In fact, he encouraged his disciples to master these poems, as recorded in other passages of the *Analects* (see 16.13, 17.9, 17.10).[26] Rather, Confucius was saying that one should learn the Odes *with understanding* rather than mindlessly; only then can a person apply the moral lessons from the Odes to daily life. Confucius renounced an unthinking mode that was over-determined by categories drawn in the past. Although Confucius supported the learning and memorization of the canon, he was not thereby endorsing mindless learning and behaviour.[27]

A failure to consider alternative perspectives and contexts

The second feature of mindlessness, which closely relates to the first, is an outlook that fails to consider alternative viewpoints and contexts. Confucius opposed a lack of capacity and initiative to explore fresh viewpoints based on circumstantial information.[28] This is illustrated in his call for a judicious selection of relevant traditional resources to match present developments and needs. Tradition, for Confucius, was not sacrosanct and fossilized, and should instead be appropriated and adapted to suit changing times.

An example is his advice to rulers on governing a state: 'Follow the calendar of the Xia, ride in the carriage of the Yin, and wear the ceremonial cap of the Zhou, but, as for music, adopt the *shao* and the *wu*' (行夏之時，乘殷之輅。服周之冕。樂則韶舞 15.11). It is apparent that Confucius advocated a fine mix of practices rather than a wholesale and indiscriminate acceptance of traditional ways.[29] A major consideration for the selection is whether the practice promotes virtues and moral living. In the case of music, the lyrics and tune should inspire values such as love, compassion and loyalty, and not instigate licentious thoughts and actions. That is why Confucius, in the same passage (15.11), argued that the tunes of Zheng should be 'banished' (放 *fang*) because they were 'wanton'

(淫 *yin*). All in all, Confucius desired a return to an ideal state ruled by sage-kings, who were known for their outstanding character and selfless service for the masses.

> Confucius advocated a fine mix of practices rather than a wholesale and indiscriminate acceptance of traditional ways.

Instead of mindlessness, Confucius supported and modelled mindfulness. More will be said about what Confucius meant by mindfulness (and by extension, mindful leadership) in subsequent chapters. It is helpful, as a preamble, to make two preliminary observations about Confucius's approach to mindfulness: (1) it integrates Western and Eastern traditions of mindfulness and (2) it comprises three forms of mindfulness: as a trait, state and practice. These two aspects are elaborated on in the next segment.

Confucian mindfulness: Western and Eastern

We have learnt in the previous chapter that mindfulness is essentially about the present-moment attention to and engagement with oneself, people, things and events. It has also been noted that there are two broad origins and orientations of mindfulness in the existing literature and discourses.[30] The Eastern traditions of mindfulness, exemplified by the ideas of Kabat-Zinn, are associated with Buddhism, meditation or contemplation, and a non-judgemental awareness of the present. The Western traditions, represented by the research of Langer, give prominence to the cognitive and social dimensions, such as organizing ideas and making distinctions.[31] Confucius's postulation of mindfulness challenges the above dichotomy by displaying and integrating elements from both Eastern and Western traditions. Specifically, his approach to mindfulness incorporates and harmonizes (1) the Western focus on contextualized judgement and innovation and (2) the Eastern emphasis on constant, cultivated present attention. These two points are amplified in the next section.

Confucius and the Western focus on contextualized judgement and innovation

Consistent with the Western/Langer's conceptions of mindfulness, Confucius underscored a flexible mindset that is manifested in the following three ways: (1) active engagement, (2) observation and construction of new things and (3) sensitivity to context.

First, Confucius welcomed *active engagement*. He remarked: 'Is it not a pleasure, having learned something, to try it out at due intervals?' (學而時習之，不亦說乎 1.1). This statement complements and affirms passage 13.5, which was cited earlier, where Confucius questioned the usefulness of memorizing three hundred Odes without putting them to good use. To Confucius, academic or book learning should not be divorced from application. He valued the theory-practice nexus and considered 'trying out what one has learnt' a pleasure. The process of constantly practising what one has studied implies learner involvement, which is the first characteristic of mindfulness.[32]

Second, Confucius privileged *the observation and construction of new things*. He felt that students should regularly build on what they have learnt (2.11) and partake in reflection (2.15). Confucius's teaching method supported the awareness and creation of new ideas. Rather than having his students rely on knowledge transmission and spoon-feeding, he promoted inferential thinking and engaged in spontaneous discourses with them. He articulated his educational philosophy thus:

7.8 不憤不啟，不悱不發。舉一隅不以三隅反，則不復也。

I never enlighten anyone who has not been driven to distraction by trying to understand a difficulty or who has not got into a frenzy trying to put one's ideas into words. When I have pointed out one corner of a square to anyone and the person does not come back with the other three, I will not point it out to that person a second time.

> Confucius propagated what is known today as 'student-centred education' and 'self-directed learning', long before these became popular in schools.

In this passage, Confucius used the analogy of a square, which, as we all know, has four points or corners. Confucius stated that he would only teach 'one corner' or the basic content to students. With this foundational knowledge, the students were then expected to do their own thinking and analysis and discover the other three corners by themselves. Confucius propagated what is known today as 'student-centred education' and 'self-directed learning', long before these became popular in schools. He desired that his students engage in deep learning, which was achieved when they connected the dots under the guidance of the teacher. Confucius did not present himself as an infallible source or a 'know-it-all'. Instead, he aspired to be a lifelong learner, and shared this about himself: 'I use my ears widely and follow what is good in what I have heard; I use my eyes widely and retain what I have seen in my mind.' (多聞，擇其善者而從之；多見而識之；知之次也 7.28).

Finally, Confucius was *sensitive to the context*, thereby modelling an open, creative and probabilistic mental state. By combining the qualities of active engagement as well as the observation and construction of new things based on specific contexts, Confucius was mindful of prevailing needs, problem-situations and developments. A historical account fittingly illustrates Confucius's investigative powers. A duke was puzzled to find a dead falcon shot by a foreign-looking arrow. He asked Confucius for an explanation and the latter correctly deduced the arrow as belonging to the tribe of Jurchen that lived at the northernmost state of China. A biographer of Confucius elaborates:

> Confucius went on to tell the story of the Martial King of the early Zhou dynasty, who had established contact with many outlying tribes, and demanded gifts from them. The Jurchens had sent such arrows as part of their tribute, and the arrows had eventually formed part of the dowry of the king's eldest daughter. Her husband, the current duke's ancestor, had also received the state of Chen itself as his wedding present. It was a moment of Holmesian deduction, as Confucius solved an apparent mystery, not by hunting and tracking down the falcon's killer, but instead locating him with the aid of nothing but a good grasp of history.[33]

In the above episode, Confucius directed his attention to the problem by scrutinising the falcon and arrow. He then noticed what was unusual about the arrow, and inferred that it was a weapon used by the Jurchens. He further linked the arrow to his recollection of a past event about the arrows as dowry gifts. He also extended knowledge by telling the duke that he should expect to find more Jurchen arrows in the state armoury, which turned out to be the case.

Confucius and the Eastern emphasis on constant, cultivated present-moment attention

The foregoing has explained that Confucius's approach to mindfulness is congruent with the Western traditions, with its insistence on localized judgement and innovation. That said, his conception of mindfulness is not simply Western; it also includes an Eastern focus on constant, cultivated present-moment attention. Confucius espoused the need for whole-hearted attentiveness in all areas of life; he modelled mindfulness when visiting his home village (10.1), conversing with higher officials (10.2), eating (10.10), sleeping (10.10, 10.24), riding on a carriage (11.26) and receiving a gift (10.16, 10.18, 10.23).[34] I shall return to and give details on Confucius's understanding of mindfulness in the next section.

However, Confucius's interpretation of mindfulness is not totally Eastern in the sense that it does not involve meditation; he did not propound formal breathing exercises, body scans, loving-kindness meditation or other practices associated with Buddhism. Furthermore, Confucius's mindfulness, though involving an awareness of the present moment, is not non-judgemental – another feature that is widely attributed to Buddhism.[35] He did not prescribe experiencing the present moment dispassionately or withholding one's value judgements about people and things. Far from being values-neutral and simply accepting things as they are, Confucius's conception of mindfulness is necessarily ethical, where attentiveness is part and parcel of moral cultivation, and is anchored upon the virtue of respect. I shall expand on the moral basis of Confucian mindfulness in the next chapter.

Moreover, Confucian mindfulness, unlike the dominant Eastern formulations that revolve around individual experiences, is inescapably interpersonal. For Confucius, personal mindfulness is inseparable from collective mindfulness because the self is intertwined with others and thus interdependent. I shall clarify these themes of Confucian mindfulness and mindful leadership in subsequent chapters.

> For Confucius, personal mindfulness is inseparable from collective mindfulness because the self is intertwined with others and thus interdependent.

Confucian mindfulness: A trait, state and practice

The second preliminary observation of Confucian mindfulness is that it comprises three forms of mindfulness: a state, trait and practice.

Mindfulness as a state and trait

Confucius's viewpoint on mindfulness is aligned with *state mindfulness*; he stressed the importance of being aware of what is taking place in the present. State mindfulness occurs when a mindful person varies one's reactions according to the specific circumstances. For instance, a person is likely to pay greater attention to one's movements when officiating a special ritual, than when engaging in daily routines such as drinking a cup of tea. Confucius demonstrated state mindfulness when, upon entering the outer gates of his lord's court, he 'drew himself in, as though the entrance was too small to admit him' (鞠躬如也，如不容 10.4). The act of 'drawing oneself in' is to make oneself smaller, thus expressing humility and deference towards one's lord. In the contemporary world, Confucius's act is analogous to curtsying to the queen as a mark of respect. Confucius's response, a reflection of state mindfulness, was tailored to the occasion and showed his sensitivity to contextual needs.

It would be simplistic to describe Confucian mindfulness as a mere state; it is also and basically, a trait. Unlike state mindfulness, which may fluctuate and is object-dependent, *trait mindfulness* is relatively stable; it is about *being* rather than doing. The *Analects* notes that Confucius 'remained correct though relaxed' (申申如也，夭夭如也 7.4) even during moments of leisure. 'Remaining correct' suggests that his present-moment awareness was a disposition; 'being relaxed' indicates that he was consistently mindful in a natural rather than contrived way.

Confucius's version of mindfulness can alternatively be viewed not simply as *an intentional state*, but also *a frame of mind*.[36] A frame of mind corresponds to trait mindfulness whereas an intentional state correlates with state mindfulness. The key differences between the two manifestations depend on two criteria: (1) whether one's mental state is aimed at a specific object and (2) the degree to which one's mental state dominates one's consciousness. Table 2.1 summarizes the major divergences between a frame of mind and an intentional state.

> By his declaration, 'At seventy I followed my heart-mind's desire', Confucius articulated his ability to harmonize his thoughts with his feelings and actions.

Table 2.1 Main Differences between a Frame of Mind and an Intentional State

	Is one's mental state aimed at a specific object?	*Does one's mental state dominate one's consciousness?*
A frame of mind (trait mindfulness)	No	Yes
An intentional state (state mindfulness)	Yes	No

A frame of mind is an overall condition of the mind that is determined by a prevalent attitude such as seriousness, calmness or anxiety. A frame of mind concentrates on the subject-regarding component of one's responses. For example, a serious-minded person (the subject) looks at everything in earnest. In contrast, *an intentional state* is targeted at a particular object and plays up the object-regarding component of one's responses. To illustrate, a person who attends an important function would carry oneself with seriousness, because the event calls for such a mental state. This is exemplified in how Confucius drew himself in upon entering the lord's residence, as recounted earlier (10.4). He was adept at adjusting the level and nature of his mindful responses based on contingent demands. Confucius's approach to mindfulness as a trait and frame of mind points to the subject-regarding nature of a mindful person. Such a person is predisposed to mindfulness as an attitude at all times, as illustrated in the passage 7.4.

A more accurate way of describing Confucius' orientation of mindfulness is to call it 'a frame of *heart-mind*'.[37] The word 'heart-mind' or 'heart-and-mind' (心 *xin*) is a distinctive concept in Confucian philosophy. The English translation of *xin* (心) is 'heart-mind' and not just 'heart', as it captures the synthesis of the heart (affective) and mind (cognitive). Confucius and other ancient Chinese philosophers did not support Cartesian mind-body dualism: they did not regard the body and mind as substantially different kinds of existence.[38] By his declaration, 'At seventy I followed my heart-mind's desire' (七十而從心所欲 2.4), Confucius articulated his ability to harmonize his thoughts with his feelings and actions.[39] The notion of heart-mind accords well with mind-body monism that underpins mindfulness.[40]

The paragon of mindfulness as a frame of heart-mind, or trait mindfulness, is a *junzi* 君子, a term that historically referred to aristocrats and their offspring. Confucius reappropriated this term to denote nobility in a ethical sense – a *junzi* is a morally excellent or exemplary person. In so doing, Confucius discarded the hereditary status of *junzi*; anyone could become a *junzi* through self-cultivation.[41] A *junzi* 'cherishes virtue' (懷德 4.11) and is 'at ease' (泰 13.26), possessing mindfulness as a frame of heart-mind. Such a person acts morally, not in a self-conscious, pretentious or anxious manner, but spontaneously as a character trait.

Confucius's spotlight on the *junzi* as a virtuous person explains why his philosophical thought is classified under *virtue ethics* in Western philosophy.[42] Virtue ethics, broadly speaking, defines the goodness of a person not on the basis of the outcome of one's moral actions, moral rules or absolute moral duties. Rather, this theory is more interested in the character of the person performing the moral act. Expressed otherwise, the accent is on virtues, which are the flexible aspects of our character that are tied to our sense of self, and revealed through our choices and social interactions.[43] Virtues constitute human excellence and advance human flourishing. A person is virtuous, according to Confucius, when they internalize and exhibit humane conduct, attitudes and values appropriately at all times.[44]

Following Confucius's emphasis on the centrality of morality, Confucian mindfulness (and mindful leadership, as we shall see later), is necessarily moral.[45] This serves to remedy the insufficient attention to the ethical foundations and ramifications of mindfulness and mindful leadership, which was noted in the previous chapter.[46] Confucius's ideal of a *junzi* also repudiates McMindfulness that pervades mindfulness in contemporary times – a point I shall return to in a later chapter.

> Practice is a cardinal belief in Confucianism, as seen in the opening passage of the *Analects*: 'Is it not a pleasure, having learned something, to try it out at due intervals?'.

Mindfulness as a practice

Confucian mindfulness is not just a state or a trait but also *a practice*. This point follows logically from Confucius's teaching on cultivating oneself to become a *junzi*. No one, according to Confucius, is born morally perfect. Had Confucius argued that a person's moral quality depended on one's birth, his concept of *junzi* would be no different from the traditional definition of *junzi*.[47] Instead, Confucius forwarded the notion that a person becomes an exemplary person through mindful practice – moral cultivation is something that can (only) be learned incrementally.

The nature and extent of mindfulness practice that one engages in account for the different levels of moral attainment among people. Confucius observed that human beings 'are close to each other by nature' but 'diverge as a result of repeated practice' (性相近也，習相遠也) (17.2). Practice is a cardinal belief in Confucianism, as seen in the opening passage of the *Analects* that extols the theory-practice nexus: 'Is it not a pleasure, having learned something, to try it out at due intervals?' (學而時習之，不亦說乎 1.1). The word 'pleasure' shows Confucius's conviction that we can – and should – derive joy from learning (6.20). The theme of joyful learning reiterates the earlier point about the integration of the heart-mind: from a Confucian perspective, to 'know' something is not purely cognitive but also affective.[48] In 1.1, Confucius highlighted the pleasure one derives from synthesising one's actions ('practise what you have learnt') and one's attitudes and values ('to learn').

Mindfulness as a practice is epitomized in self-cultivation, which is both the basis and means of moral development, authentic motivation, self-actualization and self-transformation. Confucian self-cultivation involves disciplining oneself to develop and display *ren* (humanity or benevolence). *Ren* is about being authentic, fully human and perfectly realized. Although the word 'self' is mentioned in self-cultivation, this form of personal development is not individualistic, but rather, interpersonal.[49] There is a symbiotic relationship between helping oneself and helping others in Confucianism. As Confucius said, 'A person of *ren* establishes others in seeking to establish oneself and gets others there in so far as one wishes to get there' (夫仁者，己欲立而立人，己欲達而達人6.30).

It follows that human beings, in the Confucian traditions, are not atomistic or pre-social, but communal beings who perform social roles. Self-cultivation, from a Confucian perspective, is really *selves*-cultivation; one practises mindfulness not by oneself, but within a community of *junzi* (exemplary persons). Confucius's worldview may be illustrated by four concentric circles, with the cultivation of the self in the innermost circle, and the bigger circles representing the performance of social roles in the family, community and finally the world.[50]

Conclusion

The preceding has introduced Confucius in terms of his life, achievements and philosophy. He dedicated his life to persuading rulers to emulate the sage-kings so as to end the political and social chaos of his time. As a teacher, he distinguished himself by providing mass education, and assuring all and sundry that everyone can become an exemplary person through moral self-cultivation.

On the topic of mindfulness, Confucius rejected mindlessness, which is a simplistic and rigid mentality that clings on to the past. His conception of mindfulness challenges the dichotomy between Eastern and Western traditions of mindfulness. Confucius set forth a flexible attitude that is exhibited through active engagement, observation and construction of new things, and sensitivity to context. At the same time, his formulation of mindfulness is compatible with an Eastern approach that centres on sincere, serious, moment-by-moment attention. Confucian mindfulness also embodies and supports mindfulness as a state, trait and practice; it is basically a trait or a tendency that is relatively stable in a person.

As a state, Confucian mindfulness is about the primacy of being aware of what is taking place in the present. Finally, Confucius's construal of mindfulness is also a practice in the sense that moral development can be learnt and mastered.

In the rest of the book, I shall make clear the notion of Confucian Mindful Leadership (CML) that is drawn from Confucius's thought and example. The word 'leadership' in CML refers to influencing others towards the attainment of a shared goal, through the leader's example and interactions with one's followers.[51] The context for CML is 'schools', which is defined broadly to refer to educational institutions for all forms of learning and across all age groups. In the educational settings, 'leaders' include not just the school principals, head teachers, administrators and other synonyms, but also other staff in the senior management team, such as senior leaders and middle-level leaders.[52] A Confucian leader's aspiration is for everyone to realize moral excellence, thereby becoming a *junzi* (exemplary person). CML, it may be concluded, is fundamentally about *moral influence through moment-by-moment attention to and engagement with oneself, people, things and events*. The various chapters shall explain how CML centres around influencing others towards the achievement of the common goal of becoming moral persons through R|E|S|T. R|E|S|T is an acronym for **R**espectful mindfulness, **E**xemplary living, **S**erving others and **T**ransforming society (see Figure 2.1).

Each characteristic of R|E|S|T is encapsulated by a cardinal Confucian concept, as shown below.

R | **R**espectful mindfulness (敬 *jing*)
E | **E**xemplary living (君子 *junzi*)
S | **S**erving others (仁 *ren*)
T | **T**ransforming society (道 *dao*)

Although the four components of R|E|S|T are detailed sequentially in this book for the purpose of explanation, they are neither mutually exclusive nor should they be practised in a linear fashion. A Confucian Mindful Leader is one who learns and displays all the four components of R|E|S|T concurrently. It follows that acquiring the four components of R|E|S|T is a progressive and lifelong endeavour.

> I have become convinced that Confucius can be a teacher to us today – a major teacher, not one who merely gives us a slightly exotic perspective on the ideas already current. He tells us things not being said elsewhere; things needing to be said. He has a new lesson to teach.
> –Herbert Fingarette, author of *Confucius: The Secular as Sacred*.

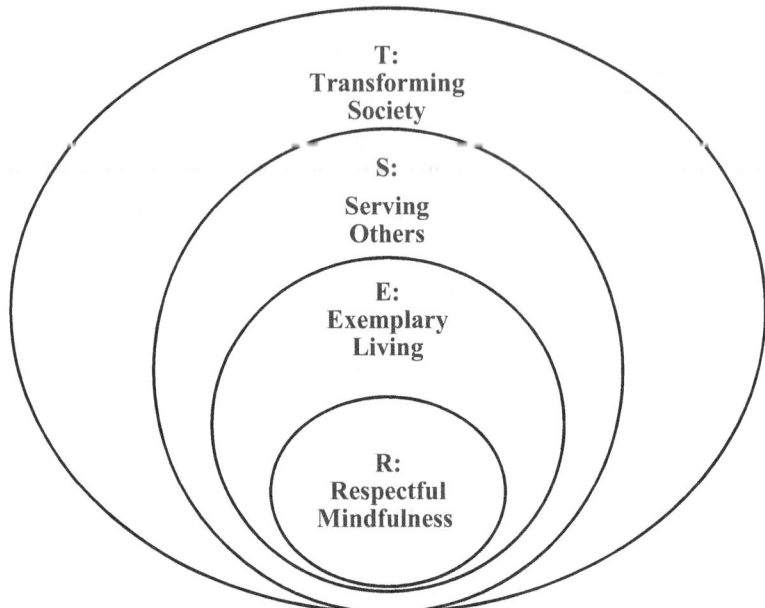

Figure 2.1 R|E|S|T.

The philosopher Herbert Fingarette who is known for his influential book, *Confucius: The Secular as Sacred*, posited in the above quote that we can learn 'a new lesson' from Confucius.[53] The next chapter begins our exploration of the new lessons offered by Confucius, beginning with 'R' in R|E|S|T.

3

Respectful Mindfulness

Cultivates oneself by being respectful 修己以敬 *(Confucius, Analects 14.42)*

As mentioned in the previous chapter, Confucian Mindful Leadership (CML) is about influencing others towards the achievement of a common goal through R|E|S|T. The acronym R|E|S|T represents **R**espectful mindfulness, **E**xemplary living, **S**erving others and **T**ransforming society. This chapter begins with an exposition of R|E|S|T by focusing on the first component of respectful mindfulness (see Figure 3.1).

I shall explain how mindfulness, as taught and modelled by Confucius, is based on and informed by the quality of *jing* (敬 respect). Two points of clarification are needed at the outset. First, although R|E|S|T begins with respectful mindfulness, CML does not need to be developed in this order. In reality, it is likely that all the four components of R|E|S|T coexist at the same time. In executing one's responsibilities and interacting with people, a Confucian mindful leader learns and experiences respectful mindfulness and exemplary living, and is engaged in serving others and transforming society. This being so, why begin with respectful mindfulness? This brings us to the second clarification. A mindful leader is – and needs to be – first and foremost, a mindful *practitioner*. Mindfulness is not simply a tool or technique that is used by a Confucian mindful leader occasionally or strategically. Rather, such a leader begins with, and continues to exhibit, the attitude, disposition and lifestyle of mindfulness. Mindfulness, or more precisely for Confucius, respectful mindfulness, is the basis and engine that motivate and sustain a Confucian mindful leader throughout their leadership journey.

The chapter begins with an examination of Confucius's concept of respect based on a textual study of the *Analects*. This is followed by a sketch of the salient characteristics of respectful mindfulness and guidelines for cultivating it. The last segment relates the notion of respectful mindfulness to the dominant understandings of mindfulness and mindful leadership.

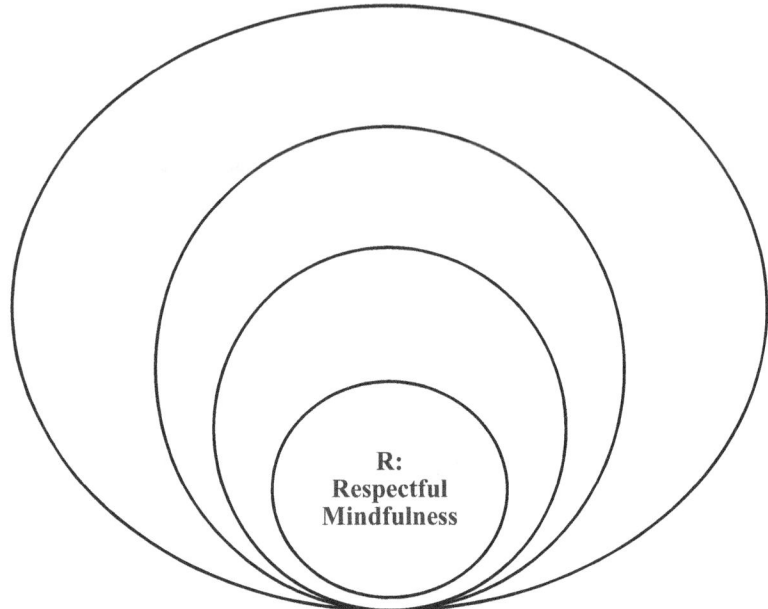

Figure 3.1 Respectful mindfulness.

What is respect?

As Confucius's idea of mindfulness is predicated on respect, it is necessary to begin with the latter. The English word 'respect' comes from the Latin word *respicere*, which means 'looking at' (*specere*) and 'back' (*re*). Originally a descriptive word, 'respect' has acquired a positive connotation since the sixteenth century; it refers to looking at someone or something favourably. 'Respect' today denotes holding someone or something with esteem or admiration, attributing importance, honour and care to the object of one's attention.

In the Chinese language, respect is primarily conveyed by the word *jing* 敬 and by cognates such as *gong* 恭. The quality of respect has had a long history in China. In the pre-Confucian era, *jing* described a ruler's commitment to the ceremonial sacrifice to Heaven and his ancestors.[1] Similar to the English meaning, *jing* suggests an attitude of seriousness, with honour and reverence given to an object. Confucius continued the tradition of interpreting *jing* as an appreciation of something or someone, but he expanded its original focus on actions and consequences to include the character of the person performing the act. This meant that respect is no longer tied to an external object or purpose, such as when one is in the presence of important guests or officiating a ceremony, and instead reflects the person as a moral agent.

Respect, as conceived by Confucius, was also not to be restricted to religious rituals or the prerogative of rulers, which was the historical context of respect in ancient China. Respect is more about who a person is in everyday life rather than purely what a person does only on special occasions. From a Confucian perspective, people ought to be respectful all the time, even when doing mundane and seemingly insignificant things such as eating and sleeping.

> Confucius expanded the original focus of respect in China, from actions and consequences to the character of the person performing the act.

This chapter draws upon Confucius's views on respect to formulate the notion of respectful mindfulness. We have already noted, from a review of literature in Chapter 1, that mindfulness is essentially about the present or moment-by-moment attention to and engagement with oneself, people, things and events. I shall explain in this chapter that respectful mindfulness, following Confucius's idea of respect, refers to the moment-by-moment, appreciative and whole-hearted attentiveness to oneself, people, things and events. For the sake of clarity, I have juxtaposed the two definitions, with the differences in italics, as follows:

1. **Mindfulness**: The moment-by-moment attention to and engagement with oneself, people, things and events.
2. **Respectful mindfulness**: The moment-by-moment, *appreciative* and *whole-hearted attentiveness* to oneself, people, things and events.

When we compare the generic definition of mindfulness with that of respectful mindfulness, we can observe some noteworthy similarities and differences. The first commonality is that both concepts oppose mindlessness by focusing on present-moment awareness. Second, both definitions go beyond paying attention within oneself to being conscious of other people, things and happenings.

However, there are two basic differences between the two definitions. First, I have replaced 'attention' and 'engagement' with 'attentiveness'. The aim is to stress that respectful mindfulness goes beyond what one does – paying attention and being engaged – to one's disposition and character, which is conveyed by the word 'attentiveness'. The second dissimilarity is the addition of the words 'appreciative' and 'whole-hearted' for respectful mindfulness, which mark out a person's moral values and worldview. The term 'whole-hearted' is a reference to the Confucian notion of 'heart-mind' (心 *xin*) discussed in the previous chapter. Confucian mindfulness necessarily involves the complete synthesis of one's thoughts and feelings.[2] I shall amplify the concept of 'heart-mind' in the next section. The adjective 'appreciative' is a generic term that encapsulates all types and degrees of respect, such as regard, recognition, admiration, favour, homage and veneration.

The explanation of respectful mindfulness in the rest of this chapter is organized around four 'W's and one 'H': what, why, who, when and how.

What is Confucius's idea of respectful mindfulness?

There are four key features of respectful mindfulness: (1) it reflects a person's frame of heart-mind and intentional state; (2) it is embodied; (3) it is context-sensitive and (4) it is an intrinsic part of self-cultivation.

Figure 3.2 illustrates how the four features are linked to the definition of respectful mindfulness, that is, the moment-by-moment, appreciative and whole-hearted attentiveness to oneself, people, things and events. The absence of any sharp boundaries between the three facets – whole-heartedness, appreciation and attentiveness – shows that they are not discrete, but overlap in practice.

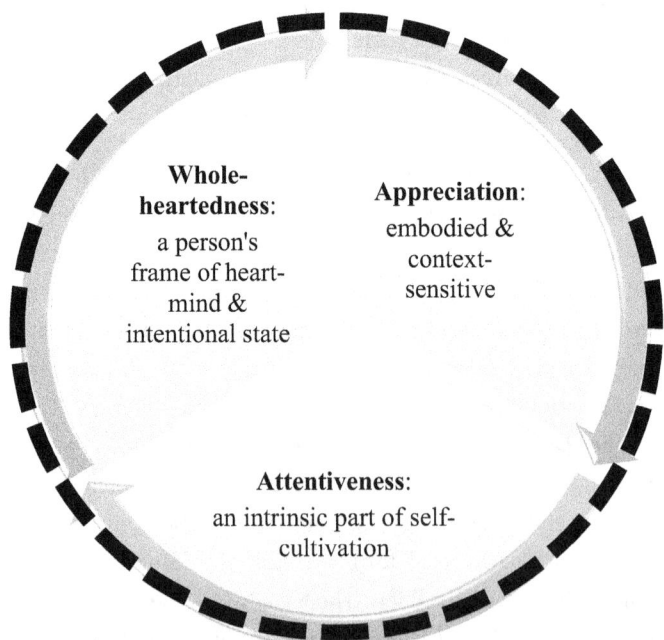

Figure 3.2 Salient features of respectful mindfulness.

The arrows signal how the facets are connected and reinforce each other in a continuous process of respectful mindfulness. Finally, the broken lines signify the time factor: the moment-by-moment experience of attending to self and one's surroundings. The next segment elaborates on the four striking properties of respectful mindfulness.

> Confucian mindfulness necessarily involves the complete synthesis of one's thoughts and feelings.

Respectful mindfulness reflects a person's frame of heart-mind and intentional state

> Respectful mindfulness is inherently subject-regarding – a respectful person is predisposed towards being respectful, regardless of the object of attention.

Respectful mindfulness, for Confucius, is whole-hearted in the sense of being both a frame of heart-mind and an intentional state.[3] I have already discussed these two concepts in the previous chapter. Briefly, a *frame of heart-mind* is an overall condition that is dominated by the prevalent attitude of respect. It is subject-regarding, where a person maintains one's respectful tendency irrespective of the object of attention. Such a person looks at people, things and happenings appreciatively, regardless of external factors. An *intentional state*, in contrast, is object-regarding in the sense that a person's respectful response (or the lack of) depends on the focus of one's attention. For instance, a person who appears before a dignitary would show visible deference, such as standing upright, as compared with a more relaxed posture that they would adopt when with their friends. In what follows, I shall explain how respectful mindfulness, as intended by Confucius, is both a frame of heart-mind and an intentional state.

Jing 敬 (respect), which is cited twenty-one times in the *Analects*, refers to a frame of heart-mind fifteen times, and an intentional state six times.[4] The greater emphasis of *jing* as a frame of heart-mind indicates that Confucius construed respect primarily as a general condition of one's heart-mind (心 *xin*).[5] Respectful mindfulness, in other words, is inherently subject-regarding – a respectful person is predisposed towards being respectful, regardless of the object of attention. As a frame of heart-mind, Confucian respect is not just about thinking about respect but also being respectful all the time, as part of a person's traits.

Confucius exemplified respectful mindfulness as *a frame of heart-mind*. The *Analects* describes him as a person who was 'deferential yet at ease' (恭而安 7.38).[6] The paradoxical coupling of deference and being at ease points to a person who is always respectful in a spontaneous way, and is not self-conscious when doing so.

Another passage reiterates: 'During his leisure moments, the Master remained correct though relaxed' (子之燕居，申申如也，夭夭如也 7.4). The expression 'correct though relaxed' (申申如也，夭夭如也) has also been translated as 'dignified, … good-natured and agreeable' and 'composed and yet fully at ease'.[7] What is portrayed here is a person whose heart-mind is permeated by an attitude of respect, which is exhibited through a dignified and composed disposition. The *Analects* gives examples of Confucius's respectful mindfulness in his daily living, such as when he was sleeping (10.10, 10.24), receiving a gift (10.16, 10.18, 10.23), visiting the ancestral temple (10.1), relating to his lord and colleagues (10.3), meeting someone from another state (10.15) and interacting with people in the community (10.1).

Although Confucius's practice of respect was predominantly a frame of heart-mind, it was also *an intentional state*. Respectful mindfulness, in this case, is object-regarding, where the external circumstances shape one's mental state and affect how a person reacts.[8] An example is when Confucius was at his lord's hall, which was the object of his attention. The *Analects* records: 'When he had come out [of his lord's hall] and descended the first step, relaxing his expression, he seemed no longer to be tense' (出降一等，逞顏色，怡怡如也 10.4). Confucius initially appeared 'tense', that is, serious and respectful, when he was in the hall. When he left the place, however, he relaxed noticeably. His respectful responses varied according to where he was and the situation he was in.

Summarizing the foregoing, Confucian respect is both a frame of heart-mind and an intentional state. As a frame of heart-mind, respect is a distinguishing attribute of a mindful person. While such a person is always respectful, they also skilfully adjust their respectful responses based on external factors (i.e. the 'object') – they manifest respect as an intentional state. In all, Confucius's notion of respectful mindfulness refers to the moment-by-moment, appreciative and whole-hearted attentiveness, both inwardly (subject-regarding) and outwardly (object-regarding).

Respectful mindfulness is embodied

The second essential aspect of respectful mindfulness, which pertains to appreciative attentiveness, is that it is necessarily embodied. Appreciation, for Confucius, is not just a thought or an emotion that is hidden or sporadically displayed. Rather, it is tangibly presented through the harmonization of one's thoughts, feelings and actions. Confucius's visit to his lord's court, as described below, demonstrates this.

> 10.4 入公門，鞠躬如也，如不容。立不中門，行不履閾。過位，色勃如也，足躩如也，其言似不足者。攝齊升堂，鞠躬如也，屏氣似不息者。
>
> On going through the outer gates to his lord's court, he drew himself in, as though the entrance was too small to admit him. When he stood, he did not occupy the centre of the gateway; when he walked, he did not step on the threshold. When he went past the station of his lord, his face took on a serious expression, his step became brisk, and his words seemed more laconic. When he lifted the hem of his robe to ascend the hall, he drew himself in, stopped inhaling as if he had no need to breathe.

> Appreciation, for Confucius, is not just a thought or an emotion that is hidden, or sporadically displayed. Rather, it is tangibly presented through the harmonization of one's thoughts, feelings and actions.

At first glance, Confucius's actions, such as hunching, occupying one side of the gateway, walking quickly and not breathing, may appear weird or even nonsensical to modern readers. His carefully executed actions, however, were expected of anyone who wished to show their respect for their lord in the olden days. For instance, according to the custom of that period, to stand at the centre of the gateway was regarded as rude.[9] A contemporary example is showing the sole of one's feet to another person, which is a sign of disrespect in modern-day Arab countries. The thoughts and feelings of appreciation, from a Confucian perspective, are necessarily tied to and reflected in one's actions. Photo 3.1 gives modern readers an idea of the solemn demeanour shown by officials attending an important ceremony in ancient China.

Respectful mindfulness is context-sensitive

Closely related to the previous point is that the demonstration of appreciation is *context-sensitive*. The ability to express one's regard for someone or something

Photo 3.1 Officials attending an important ceremony in ancient China.

appropriately relates to respectful mindfulness as an intentional state. Recall that state mindfulness is about responding to specific objects and adjusting the nature and degree of one's respect based on environmental and evolving demands. The following passage illustrates this (also see 1.10).

> 9.10 子見齊衰者，冕衣裳者，與瞽者，見之雖少必作；過之必趨。
>
> When the Master encountered people who were in mourning or in ceremonial cap and robes or were blind, he would, on seeing them, rise to his feet, even though they were younger than he was, and, on passing them, would quicken his step.

In ancient China, rising to one's feet and quickening one's step are expressions of respect.[10] We see here that Confucius evinced respectful mindfulness towards three groups of people: the bereaved, officials and the visually impaired.[11] Collectively, these three groups represented the three main categories of people in society: the masses (mourning is an emotion common to all), those in power (who figuratively wear a ceremonial cap) and those in need (e.g. the blind). In all three cases, Confucius expressed context-sensitivity through his deliberate responses; he showed his awareness of his target audience, gave honour to them and felt affinity with them. His calibrated actions were thus subject-regarding: he was conscious of the people he was with (such as with the blind or the young) and the occasion (such as a funeral procession).[12]

To sum up this section, respectful mindfulness, as advocated and modelled by Confucius, reflects a person's frame of heart-mind and an intentional state;

it is embodied and context-sensitive. The fourth characteristic of respectful mindfulness – as an intrinsic part of self-cultivation – will be covered in the next segment.

> Confucius exhibited context-sensitivity through his deliberate responses; he showed his awareness of his target audience, gave honour to them and felt affinity with them.

Why the need for respectful mindfulness?

Respectful mindfulness is an intrinsic part of self-cultivation

The foregoing has noted that Confucius's idea of respectful mindfulness mirrors a person's heart-mind, and is manifested through concrete and situated responses. The fourth salient feature addresses the question of why respectful mindfulness is needed in the first place. Confucius's answer is that moment-by-moment, appreciative and whole-hearted attentiveness is *an intrinsic part of self-cultivation* 修己 (*xiuji*). This point is noted in his conversation with a disciple:

> 14.42 子路問「君子」。
> 子曰：「修己以敬。」
> 曰：「如斯而已乎？」
> 曰：「修己以安人。」
> 曰：「如斯而已乎？」
> 曰：「修己以安百姓。」

Zilu asked about the *junzi* (exemplary person).

The Master said: 'Such a person cultivates oneself by being respectful.'

'Is that all?'

'Such a person cultivates oneself by bringing peace and security to others.'

'Is that all?'

'Such a person cultivates oneself by bringing peace and security to the people.'[13]

> Confucius singled out respect as a determining mark of an exemplary person.

In the above example, Confucius singled out respect (敬 *jing*) as a determining mark of a *junzi* (君子 exemplary person). An exemplary person internalizes and demonstrates respectful mindfulness through present-moment, enthusiastic and positive consideration. Such a person is 'deferential when it comes to one's demeanour' (貌思恭 16.10) and 'respectful when one performs one's duties' (事思敬 16.10).

The exemplary person mentioned by Confucius in the above passage (14.42) is someone in a leadership position, who can bring peace and security to the masses.[14] Confucius's advice to Zilu who aspired to leadership was to start by cultivating respect in himself. A leader should model respectful mindfulness before expecting the same from their followers. A leader who does so walks in the footsteps of the sage-kings, such as Shun who developed deference within himself (恭己 15.5).

How then can a person, especially a leader, cultivate oneself by being respectful? To answer this question, it is necessary to introduce the Confucian concept of *li* (禮). Confucius linked respect to *li*:

> 4.13 能以禮讓為國乎，何有！不能以禮讓為國，如禮何！
>
> If a person is able to govern a state by observing *li* (禮) and yielding to others, what difficulties will one have in public life? If such a person is unable to govern a state by observing *li* and showing deference, what good are *li* to that person?

In the above passage, Confucius posited that a successful leader is one who yields to others and shows deference. Yielding to others is an indication of respect; someone who is powerful is not obliged to give in to others. Confucius was not saying that leaders should give in to others all the time; there are certainly times when a leader needs to stand firm and not submit to others. He was referring instead to leaders who were arrogant and condescending, who refused to yield to others and show deference *even when* it was morally right to do so.

Given that Confucius associated respect with observing *li*, more has to be said about this term. *Li* is traditionally translated as rites or rituals, but such a rendering does not capture its full meaning as intended by Confucius. The following exhortation of Confucius clarifies the quality of *li*:

> 12.1 非禮勿視，非禮勿聽，非禮勿言，非禮勿動。
>
> Do not look unless it is in accordance with *li*; do not listen unless it is in accordance with *li*; do not speak unless it is in accordance with *li*; do not move unless it is in accordance with *li*.

> According to Confucius, normative behaviours stem from and reflect one's moral values, attitudes and disposition in all aspects of life.

It is apparent from the above passage that *li*, as understood by Confucius, is not confined to customary observances, nor is it only performed on special occasions. Instead, *li* takes place all the time and in all areas of one's life.¹⁵ That all human beings should act according to *li* shows its prescriptive nature. It is by being acquainted with *li* and practising it that one learns to 'take a stand', that is, establish oneself as a member of society (8.8). It follows that *li* should not be observed in a mechanical or rigid manner, but spontaneously and without self-consciousness. *Li* is needed for the cultivation of virtues, which are excellent character traits and habituated dispositions. An exemplary person adheres to *li* by thinking and acting morally, autonomously and judiciously in every waking moment.

All things considered, *li* transcends rites or rituals, and is more accurately understood as *normative behaviours that stem from and reflect one's moral values, attitudes and disposition in all aspects of life*.¹⁶ The expression 'normative behaviours' refers to conduct that conforms to a norm or standard. The 'norm', for Confucius, is not equivalent to social conventions, traditions or customs. In other words, *li* is not always synonymous with the prevailing cultural norms, as seen in how Confucius criticized the common beliefs and practices of his time. An example is the widespread assumption that filial piety is only about providing for parents' material needs. Rejecting this interpretation, Confucius taught that filial piety is fundamentally about respecting one's parents:

2.6 子游問孝。

子曰："今之孝者，是謂能養。至於犬馬，皆能有養；不敬，何以別乎？"

Ziyou asked about being filial.

The Master said: 'Nowadays for a person to be filial means no more than that one is able to provide one's parents with food. Even hounds and horses are, in some way, provided with food. If a person shows no respect, where is the difference?'¹⁷

It is evident that the 'norm' that Confucius had in mind for *li* was not based on popular practice, but solely on respect which is part of the virtue of *ren* 仁. *Ren* has been variously translated as humanity, benevolence, humaneness, love, goodness, altruism, among others, and is epitomized by the lives of the sage-kings. I shall elaborate on the topic of *ren* in a later chapter. For now, it suffices to note that Confucius underscored the primacy of conducting oneself mindfully, in accordance with *li*. Given the lengthy English definition of *li*, it shall henceforth simply be referred to as 'normative behaviours'.

With regards to the relationship between respect and observing *li* in 4.13, an exemplary person shows respect *in accordance with normative behaviours*. The demonstration of respect through normative behaviours is shown in an instance where Confucius chided a disciple Yuanrang for sitting on the floor with his legs splayed out – a sign of disrespect in the old days (14.43). In another incident, Confucius disapproved of a youth from the Que village who sat in places reserved for seniors and walked abreast of them – all indications of a blatant disregard of his elders at that time (14.44). The flippant and rude behaviour of Yuanrang and the youth from the Que village is contrasted with Confucius's respectful conduct to everyone, including the bereaved and the blind, as mentioned earlier in this chapter.

> Respectful mindfulness applies to oneself, people, things and events. Confucius demonstrated respectful mindfulness in his daily activities.

Expanding on the link between respect and *li*, Confucius cautioned: 'Unless a person has the spirit of normative behaviours (*li*), in being deferential one will wear oneself out' (恭而無禮則勞 8.2, also see 3.26).[18] Confucius's point was that without the guidance provided by *li*, a person who aspires to be respectful would not know the proper expressions of respect. Such a person will end up experiencing confusion, toil and exasperation. In the example of Confucius's entrance into his lord's court (see 10.4), each location he was at – be it the outer gates, inside the hall or at the bottom of the steps – required precise actions to demonstrate his respect for his lord. Confucius's adjustment of his facial expression, breathing and attire were in accordance to *li*, and testified to his respectful mindfulness. Without the awareness of *li*, one would be unable to show respectful appropriately, and would likely end up trying too hard and consequently feel worn out.

In sum, respectful mindfulness is paramount as it is a mark of exemplary personhood and leadership, and is expressed by observing *li*, which is required of all human beings.

To whom and when should respectful mindfulness be given?

Turning to the question of to whom should respectful mindfulness be shown, the object of respectful mindfulness can be grouped under the following broad categories: Self, people, things and events.

First, respectful mindfulness towards *oneself* is needed for one to become an exemplary person. This involves rejecting an auto-pilot mode and being aware of one's thoughts, feelings and actions, moment-by-moment, appreciatively and whole heartedly. The value of respect in Confucian mindfulness reminds us not to be overly critical of oneself, but to practise self-care and self-compassion. Confucius stressed that we need to be mindful of respect even when we are alone – respect is not just a social etiquette but a habit of heart-mind and way of life.[19] Confucius advised a disciple to exercise present-moment mindfulness even when performing mundane activities such as standing and sitting inside a carriage: 'When you stand you should have this ideal [of being respectful in deed] there in front of you, and when you are in your carriage you should see it leaning against the handle-bar' (立，則見其參於前也；在輿，則見期倚於衡也 15.6).[20]

Confucius demonstrated respectful mindfulness in his daily activities. To list some examples from the *Analects*, 'When in bed, he did not lie like a corpse' (寢不尸 10.24); 'When in the carriage, he did not turn towards the inside, nor did he shout or point' (車中不內顧，不疾言，不親指 11.26). Respectful mindfulness brings out a person's frame of heart-mind, which is a generally stable tendency to be mindful. In being 'deferential yet at ease' (恭而安, 7.38), Confucius's respectful mindfulness was not contrived or episodic, but natural and continuous. To use the language of present-day mindfulness, Confucius's respectful mindfulness was displayed moment by moment, which is represented by the broken line in Figure 3.2.

> Respectful mindfulness starts at home, before being extended to other people in the community and ultimately the world.

The second category is respectful mindfulness towards *other people*. This point has already been discussed earlier, when we noted Confucius's respectful mindfulness to all and sundry.[21] The *Analects* underlines the primacy to show respect to everyone, in both the private and public spheres. Respectful mindfulness starts at home, before being extended to other people in the community and ultimately the world. Focusing on respectful mindfulness in the family, Confucius maintained: 'While at home, hold yourself in a deferential attitude' (居處恭 13.19). Another passage adds that 'being good as a son or daughter, and obedient as a young person is, perhaps, the root of a person's exemplary character' (孝弟也者，其為仁之本與 1.2).[22] Beyond the private sphere, respectful mindfulness should also be accorded to people in the public sphere, such as one's friends (5.17), clients (12.2) and employer (5.16).

On showing respect to one's employer, it is worthy of note that respectful mindfulness is not one-way or top-down. Instead, Confucius underscored mutual respect between two parties, even in a hierarchical relationship. Confucius advised a disciple who was an office bearer to assume this leadership practice: 'When employing the services of the common people behave as though you were officiating at an important sacrifice' (使民如承大祭 12.2). In ancient times, officiating at an important sacrifice was a sacred task that demanded seriousness, devotion and undivided attention. By comparing the employment of the services of the masses with the officiation of a religious ceremony, Confucius was highlighting how employers should show respect to their employees. It is for this reason that Confucius approved of a leader, Zisang Bozi, for rendering respect to the common people (6.2).

In the public sphere, respectful mindfulness is not restricted to people we are acquainted with. The *Analects* states that respectful mindfulness should be extended to all human beings: 'An exemplary person is respectful and does nothing amiss, is deferential towards people' (君子敬而無失，與人恭而有禮 12.5, also see 15.6). Respectful mindfulness should also be shown to the gods and spirits (6.22). In a nutshell, the cultivation of respectful mindfulness starts at home, before progressing to the community and the world (see Figure 3.3).

Finally, respectful mindfulness also applies to *things* and *events*, a conclusion that follows naturally from the need to show respect in everyday life. Confucius's respectful mindfulness extends beyond human beings to *things* such as objects and animals. An example is the following description of his handling of a jade tablet:

10.5 執圭，鞠躬如也；如不勝。上如揖，下如授，勃如戰色，足蹜蹜如有循。

When he held the jade tablet, he drew himself in as though its weight was too much for him. He held the upper part of the tablet as though he was bowing; he held the lower part of the tablet as though he was ready to hand over a gift.

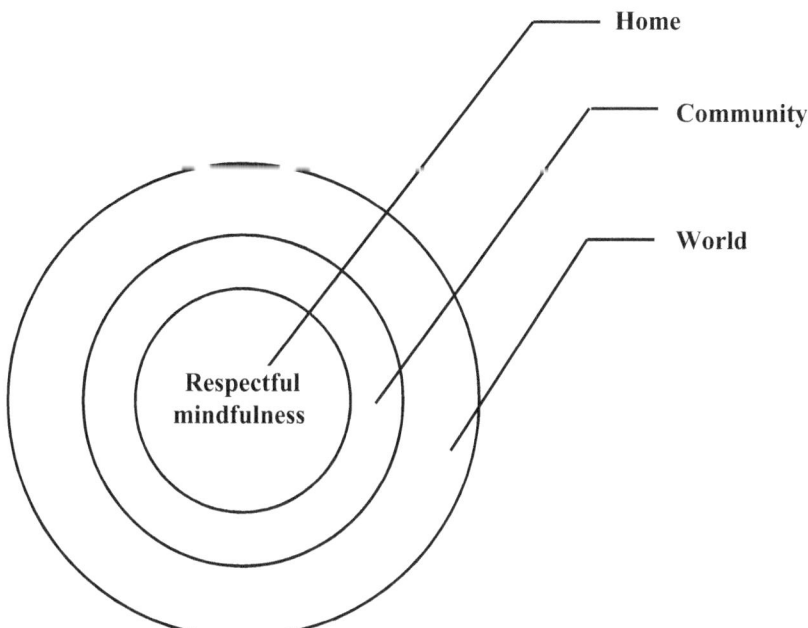

Figure 3.3 A Confucian worldview of respectful mindfulness.

> His expression was solemn as though in fear and trembling, and his feet were constrained as though following a marked line.

The jade tablet was a symbol of authority given to a minister by one's ruler, and presented by an envoy to the sovereign one was sent to meet in a foreign state.[23] In the above passage, Confucius demonstrated the careful, almost reverential treatment he gave to the jade tablet. Elsewhere in the *Analects*, Confucius also expressed his whole-hearted and appreciative attentiveness to everyday items, such as his food (10.10), carriage (11.26), gifts received (10.16, 10.18, 10.23) and the classics (7.18). He also showed respectful mindfulness to animals. A case in point is his treatment of fish and birds, choosing to fish and hunt them using humane ways (7.27).

As for *events*, Confucius called attention to respectful mindfulness when carrying out one's duties at work (1.5, 13.19, 15.6, 15.38), partaking in mourning rituals (3.4), performing sacrifices to the spirits (3.12, 3.17), wearing the correct ceremonial cap (9.3), participating in archery (3.7) and reciting the *Book of Songs* and *Book of History* (7.18).

As to when respectful mindfulness should be given, it should be expressed at all times. This point proceeds from our understanding that respectful mindfulness is a frame of heart-mind. Cultivating respect, as noted earlier, characterizes an exemplary person (14.42) and an outstanding leader (4.13). Although respectful mindfulness should be present all the time (as a frame of heart-mind), its specific form and degree depend on a host of contextual factors, such as the object of one's respect, the purpose, the task at hand and the people involved. In other words, respectful mindfulness is also an intentional state. An example is Confucius's varying reactions, as noted in this passage:

> 10.2 與上大夫言，闇闇如也。君在，踧踖如也，與與如也。
>
> When speaking with counsellors of upper rank, he was frank though respectful.
> In the presence of his lord, his bearing, though respectful, was composed.

Confucius differentiated his responses in the above passage according to the objects of his attention, such as more open when he was with the counsellors and more reserved when he was with his lord.[24] Despite the variations in one's respectful mindfulness, ranging from regard to admiration, reverence and worship, what is common in all instances is a fundamental appreciation towards others.

How can respectful mindfulness be cultivated?

Given the critical importance of respectful mindfulness for all people and at all times, how can one cultivate this quality? The answer to this question brings us back to *mindfulness practice* which was discussed in the previous chapter. Respectful mindfulness that comprises attitudes, knowledge and skills has to be learnt and mastered. Concerted and consistent efforts are required for a novice to grasp and practise *li* (normative behaviours) in a variety of settings. Confucius provided guidelines on how to partake in mindfulness practice, which I have classified as the three Rs: *Resolve, Revise* and *Rejoice*.

> Confucius noted: 'There is nothing I can do with a person who is not constantly saying, "What am I to do? What am I to do?"'

The first step to the attainment of respectful mindfulness is to *resolve* to do so. Commenting on self-motivation as a pre-requisite to learning, Confucius noted: 'There is nothing I can do with a person who is not constantly saying, "What am I to do? What am I to do?"' (如之何，如之何者，吾末如之何也已矣？ 15.16, also see 9.24). Having set one's heart-mind to cultivate respectful mindfulness, the person should then avail oneself to varied opportunities to practise respectful mindfulness towards oneself, people, things and events.

Throughout the process, the practitioner should constantly *revise* what they have learnt. Confucius highlighted the need to 'know what is new by keeping fresh in one's mind what one is already familiar with' (溫故而知新 2.11). Another passage in the *Analects* echoes the same message: 'A person can, indeed, be said to be eager to learn who is conscious, in the course of a day, of what one lacks and who never forgets, in the course of a month, what one has mastered!' (日知其所亡，月無忘其所能，可謂好學也已矣！ 19.5). An integral part of revision is self-reflection, self-correction, obtaining feedback from others and fine-tuning the practices. Confucius asserted: 'If one learns but does not reflect, one will be bewildered' (學而不思則罔 2.15). He added that when one realizes that one has made a mistake, 'do not be afraid of mending your ways' (則勿憚改 9.25); doing so is to 'sharpen one's tools' (利其器 15.10, also see 4.17, 5.27, 7.22).

It is not uncommon, in the course of learning, for one to become discouraged and even to consider giving up. With that being said, one should be steadfast in improving oneself (13.22) and persevere in repeated practice. Affirming the importance of celebrating small successes, Confucius shared that 'if, though tipping only one basketful, I am going forward, then I am making progress' (雖覆一簣；進，吾往也 9.19). Believing that nurture is more important than nature, he contended that human beings 'diverge as a result of repeated practice' (習相遠也 17.2).

Finally, the entire learning journey should be accompanied by an attitude of *rejoicing* in mindfulness practice. Experiencing joy entails seeing the cultivation of respectful mindfulness as not merely an obligation or even a burden. Rather, it involves finding delight in putting into practice what one has learnt about respectful mindfulness. As declared by Confucius: 'Is it not a pleasure, having learned something, to try it out at due intervals?' (學而時習之，不亦說乎？ 1.1). Confucius's testimony may surprise readers who have the (mis)conception of him as a stoic master and an authoritarian teacher who deprived himself and his disciples of pleasures in life. In actuality, Confucius urged all to go beyond head knowledge to enjoy what one does (6.20). He also described himself as someone who is 'so full of joy that he forgets his worries' (樂以忘憂 7.19).

Rejoicing entails not just studying the techniques of respectful mindfulness, such as when to bow and quicken one's pace, but also and more crucially, finding joy in being mindful. A joyful person relishes present-moment experiences, even when living a frugal life. Confucius observed: 'In the eating of coarse rice and the drinking of water, the using of one's elbow for a pillow, joy is to be found in these things' (飯疏食飲水，曲肱而枕之，樂亦在其中矣 7.16). In conclusion, respectful mindfulness is acquired when a person resolves to practise, constantly revise and rejoice in what one has learnt.

> Rejoicing entails not just studying the techniques of respectful mindfulness, such as when to bow and quicken one's pace, but also and more crucially, finding joy in being mindful.

Relevance to mindfulness and mindful leadership

Mindfulness

The preceding has explained that respectful mindfulness, from a Confucian perspective, is the moment-by-moment, appreciative and whole-hearted attentiveness to oneself, people, things and events. There are four noticeable qualities of respectful mindfulness: It shows a person's frame of heart-mind and intentional state of respect, is manifested in tangible ways, is context-dependent, and is a required part of self-cultivation. When we compare Confucius's concept of respectful mindfulness with the current understandings of mindfulness, we can observe certain considerable similarities and differences.

Major similarities

In terms of the similarities, the first parallel is that respectful mindfulness, as forwarded by Confucius, is aligned with the prevailing interpretation of mindfulness as moment-by-moment attention, awareness, memory and acceptance of one's encounters, surroundings and relationships. These characteristics of mindfulness have already been explicated in the previous chapter.

The second similarity is that Confucius's respectful mindfulness, in concert with the existing mindfulness practices, rejects Cartesian dualism where the mind and body are regarded as discrete. Mindfulness researchers have noted how the mind-body divide is dominant in the Anglo-European world, a presupposition that is rejected in mindfulness.[25] Departing from traditional psychological therapies that tend to focus on cognitive capacities, mindfulness-based therapies synthesize both the mind and body.[26] Together with mindfulness practices in the West, Confucius's respectful mindfulness is an example of *mind-body medicine* that achieves holistic healing through connecting the physical to the mental and emotional.[27]

Major differences

A basic difference between Confucius's idea of respectful mindfulness and the dominant understanding of mindfulness is that the former is not individualistic, amoral and acontextual. Rather, Confucian mindfulness is necessarily communal, ethical and context-sensitive. As noted in the previous chapter, the current mindfulness movement tends to overlook value systems, normative frameworks and cultural worldviews.[28] Stripped of its moral foundation, mindfulness practices may inadvertently support or reinforce self-centred values, where individuals privilege their personal wellbeing over their concern for others.

Confucius's notion of respectful mindfulness is not non-judgemental, that is, it is not values-neutral. Instead, it revolves around an attitude and disposition of respect, where one holds the object of attention in esteem and with admiration. As noted earlier, respecting others is a testament of one's exemplary character. Far from being unconcerned about ethics and the welfare of others, Confucius's vision of mindfulness is grounded in and motivated by, respect towards everyone without exception.

> Confucian mindfulness is relatively free of religious or other-worldly claims; it is more humanistic.

Regarding the marginalization of ethics in the mindfulness discourses, it should be acknowledged that Buddhist conceptions of mindfulness give due attention to the prescriptive dimensions of mindfulness.[29] Nonetheless, there are two notable differences between the Buddhist approach to mindfulness and that of Confucius. The first major divergence is that Buddhism situates morality within a religious worldview. Buddhist mindfulness practitioners are, on the whole, expected to accept the spiritual teachings on *duhkha* (suffering), *samsara* (cycle of life and rebirth), *karma* (actions that determine one's fate) and reincarnation, among others, before they can adequately understand the purpose of Buddhist mindfulness and reap benefits from it.

In contrast, Confucian mindfulness is relatively free of religious or other-worldly claims; it is more humanistic. To be sure, Confucius did make reference to Heaven (天 *tian*) in the *Analects*.[30] Describing Heaven in anthropomorphic terms, Confucius shared that only Heaven understood him (知我者其天乎) (14.35), and that the source of his virtue was Heaven (天生德於予) (7.23) He also cautioned against offending Heaven (罪於天) (3.13), and averred that an exemplary person is in awe of the decree of Heaven (畏天命) (16.8). Confucius claimed to have understood the decree or mandate of Heaven at the age of fifty (五十而知天命) (2.4), but he did not elaborate on the nature of Heaven and its relationship with humans, beyond what was recorded in the *Analects*. In fact, he avoided commenting on religious or supernatural matters; his lack of interest in spiritual matters is noted in the following passage (also see 7.21):

11.12 季路問事鬼神。

子曰:「未能事人,焉能事鬼?」

「敢問死?」

曰:「未知生,焉知死?」

Zilu asked how the spirits of the dead and the gods should be served.

The Master said: 'You are not able even to serve humans. How can you serve the spirits?'

'May I ask about death?'

'You do not understand even life. How can you understand death?'

Confucius's largely non-religious approach to mindfulness and mindful leadership, therefore, may be more acceptable for secular organizations, purposes and settings.

The second difference between Confucianism and Buddhism is that the former does not involve formal mindfulness practices such as mindful breathing, sitting meditation or body scanning.[31] This is not to say that Confucius did not display certain behaviours that bear a semblance to the formal exercises, such as controlled breathing and mindful walking (10.4).[32] But he did not expound on the steps or techniques involved, choosing instead to foreground the moral values that undergird his actions. For the most part, respectful mindfulness for Confucius was not about specific practices but rather an attitude, habit of heart-mind and way of life.

Mindful leadership

> Leaders need to start with themselves – by practising respectful mindfulness as part of cultivating themselves to become exemplary persons.

This final section relates Confucius's idea of respectful mindfulness to mindful leadership. As mentioned in the previous chapter, CML is about influencing others towards a common goal by paying attention to R|E|S|T. Confucius's concept of respectful mindfulness, as outlined in this chapter, enables and empowers leaders to go beyond doing to *being*. Confucian mindful leaders are distinguished by their trait mindfulness. I have noted in Chapter 1 that leaders with prominent trait mindfulness demonstrate strong leadership flexibility by maintaining equanimity and sensitivity in face of contingent demands, and possessing the capacity to make sense of, select and utilize information in their decision-making. A Confucian mindful leader embodies respectful mindfulness through moment-by-moment, appreciative and whole-hearted attentiveness to oneself, people, things and events as part of self-cultivation.

What sets CML apart from the existing theories on mindful leadership is Confucius's focus on respect as the underlying basis of mindful leadership. Respectful mindfulness is foundational for leaders because research shows that a major stressor for workers is being treated with disrespect and condescension.[33] Studies have also reported that the emotions and responses of a leader have a direct impact on their followers.[34] This makes the respect given by the leader to their followers indispensable.

Unfortunately, as noted in the previous chapter, the dominant conceptions of mindful leadership are largely instrumental in nature, and downplay the ethical values and attributes of the leader and leadership behaviour. Without sufficient regard for the moral aspect of mindfulness, school leaders may become self-absorbed, and harness mindfulness practices and strategies to further their self-interest at the expense of the followers. For the same reason, a school leader may be only interested in capitalizing on mindful leadership strategies, such as mindful organizing, to achieve high test scores while neglecting the holistic needs of students and staff.[35] Confucius's construal of respectful mindfulness rectifies a prevailing tendency to adopt technical and amoral/nonmoral mindset to mindful leadership in a neoliberal educational backdrop. A mindful leader, according to Confucius, is one who is constantly respectful towards others, and values everyone by showing deference towards them.

Suggestions

> School leaders should commit themselves not only to mindfulness but specifically *respectful* mindfulness. This means preparing and reminding oneself constantly to show respect to everyone at all times, be they students, colleagues or parents.

Respectful mindfulness can be incorporated into mindful leadership practices in three main ways: (1) setting an intention to be respectfully mindful, (2) modelling and promoting respectful mindfulness and (3) creating and sustaining a culture of respectful mindfulness.

First, the leader can lead the staff in *setting an intention* to be respectfully mindful. Take for example the following testimony from a school leader:

> I started leading my staff in setting an intention for the day or week – not what we were to accomplish but how we were going to *be* as we moved about the school. We started to be more conscious of how our facial expressions, our tone, and our body language created a powerful atmosphere in the school. We prioritised the demonstration of compassion for ourselves and others as a tool that gave us the energy and stamina to achieve our goals, instead of prioritising 'getting things done' in spite of our needs and the needs of others. The result of this reprioritisation meant that instead of reacting to student situations, we felt empowered to proactively create a climate in the school wherein students felt heard and cared for.[36]

Although it is heartening to read of the above, what is not underscored is the value of respect as part of mindfulness. It is not enough for the school leader and teachers to 'be more conscious of how our facial expressions, our tone, and our body language created a powerful atmosphere in the school'. Complementing 'the demonstration of compassion for ourselves and others' is the virtue of respect so that everyone in the school treats one another with due regard and admiration all the time.

Hence, it is suggested that school leaders commit themselves not only to mindfulness but specifically *respectful* mindfulness. This means preparing and reminding oneself to appreciate oneself, people, things and events moment by moment and whole-heartedly.[37] The intention should also include respectful mindfulness as a frame of heart-mind and an intentional state. The objective is to create a school led by a morally outstanding leader who evinces and champions respectful mindfulness through the school ethos and climate. Such a school invites everyone to be equal partners and practitioners, who resolve to attain, regularly revise what one has learnt and rejoice in respectful mindfulness.[38]

Second, the leader can *model and promote respectful mindfulness*.[39] In other words, leaders need to start with themselves – by practising respectful mindfulness as part of cultivating themselves to become exemplary persons. Mindful leaders are sensitive of how they carry themselves before others; for example, they are aware of how their usage of digital devices in a social setting can affect their teams. A supervisor who does not give full attention to their co-workers because of distractions, such as using their mobile phone when one should be listening to a colleague, is seen as less trustworthy by others; this in turn lowers employee engagement.[40]

The following is an example adapted from *CVS Morning Pause* by Jerry Murphy, a former dean of the Harvard Graduate School of Education.[41] The acronym CVS represents Count your blessings, dwell in your Victories and show up as your bigger Self. The value of respect, as well as additional questions drawn from Confucian mindfulness, has been incorporated into this practice (see words in italics).

Step 1 C – Count your blessings morning pause

1. Take a few seconds to get yourself grounded. You can sit, stand or lie down. Close your eyes, if you like.
2. Imagine your whole body rooted in the earth. Feel your feet in contact with the ground or the floor.
3. Start by asking yourself, 'How am I feeling right now? What emotions can I sense inside?' Whatever you are feeling, just let it be.
4. When you are ready, shift your attention to the blessings in your life. Ask yourself, 'What do I feel good about? What makes my life worth living? What am I grateful for?', 'Whom do I respect?' And *'Whom should I respect?'* You might identify family members, colleagues, your health – whatever comes to mind.
5. Now identify three persons or things that you want to express gratitude and *respect* for today. *Practise moment-by-moment, appreciative and whole-hearted attentiveness towards these persons or things.* 'I am so thankful for . . .' *'I really respect . . .'* Notice how you feel right now. For a moment more, count your blessings and stay with your good feelings.

Step 2 V – dwell on your Victories

1. Now, shift your attention to any victories at work – victories that perhaps are small and private, such as comforting a colleague in a moment of grief. Dwell on them, instead of dismissing them as we so often do. Notice how you feel right now.
2. Direct your attention to another *V* – your vision and core values. Ask yourself, 'What really matters to me? What do I stand for? What gives my life meaning?' *'Whom or what do I respect?'* And *'Whom or what should I respect?* Identify three core values – such as caring, fairness and

family time. For a moment, dwell on them. *Practise moment-by-moment, appreciative and whole-hearted attentiveness towards your vision and core values.* Notice how you feel right now.

Step 3 S – show up your bigger Self

1. Now ask yourself, which part of me is going to show up at work this morning? My weary self? My reactive self? My small-minded self? *My disrespectful self?* Instead, imagine showing up as your bigger, *exemplary* self – calm, clear, connected, compassionate, curious, *respectful, in accordance with li* (normative behaviours). Your bigger self is able to notice your upsetting feelings, instead of getting hooked by them. Notice how you feel. Now imagine being your bigger self as you walk through the front door at work later this morning.
2. Finally, thank your body and *heart-mind* for all their hard work, and open your eyes.

Besides modelling, the leader needs to *create and sustain a culture of respectful mindfulness* for their staff. All employees need to feel respected by their school leader, and show respect to one another within a safe and nurturing work environment. Following our understanding of respectful mindfulness, the leader and all staff should approach mindfulness not as a private, values-neutral form of self-therapy. Instead, the shared mindfulness in the organization is to be anchored upon respect, where everyone holds each other in high regard. School leaders should also encourage teachers to turn classrooms into mindful spaces.

> Besides modelling, the leader needs to create and sustain a culture of respectful mindfulness for their staff. All employees need to feel respected by their school leader, and show respect to one another within a safe and nurturing work environment.

Conclusion

This chapter has delineated that respectful mindfulness, as advocated by Confucius, is the moment-by-moment, appreciative and whole-hearted attentiveness to oneself, things, people and events as part of self-cultivation. Respectful mindfulness, as the foundation of R|E|S|T, is the first step for a leader to become a Confucian mindful leader. Such a leader needs to embrace respectful mindfulness and continue with the practice of it, even after they learn and practise the other components. Respectful mindfulness enables leaders to strengthen their emotional intelligence. As noted in the previous chapter, emotionally intelligent leaders are cognisant of and regulate their feelings well. They are also sensitive to the feelings of others and the impact of one's responses on them. Respectful mindfulness encourages leaders to show present-moment, positive and undivided attention to others, thereby demonstrating mindful engagement.

Respectful mindfulness engenders empathic leadership that is marked by deep listening, relationship-building and wise judgements. In this regard, a Confucian mindful leader who espouses respectful mindfulness is similar to a resonant leader who is aware of their whole self, other people and environment. Confucian mindfulness also resonates with *caritas*-focused leadership that pivots on caring for others based on a spirit of dignity, respect and compassion. Rooted in love and compassion (the Latin meaning of *caritas*), mindful leaders rely on self-awareness obtained through reflective practices to achieve courage, purpose and joy. What differentiates a Confucian mindful leader from a resonant leader or a *caritas*-focused leader, however, is that the former, although also possessing strong emotional intelligence to connect, empathize with and inspire others, is grounded in and motivated by respectful mindfulness. Having elucidated the first component of R|E|S|T, the next chapter shall move to the second component on exemplary living.

4

Exemplary Living

Lead with virtue 道之以德 *(Confucius, Analects 2.3)*

As mentioned in the preface, Confucian Mindful Leadership (CML) is about influencing others towards the achievement of a common goal by paying attention to R|E|S|T: **R**espectful mindfulness, **E**xemplary living, **S**erving others and **T**ransforming society. Confucian leadership has been said to be essentially about moral influence. Following the prior discussion of respectful mindfulness, this chapter shifts to the second acronym, Exemplary living. The focus is on Confucius's vision of a good leader – one who cultivates oneself and inspires everyone to become a *junzi* (君子 exemplary person) (see Figure 4.1).

As illustrated in Figure 4.1, exemplary living builds upon and presupposes, the trait, state and practice of respectful mindfulness. Being respectfully mindful and exemplary in living complement and fortify each other. In conjunction with respectful mindfulness, exemplary living involves moment-by-moment, appreciative and whole-hearted attentiveness in one's journey towards virtue. Good leadership, as we shall see, revolves around the leader's moral character, rather than his or her charisma, academic qualifications, professional credentials, awards, family background, social connections or management strategies.

A clarification is that although 'exemplary living' is the second aspect of R|E|S|T, it is not practised *only after* one has mastered 'respectful mindfulness'. Conceptually, a person who is new to R|E|S|T should start with learning about and developing respectful mindfulness, as it is the foundation of CML. In practice, however, as noted in the earlier chapters, all the components of R|E|S|T are likely to be acquired and experienced at the same time. The four circles in R|E|S|T do not signify the sequential development of the four components, and represent instead the growing spheres of influence exercised by a Confucian mindful leader. Starting with becoming a respectful mindful person, the

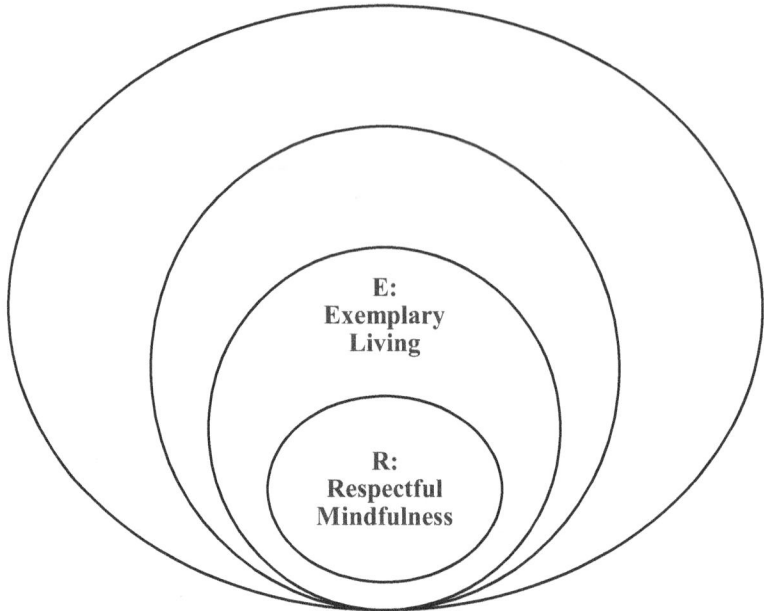

Figure 4.1 Exemplary living.

practitioner should then expand one's impact on other people and finally society at large.

> The focus of this chapter is on Confucius's vision of a good leader – one who cultivates oneself and inspires everyone to become an exemplary person.

As exemplary living is tied to Confucius's ideal of *junzi*, this chapter begins by explaining this concept. This is followed by an elucidation of two vital aspects of exemplary living: cultivating oneself and inspiring others. The last section highlights the key implications of exemplary living for mindful leadership.

Junzi (exemplary person)

What makes a good leader? For Confucius, it was not so much one's talents or achievements, important though they may be, but one's moral character. This is seen in Confucius's declaration:

8.11 如有周公之才之美，使驕且吝，其餘不足觀也已。

> Even with a person as gifted as the Duke of Zhou, if such a one was arrogant and miserly, then the rest of that person's qualities would not be worthy of admiration.

The Duke of Zhou was the founder of the state of Lu and was upheld by the Chinese as a sage-king from the Zhou dynasty. His deferential and sacrificial spirit was seen in how he rejected rulership upon the death of King Wu, who was his brother. Instead, he chose to serve as a regent for the King's son until the latter was old enough to rule.[1] The Duke of Zhou was also known for his talent in consolidating and propagating the *li* (normative behaviours) of the Zhou dynasty. This act ensured that praiseworthy traditions and resources from antiquity, such as institutions, literature and music, were passed down the generations. Returning to 8.11, Confucius's point was that even for someone as capable as the Duke of Zhou, he would not be respected by posterity if he lacked the virtues of humility and generosity.

> What makes a good leader? For Confucius, it was not so much one's talents or achievements, important though they may be, but one's moral character.

To Confucius, a sage-king such as the Duke of Zhou was indisputably a *junzi*.[2] For exemplary living to be authentic and impactful, it must come from someone who is a *junzi*. Mentioned over a hundred times in the *Analects*, the term *junzi* was meant only for aristocrats during the time of Confucius. Confucius, however, ingeniously reappropriated the term to denote moral nobility instead of hereditary nobility – a *junzi* is exalted because of their *moral excellence*.[3] Through his re-interpretation, Confucius effectively flung open the door of *junzi* to everyone; the title was now based on individual merit rather than birth. Everyone can – and should aspire to – become a *junzi* through moral self-cultivation.[4] Acknowledging the ethical nature of a *junzi*, scholars have translated the term as, among others, 'superior person', 'virtuous man', 'morally developed person' and 'paradigmatic man'.

Given that *junzi* literally means 'son of a lord', some readers may wonder whether this ideal privileges males over females. Although the term *junzi* was applied to noblemen in ancient China, there is limited historical and philosophical support to restrict this term to men only. First, the use of *junzi* during pre-Confucian times was not confined to sons of the ruling class only; it was applied to both male and female offspring of aristocrats.[5] Second, there is no textual evidence in the *Analects* to indicate that Confucius only intended for males to become *junzi*. On the contrary, *junzi* was used by him and his disciples to denote an exemplary person in a gender-neutral way throughout the *Analects*.[6] In summary, there are no tenable arguments to support the view that Confucius' notion of *junzi* is gender-specific.

Having introduced the concept of *junzi*, the rest of the chapter delineates the distinguishing characteristics of such a person and the implications for mindful leadership. As noted at the start of this chapter, exemplary living, according to Confucius, comprises two dimensions: (1) cultivating oneself and (2) inspiring everyone to become a *junzi*. The next segment focuses on the first element: self-cultivation.

> The ideal of a *junzi* (literally 'son of a lord') was used by Confucius to denote an exemplary person in a gender-neutral way throughout the *Analects*.

Exemplary living through self-cultivation

Confucius encouraged all to aspire to become exemplary persons through 'cultivating oneself' (修己 *xiuji*). I have already discussed the idea of self-cultivation in the previous chapter so I shall only summarize the main points here. Self-cultivation is inseparable from respectful mindfulness; Confucius states that an exemplary leader 'cultivates oneself by being respectful' (修己以敬 14.42). A good leader also brings 'peace and security to the common people' (安百姓), as modelled by Yao and Shun, who were legendary sage-kings in days of old (14.42). This passage sheds light on the two-fold desired outcome of self-cultivation: (1) the attainment of respect for oneself and (2) the realization of peace and security for others. I shall briefly clarify these two goals in turn.

First, the point of departure of self-cultivation is *respect* (*jing* 敬 as well as cognates such as *gong* 恭), a concept that has already been expounded on in the previous chapter. Highlighting respect as a distinctive feature of a *junzi*, the *Analects* states that 'the exemplary person is respectful and does nothing amiss, is deferential towards others' (君子敬而無失，與人恭 12.5, also see 19.1). Self-cultivation is about 'seeking within oneself' (求諸己 15.21) – a personal investment in respectful mindfulness. Respectful mindfulness, as a frame of heart-mind is all-encompassing; it synthesizes one's thought, speech and actions.

The integration of one's cognitive, affective and behavioural domains is reiterated in another passage about an exemplary person 'appearing deferential when it comes to one's demeanour, being conscientious when one speaks [and] being respectful when performing one's duties' (貌思恭，言思忠，事思敬 16.10). This outlines an exemplary person's appearance, speech, conduct and habit of heart-mind. Respectful actions, such as appearing deferential and being conscientious, proceed from one's thoughts and reflect one's disposition of respect. Confucius was foregrounding mindfulness when he observed that an exemplary person is 'sensitive to the words of others, observant of the expression on their faces [and is] *always mindful of* being modest' (察言而觀色，慮以下人 12.20, italics added).

Guided by respectful mindfulness, an exemplary person does not operate on an auto-pilot mode, but is alert and sensitive to one's experiences and surroundings at all times. The *Analects* portrays an exemplary person as having 'ease of mind' (坦蕩蕩 7.37) and being 'at ease' (泰 13.26), implying the spontaneous display of respectful mindfulness in everyday life. Confucius noted that an exemplary person is respectful in their daily communication (1.14, 4.24, 14.27) and even during recreation. He used the example of archery to highlight this:

3.7 君子無所爭。必也射乎！揖讓而升，下而飲。其爭也君子。

There is no contention between exemplary persons. The nearest to it is, perhaps, archery. In archery, they bow and make way for one another as they go up, and on coming down they drink together. Even the way they contend is exemplary.

This illustration of how an exemplary person thinks, acts and interacts with others demonstrates *li*: normative behaviours that stem from and reflect one's moral values, attitudes and tendency in all aspects of life (for further discussion of *li*, see the previous chapter). All leaders who wish to be a good influence to their followers must be fond of *li* and act in accordance with it: 'When those above love *li*, the common people will be easy to be led' (上好禮，則民易使也 14.41, also see 12.15, 17.24).

> Guided by respectful mindfulness, an exemplary person does not operate on an auto-pilot mode, but is alert and sensitive to one's experiences and surroundings at all times.

Exemplary living through role-modelling

Returning to 14.42, the second objective of self-cultivation for an exemplary person is to bring peace and security (安) to the masses (百姓). A leader who is a paradigmatic figure would inspire his followers to co-exist peacefully in contentment. Exemplary living is not so much about the mission, vision, work structures, infrastructures and appraisal systems that are in place in an organization. Rather, it is fundamentally about the leader 'walking the talk'.

This is not to say that a leader should not achieve social order and harmony through pragmatic ways, such as formulating a vision statement, enacting appropriate regulations and instructing one's followers. The point is that the most powerful way for a leader to establish and maintain social order and harmony, from a Confucian worldview, is through the leader's *role-modelling*. Confucius stressed that an exemplary person 'inspires people who see such a person with awe' (人望而畏之 20.2). He repeated this point when advising a disciple on effective governance: 'Encourage the people to work hard by setting an example yourself' (先之，勞之 13.1, also see 13.4).[7]

> Exemplary living is not so much about the mission, vision, work structures, infrastructures and appraisal systems that are in place in an organization. Rather, it is fundamentally about the leader 'walking the talk'.

It is thus unsurprising that Confucius worked tirelessly to urge political leaders of his day to be role models for their people. A case in point is the following exchange between Confucius and Ji Kangzi, who was the head of the Ji family of Lu:

12.17 季康子問政於孔子，
孔子對曰：「政者，正也，子帥以正，孰敢不正？」

Ji Kangzi asked Confucius about government.

Confucius answered: 'To govern is to correct. If you set an example by being correct, who would dare to remain incorrect?'

It is pertinent that the Chinese words for 'government' (政 *zheng*) and 'correct' (正 *zheng*) are homophones. Through a play on words, Confucius was claiming that good governance cannot be divorced from proper conduct of the leader.[8] The exhortation to set a good example by acting impeccably is a well-established

Photo 4.1 Calligraphy in a classroom that reads 'Be a teacher through study, be a role model through correct behaviour' (*xue gao wei shi, shen zheng wei fan*).

belief in Chinese education, as illustrated in Photo 4.1. It depicts calligraphy in a classroom that reminds teachers to be exemplars for their students.

The reason why Confucius placed much emphasis on leaders being models of morality is given in this passage (also see 19.21):

> 12.19 子欲善，而民善矣！君子之德風；小人之德草；草上之風必偃。
>
> Just desire the good yourself and the common people will be good. The virtue of the exemplary person is like wind; the virtue of the small person is like grass. Let the wind blow over the grass and it is sure to bend.

Here, Confucius linked the virtue 德 (*de*) of the leader to that of the followers. The pervasive moral influence of a leader on one's followers explains why Confucius did not hesitate to criticise leaders of his time for setting a bad example for the people. He castigated a greedy ruler thus: 'If you yourself were not covetous, no one would steal even if stealing carried a reward' (苟子之不欲，雖賞之不竊 12.18, also see 13.6, 13.13).[9] Exemplary living, it may be concluded, is inextricably linked to being a role model; an estimable leader's actions speak louder than words, and spurs all on to emulate them.

How then can a leader be a good influence on their followers? In the *Analects*, Confucius recommended the 'correct' (正 *zheng* cf. 12.17) or expected qualities of leaders. I have categorized these attributes into three areas: (1) motivation of the leader, (2) personal attributes of the leader and (3) the leader's relationship with one's followers. These are detailed in the next section.

Motivation of the leader

First, exemplary living starts with the leader having the right motivation, which is to serve others whole-heartedly. An exemplary leader 'puts service before the reward' (先事後得 12.21) by giving one's best (1.8, 12.14). Confucius cautioned against being driven by personal gain and materialism: 'The exemplary person seeks neither a full belly nor a comfortable home' (君子食無求飽，居無求安 1.14, also see 14.2, 16.7, 17.15). Confucius contrasted an exemplary leader with a mean fellow (鄙夫), who is insatiable. Upon obtaining power, the latter 'worries lest one should lose it, and when that happens that person will not stop at anything' (既得之，患失之；苟患失之，無所不至矣 17.15).

An exemplary leader is not fixated with how others value them. Confucius asked rhetorically: 'Is it not the mark of an exemplary person to not take offence when others fail to appreciate your abilities?' (人不知而不慍，不亦君子乎？1.1, also see 4.14). Such a person is more bothered by 'one's own lack of ability' (病無能焉 15.19, also see 14.30), which serves as a constant reminder for them to be mindful and humble, and strive towards self-improvement. The altruistic motivation of an exemplary leader is alluded to in 14.42 when Confucius described them as bringing peace and security to the masses. The ideal leader is one who cares for the underprivileged and is not self-serving. As Confucius put it, 'An exemplary person gives to help the needy and not to maintain the rich in style' (君子周急不繼富 6.4). The genuine desire of an exemplary person to do good to others explains why Confucius did not think highly of appointment-holders who pretended to be virtuous (12.20).

> Exemplary living starts with the leader having the right motivation, which is to serve others whole-heartedly.

Personal attributes of the leader

Confucius regarded *moral character* as the most important quality of a good leader. Being virtuous has nothing to do with being glib (14.4), powerful (14.33) or popular (13.24). According to Confucius, people can be classified into *junzi* (exemplary person) or *xiaoren* (小人 petty person, literally 'small person'). This point is noted in Confucius's explanation of *ru* (儒) – counsellors who have mastered the traditional rituals and classics:

6.13 女為君子儒！無為小人儒！

Be a counsellor who is an exemplary person (*junzi*), not a counsellor who is a petty person (*xiaoren*).[10]

The only difference between a counsellor who is an exemplary person (君子儒 *junzi ru*) and a counsellor who is a petty person (小人儒 *xiaoren ru*) is not their knowledge or expertise, but their moral character. A petty person is immoral and the antithesis of a virtuous person. Unlike a petty person, an exemplary person stands out for being principled (15.37), upright (3.13, 11.21, 16.1, 16.8, 19.20), humble enough to admit one's mistakes (19.8, 15.30), not gossipy or slanderous (17.24) and sensitive to the needs of others (18.10). Such a leader is trustworthy and reliable (1.8, 2.13, 15.34), modest and teachable (1.8, 1.14, 15.30, 19.7, 19.13), harmonious (13.23), prudent (14.26), agile (1.8, 2.12, 15.37, 17.23), far-sighted (12.6) and focused (19.4).

Confucius himself was portrayed as not egotistical, pretentious, dogmatic and overly critical in the *Analects* (9.4, 9.12, 14.29). He also described himself as one who leaned on *ren*, the supreme quality of humanity that is possessed by exemplary persons (7.6). His integrity was attested to when his own son died. Confucius chose not to show special favours to his son by giving him an outer coffin – a privilege reserved for high-ranking officials at that time – even though Confucius could have done so (11.8). Virtue (德 *de*), as taught by Confucius, is the embodiment of an exemplary person. As such, Confucius praised Nangong Kuo, a minister in the state of Lu, for being an exemplary person because the latter 'revere[d] virtue' (尚德 14.5).

Besides having an irreproachable character, an exemplary leader needs to *lead by virtue*. Confucius contrasted two types of leadership approaches – leading by edicts and leading by virtue – in the following passage:

2.3 道之以政，齊之以刑，民免而無恥；道之以德，齊之以禮，有恥且格。

Lead them by edicts, keep them in line with punishments, and the common people will stay out of trouble but will have no sense of shame. Lead them by virtue, keep them in line with *li* (normative behaviours), and they will, besides having a sense of shame, reform themselves.[11]

A morally outstanding leader does not require 'leading by edicts' (道之以政), that is, punitive measures, to compel compliance in one's followers. Instead, the leader galvanizes the people to emulate them in virtuous thinking, feelings, disposition and conduct. Confucius likened 'leading by virtue' (道之以德) to 'the Pole Star that commands the homage of the multitude of stars without leaving its place' (北辰居其所而眾星共之 2.1). It is through leading by virtue that a ruler inculcates a sense of right and wrong in one's followers.[12] This leadership style relies on moral suasion, where the masses observe, internalize and willingly follow the leader's value system, point of view, purpose in life and lifestyle.[13]

> Leading by virtue relies on moral suasion, where the masses observe, internalize and willingly follow the leader's value system, point of view, purpose in life and lifestyle.

Having said that, leading by virtue will not work if the leader only pretends to be virtuous. Confucius judged such a person to be 'the ruin of virtue', or literally 'a thief of virtue' (德之賊), for stealing what does not belong to them (17.13).[14] Instead, a good leader is one who consistently and convincingly demonstrates the 'virtue of the exemplary person' (12.19). The comparison of the leader to the wind and the people to grass (12.19) illustrates how a virtuous leader attracts others to them and inspires people to emulate their example.

Furthermore, exemplary leaders need to be *constant* when leading by virtue. Confucius taught that 'If one does not show constancy in one's virtue, one will, perhaps, suffer shame' (不恆其德，或承之羞 13.22). Constancy is about doing what is morally appropriate based on contextual needs. Confucius defined it as 'the excellence required to hit the mark in the everyday' (中庸之為德也 6.29).[15]

The idea of constancy as hitting the mark is fleshed out in another passage. When asked about the prerequisites for rulership, Confucius replied: 'The exemplary person is generous without being extravagant, works others hard without their complaining, has desires without being greedy, is casual without being arrogant and is awe-inspiring without appearing fierce' (君子惠而不費；勞而不怨；欲而不貪；泰而不驕；威而不猛 20.2). Here, Confucius expanded on the idea of constancy by referring to five qualities of an exemplary leader: being generous, working others hard, having desires, being casual and being awe-inspiring. For all the five attributes, the exemplary person is able to 'hit the mark' by not over-doing it, such as not being excessively generous to the point of extravagance.

It follows that virtue involves constancy or the right balance of qualities so that one's leadership behaviour is tailored to the experiences of the people and the task involved. What makes a person generous or extravagant depends on the context and other prevailing conditions. For example, a person who gives ten million dollars to starving people in a poor country would be perceived as generous, whereas a person who gives the same amount to one's niece as a birthday gift would be regarded as extravagant. Achieving constancy requires much wisdom and judgement to maintain the fine balance. Confucius elaborated on how constancy can be cultivated, using the same five qualities:

> 20.2　因民之所利而利之，斯不亦惠而不費乎？擇可勞而勞之，又誰怨！欲仁而得仁，又焉貪！君子無眾寡，無小大，無敢慢，斯不亦泰而不驕乎！君子正其衣冠，尊其瞻視，儼然人望而畏之，斯不亦威而不猛乎！

> If a person benefits the common people by giving them things that they find beneficial, is this not being generous without being extravagant? If a person, in working others hard, chooses burdens they can support, who will complain? If, desiring *ren* (humanity), a person obtains it, where is the greed? The exemplary person never dares to neglect one's manners whether one be dealing with the many or the few, the young or the old. Is this not being casual without being arrogant? The exemplary person, with one's robe and cap adjusted properly and dignified in one's gaze, has a presence which inspires people who see one with awe. Is this not being awe-inspiring without appearing fierce?[16]

In the above passage, the common thread underlying all the actions of an exemplary leader is respectful mindfulness towards oneself, people, things and events. This person evinces respectful attention to events by ensuring that they give others 'things that they find beneficial' and 'burdens they can support' on the right occasions and at the right time. Such a leader is also mindful of showing respect towards others by 'never daring to neglect one's manners' and appearing 'dignified in one's gaze'. They will not be seen as greedy because their desires are ethical, rooted in and guided mindfully by *ren* (humanity) within themselves. I shall revisit the quality of *ren* and provide greater detail in the next chapter.

> Only after one has gained the trust of the common people does the exemplary person work them hard (*Analects* 19.10).

In all, exemplary living is about being virtuous and leading by virtue, influencing and inspiring one's followers to do likewise.

The leader's relationship with one's followers

Finally, exemplary living requires the leader to build and sustain a culture of trust. On engendering an ethos of confidence, reliability and hope, Confucius stated that 'when there is no trust, the common people will have nothing to stand on' (民無信不立 12.7). This was affirmed by a disciple of Confucius: 'Only after one has gained the trust of the common people does the exemplary person work them hard' (君子信而後勞其民 19.10).

The establishment of a culture of trust necessitates three measures: (1) replacing favouritism with fairness, (2) promoting those who are upright and (3) maintaining a positive and nurturing environment. On *refraining from favouritism*, Confucius exhorted: 'The exemplary person enters into associations but not cliques' (君子周而不比 2.14, also see 15.22). Rather than encouraging cronyism, which is what a petty person (*xiaoren*) does, an exemplary leader *fosters fairness*. This is achieved by making good judgements (15.23) and upholding justice through decisions such as giving rewards and punishment appropriately (14.34).

The principles of equity and fair-mindedness extend to the deployment of one's subordinates. Confucius averred that 'when it comes to employing the services of others', an exemplary leader 'does so within the limits of their capacity' (及其使人也，器之 13.25). This requires the leader to know the strengths and weaknesses of each employee, and endeavour to bring out the best in each of them. That is why exemplary living is predicated upon respectful mindfulness – a leader needs to be constantly aware of each and every staff, appreciating their individual talents and contribution to the organization.

Second, and in connection with the first point, Confucius placed great importance on *promoting those who are upright* (also see 13.2). As he put it,

12.22 舉直錯諸枉，能使枉者直。

Raise the upright and set them over the crooked. This can make the crooked straight.

> That is why exemplary living is predicated upon respectful mindfulness – a leader needs to be constantly aware of each and every staff, appreciating their individual talents and contribution to the organization.

A disciple of Confucius, Zixia, illustrated this teaching by providing historical examples of how the sage-kings Shun and T'ang selected righteous people for office:

> 12.22　富哉言乎！舜有天下，選於眾，舉(皋)陶，不仁者遠矣；湯有天下，選於眾，舉伊尹，不仁者遠矣。
>
> Rich, indeed, is the meaning of these words [of Confucius]. When Shun possessed the Empire, he raised Kao Yao from the multitude and by so doing put those who were lacking in humanity (*ren*) at a great distance. When T'ang possessed the Empire, he raised Yi Yin from the multitude and by so doing put those who were not *ren* at a great distance.[17]

The idea of promoting the upright, for Confucius, works on the same principle as the leader being a role model. When the government is comprised of honourable appointment-holders, their incorruptible conduct is a testament to the virtue of *ren* (humanity) and other moral qualities. As actions speak louder than words, the integrity of the leaders will inspire the people to do likewise, and keep those who are not humane at bay.

Being upright and benevolent was a maxim that Confucius abided by. Although he eagerly sought an official position, he refused to accept any offer that required him to do what was unethical. In his words,

> 7.12 富而可求也，誰執鞭之士，吾亦為之。如不可求，從吾所好。
>
> If wealth were a permissible pursuit, I would be willing even to act as a guard holding a whip outside the market place. If it is not, I shall follow my own preferences.

Confucius also imprinted in his disciples the primacy of modelling exemplary behaviour by serving the common people. He was expectedly disappointed when his disciples, who were office-bearers, failed to live up to this ideal. A case in point was a disciple Ranyou, who assisted his covetous employer, the Ji family, to collect high taxes on the people. When Confucius realized that such an act merely enriched the Ji family and caused hardship for the people, he told his other disciples that Ranyou 'is no disciple of mine; you, my young friends, may attack him openly to the beating of drums' (非吾徒也，小子鳴鼓而攻之可也 11.17).[18]

Third, a leader establishes trust with one's followers by *maintaining a positive and nurturing environment*. Confucius advanced trust with his disciples by being open, honest and collegial, holding nothing back from them in his teaching (16.13). He was warm-hearted and generous in praising his disciples, and even declared that his disciple Yan Hui had surpassed him in virtue (5.9). The power dynamics between Confucius and his disciples was not coercive or oppressive, and was instead characterized by consultation and mutual learning. For example, Confucius complimented a disciple for enlightening him about the classics:

> 3.8 起予者商也！始可與言詩矣。
> It is you, Shang, who have thrown light on the text for me. Only with a man like you can one discuss the Odes.

> Confucius advanced trust with his disciples by being open, honest and collegial, holding nothing back from them in his teaching.

The *Analects* also records instances where Confucius admitted his errors to another. Confucius exclaimed that he was 'fortunate' (幸) that 'whenever [he made] a mistake, other people were sure to notice it' (苟有過，人必知之 7.31, also see 17.4).

Implications for mindfulness and mindful leadership

An ethics-centric approach to mindful leadership

A major implication arising from our exploration of Confucius's idea of exemplary living is its ethics-centric approach to mindful leadership. The quality of exemplary living counters two major critiques of mindfulness and mindful leadership in the extant literature: (1) a neglect of ethics and (2) the trend of McMindfulness. First, the prevailing mindfulness movement tends to de-emphasize ethical considerations, a point that was noted in Chapter 1. The popularity of mindfulness lies in its potential to alleviate stress and increase employee productivity or, in the school context, improve test scores in a neoliberal world.[19] Consequently, mindfulness practices may lead to or condone passivity and acquiescence, rather than critical engagement and the consideration of ethics.[20]

Second, the mindfulness programmes in schools and other learning organizations have been increasingly influenced by McMindfulness – the instrumentalization of mindfulness as a technique to deliver quick results.[21]

The phenomenon of McMindfulness questions the assumption that the predominating mindfulness movement is really amoral. A case can be made that McMindfulness presupposes certain normative beliefs, such as the premise that success or failure lies in individual effort rather than social structures or family backgrounds.[22]

From a Confucian viewpoint, mindfulness and mindful leadership are not values-neutral. That is why Confucius puts forward the ideal of a *junzi* as a respectful mindful leader.[23] Confucian mindfulness is not simply 'bare attention' but rather respectful attention. Confucius's accent on exemplary living places ethics, specifically virtue (*de*), at the heart of leadership. Research has shown how ethical leadership has a positive impact on the followers' discretionary work behaviour.[24] The International Successful School Principalship Project has highlighted the trait of respect in outstanding school leadership. A prominent feature of effective school principals is the extent to which they are looked up to and depended on by the educational stakeholders in their school communities; the trusting relationships make it easier for top-down decisions to be accepted based on the cornerstone of mutual reliance.[25]

The Confucian presupposition of respect and interdependence ensures that all educational stakeholders work together in a spirit of deference, empathy and harmony. An exemplary leader leads a school not simply by taking care of the instructional aspects of the school, but also and more fundamentally, models and advances respectful mindfulness in accordance with *li* (normative behaviours). Such a leader does not ignore, manipulate and oppress the staff but is instead attentive, accommodating and kind.[26] Consistent with the goal of a *junzi* to be filled with respect and bring peace and security to all, an exemplary leader promotes better student outcomes academically but also holistically.[27] Exemplary leading is aligned with '*metta*-based leadership'; the word '*metta*' is a Pali word that refers to kind-heartedness, compassion, geniality and other attributes that remind us of virtue.[28]

The promotion of Confucian exemplary living in schools is consistent with both the awakening view and the enlightenment view of the nature of mind. Mindful-based programmes can be designated according to their positions and assumptions about the nature of mind.[29] The key difference between the awakening view and the enlightenment view lies in whether the desired outcome of awakening or enlightenment is inherent in individuals, or whether they need to be developed.

Confucius is famously silent about whether human nature is good or evil.[30] His belief in human potential and perfection through self-cultivation, however, makes the leader's goal of instilling exemplary living in their followers compatible with both views. On the one hand, Confucius's belief – that everyone possesses *ren* (humanity) and can become a *junzi* (exemplary person) regardless of social status or family background – makes the desired result of Confucian exemplary living in students and staff harmonious with the *awakening view*. This view, as noted earlier, assumes that the qualities of healing in mindfulness therapy are innate in each individual. On the other hand, Confucius's accent on self-cultivation, memorization of the classics and receiving inspiration and coaching from an exemplary person is in tandem with the *enlightenment view*, which involves guidance from the instructor.

Confucius's conviction that everyone has the potential to become an exemplary person further supports the *developmental model* of ethical cultivation. This approach sees ethics as inherent in mindfulness, as evident in the notion of respectful mindfulness and exemplary living for CML. Confucian mindfulness is the means by which a person begins, and continues to be, an exemplary person who is satiated with mindfulness as a frame of heart-mind and an intentional state.[31] In sum, exemplary leading is not inborn and needs to be deliberately cultivated by anyone who aspires to be a leader. It is only through personal and consistent effort that a school leader may succeed in demonstrating virtue, thereby serving as a role model for everyone in the school community to do likewise.[32]

> Exemplary leading is aligned with '*metta*-based leadership'; the word '*metta*' is a Pali word that refers to kind-heartedness, compassion, geniality and other attributes that remind us of virtue.

Suggestions

This section proposes three main suggestions for exemplary living to be enacted in schools: (1) role-modelling by school leaders, (2) infusing exemplary living into the total curriculum and (3) collaborating with parents.

First, it is paramount for school leaders to be moral exemplars in the school community. An instance of role-modelling is for the leaders to express and model virtues such as gratitude in their social interactions with students, staff, parents and other educational stakeholders. Gratitude can be reinforced by the school leaders through various means, such as setting up an online sharing platform where staff and students are invited to write about things they are thankful for.

One school has started a gratitude project, where the school leaders begin faculty meetings with a gratitude circle, and staff members share what they appreciate or are delighted by.[33] The leadership team and interested staff also keep gratitude journals to record things they are thankful for daily. Extending gratitude to the whole school, the school leaders succeeded in changing the mindset of the staff and students by incorporating gratitude and other virtues into the school programmes and activities.[34]

Closely related to the first strategy is the recommendation to infuse exemplary living into the total curriculum. In a school marked by exemplary living, learning would take place both in and outside the classroom, with everyday life providing lessons for moral self-cultivation. Students would perform every activity mindfully, be it reading a textbook, discussing ideas with one's classmates or helping an elderly person as part of community service. School leaders can also promote exemplary living through Social emotional Learning (SEL) in students. SEL develops students' self-awareness, self-management, social awareness, relationship skills and responsible decision-making, ultimately guiding them to become moral persons.[35] A strong SEL programme also engenders empathy in students and enables them to esteem others and build strong bonds with them. SEL focuses on the process through which learners understand and manage their own emotions, make and attain positive goals, experience genuine concern for others, build and preserve healthy relationships, and formulate responsible choices in life.[36]

> In a school marked by exemplary living, learning would take place both in and outside the classroom, with everyday life providing lessons for moral self-cultivation.

Finally, a Confucian mindful leader should also not neglect the critical role of parents in their children's education.[37] After all, value inculcation does not begin in the schools but at home; educators therefore need to partner with the parents to inculcate virtues in students. Research has reported that the following features of the home contribute substantially to students' success at school: parent expectations for children's success at school and beyond, forms of communication between parents and children, and parents' social and intellectual capital about schooling.[38] Schools can maintain close contact with parents through meaningful ways such as school newsletters, curriculum nights at school and online messaging systems to stimulate parent engagement, involvement and assistance in student learning and school activities. Workshops on respectful mindfulness in general and mindful parenting in particular can also be conducted for parents.

Conclusion

The preceding has explained the essence of exemplary living, which is the second component of R|E|S|T. This chapter has outlined Confucius's vision of exemplary living that is determined by cultivating oneself and inspiring others to become exemplary persons. The foundation of self-cultivation is respectful mindfulness, through which an exemplary person appreciates and benefits others. An exemplary leader rules by virtue rather than by law, and goes beyond *doing* good to *being* good.

Confucius further identified the requisite qualities and practices of a praiseworthy leader, which can be organized into the leader's motivation, personal attributes and relationship with one's followers. Exemplary living starts with the leader seeking to serve others rather than themselves. A Confucian exemplary leader brings peace and security to others through respectful mindfulness and role modelling. The establishment of a culture of trust requires three measures: replacing favouritism with fairness, promoting those who are upright and maintaining a positive and nurturing environment. Exemplary living, as envisaged by Confucius, challenges the predominantly amoral presupposition of mindful leadership and the trend of McMindfulness. Mindful school leaders propagate exemplary living through role-modelling, enacting a virtue-centred curriculum and working closely with parents. The verb 'living' in exemplary living reminds school leaders to practise *embodied mindfulness* by leading continuously, moment by moment, through self-cultivation and role-modelling.[39] Such a leader goes beyond 'doing' to focus on 'being', and exhibits emotional intelligence and mindful engagement.

Having examined exemplary living, the next chapter shifts our focus to serving others, which is the third component of R|E|S|T.

5

Serving Others

Get others there in so far as one wishes to get there 己欲達而達人
(Confucius, Analects 6.30)

We have discussed the first two components of R|E|S|T in previous chapters: **R**espectful mindfulness and **E**xemplary living. This chapter turns our consideration to the third quality, namely **S**erving others. Serving others follows naturally from respectful mindfulness and exemplary living (see Figure 5.1). While the first two components of R|E|S|T focus more on *being* respectfully mindful and exemplary, the next two components emphasize *doing* by explicating one's relationships with others and one's contributions to society. To put it in another way, the first two dimensions of R|E|S|T underline self-cultivation and personal mastery, whereas the next two aspects of R|E|S|T broaden the sphere of influence to one's relationships with others and larger impact on society.

An important clarification is that serving others does not apply only after one has attained respectful mindfulness and exemplary living. Rather, as noted in the previous chapters, all the components of R|E|S|T are likely to be developed and experienced at the same time for a mindful leader. Serving others overlaps with and mutually supports exemplary living, with both resting on the foundation of respectful mindfulness. This chapter shall explain how a Confucian mindful leader serves others on the basis of the Confucian value of *ren* (仁 humanity), which is an all-encompassing virtue that includes *shu* (恕 empathy).

The chapter begins by sketching the relationship between serving others and the Confucian virtues of humanity and empathy. Next, the chapter elucidates how serving others is enacted through two Cs: community-building and coaching. The last part distils the major implications of Confucius's teachings on serving others for mindfulness and mindful leadership.

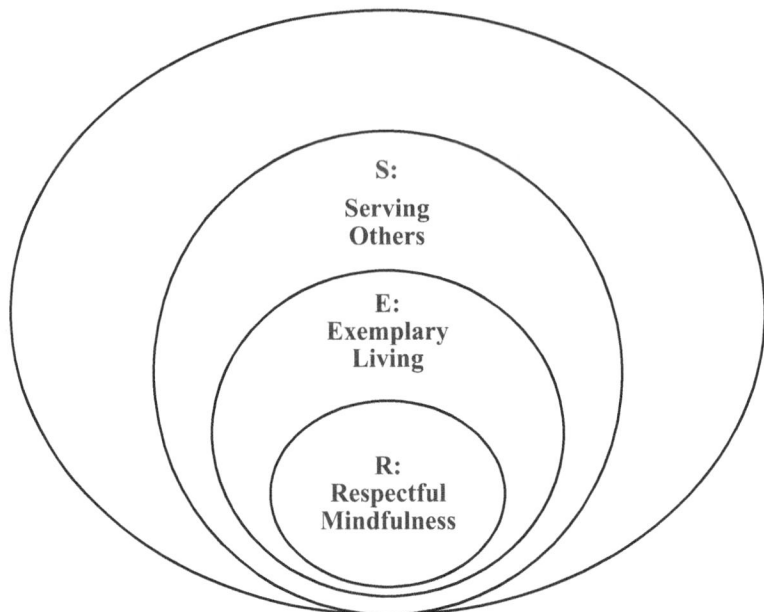

Figure 5.1 Serving others.

Serving others through *Ren* (humanity)

An exemplary leader, as noted in the previous chapter, is not self-serving. The *Analects* records occasions where Confucius chastised rulers of his time for failing to put the interests of the people first and seeking instead to enrich themselves (5.18, 11.17). A Confucian leader, to put it simply, *serves others*. Demonstrating the aspiration to serve others, Confucius shared his utmost desire to 'bring peace to the old, to build trust with my friends, and to cherish the young' (老者安之，朋友信之，少者懷之 5.26).

> The *Analects* records occasions where Confucius chastised rulers of his time for failing to put the interests of the people first and seeking instead to enrich themselves.

Ren (humanity) as loving others

More needs to be said about the Confucian call to serve others, but in short, serving others is not just about actions. It springs from and is motivated by the value, feeling and attitude of *ren* 仁. *Ren* is the hallmark of a *junzi* (君子 exemplary person), as articulated by Confucius (also see 20.2):

> 4.5 君子去仁，惡乎成名。君子無終食之間違仁，造次必於是，顛沛必於是。
>
> If the exemplary person (*junzi*) forsakes *ren*, in what way can one make a name for oneself? The exemplary person never deserts *ren*, not even for the time it takes to eat a meal. If one hurries and stumbles, one may be sure that it is in *ren* that one does so.

So indispensable is *ren* for the exemplary person, Confucius added, that they are even prepared 'to accept death in order to have *ren* accomplished' (有殺身以成仁 15.9, also see 15.35).

Mentioned more than a hundred times in the *Analects*, which bears witness to its importance, *ren* is a central virtue for Confucius. Like *li* (normative behaviours), the term *ren* already existed before Confucius' time. Its exact original meaning, though, is unclear, with scholars suggesting that it describes characteristics associated with the noble, powerful or mighty.[1]

Confucius's contribution to the ideal of *ren* was twofold. First, he borrowed this hitherto insignificant term and imbued rich, ethical meanings to it. Second, Confucius 'democratized' *ren* as he did with the notion of *junzi*. *Ren*, as envisaged by him, is not a supreme quality reserved for special people. Rather, *ren* is an ideal that is attainable by all. Confucius assured all: 'Is *ren* really far away? No sooner do I desire it than it is here' (仁遠乎哉？我欲仁，斯仁至矣 7.30). Confucius's comment that *ren* 'is here' does not mean that we are born with *ren*. What he meant was that *ren* is within reach of everyone who 'sharpens one's tools' (利其器 7.30), that is, is committed to cultivating *ren*. That is why Confucius exhorted all, especially those who aspire to become outstanding leaders, to develop and obtain *ren* (4.6, 15.36). What then is *ren*?

> *Ren* (humanity), which is loving others, is the groundwork for serving others.

It is difficult to translate *ren* as it is a comprehensive and multidimensional quality. In his exposition of *ren* in the *Analects*, Confucius defined it in a plurality of ways. He offered different explanations and applications of *ren*, depending on who he was speaking with, the purpose of the dialogue, the setting and other context-dependent factors. All things considered, scholars have rendered *ren* as 'benevolence', 'goodness', 'perfect virtue', 'humaneness' and 'authoritative conduct', among others. I have chosen to translate *ren* as 'humanity' to reflect the logogram of *ren* in the original language. *Ren* in Chinese is 仁 which comprises 'a person' (人) and the number two (二). It is also worthy of note that 仁 (*ren*) and 人 (*ren*) are homophones. Hence, *ren* is about *being human through co-humanity*. Confucius stressed the identification with and affinity to fellow humans when he declared that *ren* is 'to love others' (愛人 12.22). Speaking to leaders, as signified by his mention of people who are 'guiding a state of a thousand chariots' (道千乘之國), Confucius exhorted them to 'love the people' (愛人 1.5, also see 1.6). In the main, *ren*, which is loving others, is the precursor to serving others.

Linking *ren* to the service of others means that love, for Confucius, is not a fuzzy, volatile feeling towards people. Instead, *ren* is an attitude, tendency and motivation that is manifested through acts of service. Confucius advised a disciple on *ren* leadership:

17.6 子張問「仁」於孔子。

孔子曰：「能行五者於天下，為仁矣。」

「請問之？」

曰：「恭、寬、信、敏、惠：恭則不侮，寬則得眾，信則人任焉，敏則有功，惠則足以使人。」

Zizhang asked Confucius about *ren* (humanity).

Confucius said: 'There are five things and whoever is capable of putting them into practice in the Empire is certainly *ren*'.

'May I ask what they are?'

'They are deference, tolerance, trustworthiness in word, diligence and generosity. If a person is deferential, such a one will not be treated with insolence. If a person is tolerant, such a one will win the multitude. If a person is trustworthy in word, others will entrust such a one with responsibility. If a person is diligent, such a one will achieve results. If a person is generous, such a one will be good enough to be put in a position over others.'[2]

Confucius's counsel in the above passage was meant for leaders, as he referred to putting in place five things 'in the Empire', that is, within the territory governed by a ruler. It is noteworthy that *ren* has nothing to do with a leader's academic credentials, material possessions, professional knowledge or organizational expertise.[3] Elsewhere, Confucius maintained that *ren* has nothing to do with leadership capabilities, such as 'managing the military levies in a state of a thousand chariots' (千乘之國，可使治其賦也), being 'a steward in a town with a thousand households or in a noble family with a hundred chariots' (千室之邑，百乘之家，可使為之宰也) or 'conversing with the guests' (可使與賓客言也 5.8, also see 5.19). This is not to say that the aforementioned competences are unimportant for responsible and effective leadership. Confucius's emphasis, rather, was that *ren* leadership, taken as a whole, is about a person's moral character, which is authenticated through their actions.

Returning to 17.6, *ren* is an all-inclusive virtue that includes, among others, deference, tolerance, trustworthiness, diligence and generosity. The reference to deference 恭 (*gong*) reminds us of the attribute of respectful mindfulness, which is the starting point of a Confucian mindful leader. Besides these five qualities highlighted in 17.6, other desirable attributes of *ren* include sincerity, reverence, dutifulness and empathy (12.2), courage (14.4), strength, decisiveness, simplicity and deliberateness in speech (13.27; also see 1.3, 12.2, 17.17). To conclude this segment, *ren* is humanity and is comprised of a cluster of moral values that are identifiable through one's attitude, disposition and behaviour.

> Confucius's message was that humane (*ren*) leadership, taken as a whole, is about a person's moral character, which is authenticated through their actions.

Ren (humanity) and mindfulness

Relating *ren* to mindfulness, *ren* is both a frame of heart-mind and an intentional state. As a *frame of heart-mind*, *ren* is a pervasive attitude and disposition of loving others, regardless of changing circumstances. Confucius noted that 'an exemplary person never deserts *ren*, not even for the time it takes to eat a meal' (君子無終食之間違仁 4.5). Governed by *ren* as trait mindfulness, such a person enjoys safety (4.2), joy (6.23) and freedom from worries (9.29). The spontaneous and stable character of *ren* makes such a person appealing (4.1), keen to learn (17.8), steadfast (6.22), long-suffering (14.9) and free from evil (4.4).

Ren is also an *intentional state*: a *ren* person is adept at loving others in diverse ways and to varying degrees. To cite an example, the love a *ren* leader has for their followers differs from the love the same person has for their parents. *Ren* as state mindfulness reminds us of, and goes hand in hand with, *li* (normative behaviours). Confucius underlined the intertwined relationship between *ren* and *li* when he asked rhetorically, 'What can a person do with *li* who is not *ren*?' (人而不仁，如禮何 3.3). A *ren* person is mindful of responding appropriately to the object of one's attention by thinking, feeling and acting according with *li* (normative behaviours). Returning to 17.6 cited earlier, a *ren* person may express love for another person by showing deference, tolerance, trustworthiness in word, diligence or generosity, depending on who one is with and the circumstantial needs. Such a person may also demonstrate other aspects of *ren*, such as discernment (4.3, 6.26), wisdom (14.31) and courage (14.4) as they see fit.

Taking everything into account, *ren* is a frame of heart-mind that predisposes a person to love others, as well as an intentional state that enables one to be mindful of how and when to express love in specific situations.

Shu (empathy)

Among the attributes of *ren*, a quality that is closely associated with the love of others and integral to the service of others is *shu* (恕). *Shu* is highlighted by Confucius in this passage:

> 15.24 子貢問曰：「有一言而可以終身行之者乎？」
> 子曰：「其恕乎！己所不欲，勿施於人。」
>
> Zigong asked: 'Is there a single word which can be a guide to conduct throughout one's life?'
>
> The Master said: 'It is perhaps the word *shu* (empathy). Do not impose on others what you yourself do not desire.'

Shu 恕 has been variously translated as 'using oneself as a measure to gauge the likes and dislikes of others', 'putting oneself in the other's place' and 'understanding', among others.[4] Regardless of the different interpretations, the consensus is that *shu* revolves around a thoughtful consideration of others based on the principle of reciprocity.[5] I have henceforth rendered *shu* simply as empathy.

> Confucian empathy revolves around a thoughtful consideration of others based on the principle of reciprocity.

Confucius's notion of empathy is not a passive one, despite the impression given in the above passage ('Do not …'). Rather, his concept of empathy requires active participation, where a person uses oneself as a measure when relating with others and responding to them. Confucius elaborated on this approach:

> 6.30 夫仁者，己欲立而立人，己欲達而達人。能近取譬，可謂仁之方也已。
>
> A person of *ren* establishes others in seeking to establish oneself and gets others there in so far as one wishes to get there. The ability to take as analogy what is near at hand can be called the method of *ren*.

In the above passage, 'to take as analogy' refers to comparing oneself with another person. The expression 'what is near' denotes one's own thoughts, feelings and actions. Hence, the clause 'the ability to take as analogy what is near at hand' points to using oneself as a benchmark to understand others, which is essentially what empathy is about.[6]

The cognitive, affective and moral dimensions of empathy

Shu, as the extension of self to others, encompasses the cognitive, affective and moral dimensions of empathy. Cognitively, *shu* involves *perspective taking*, where a person places themselves in the shoes of another person, so as to appreciate what the latter thinks or feels.[7] *Shu* also includes *affective empathy*, also known as emotional contagion, where one feels how another person feels, although not necessarily with the same intensity.[8] Finally, *shu* brings to the fore the moral dimension of empathy, also known as *empathic concern* that signals one's motivation to care for the welfare of others.[9] Empathic concern generates altruistically motivated behaviour by producing shared feelings and prompting an intrinsic desire to alleviate the suffering of others.[10]

Returning to 6.30, the overall message is about going beyond one's personal interests to care for and further the interests of others.[11] A *ren* person loves others by wishing for others what they wish for themselves, and establishing others in the same way they establish themselves. The Chinese word 立 (*li*) for 'establish' in 6.30 is literally 'take a stand', which is a Confucian expression for observing *li* (normative behaviours) (c.f. 8.8, 14.14).[12] Hence, 6.30 means that those who wish to conduct themselves morally must enable others to do likewise. Another passage reiterates that loving others entails 'helping others to be their best, not their worst' (成人之美，不成人之惡) (12.16). The central theme of

Confucius is that empathy is necessary for a person of *ren* to serve others within a network of intertwined interests. Putting together 15.24 and 6.30, *shu* refers to extending the love for oneself to others, by correlating one's thoughts, feelings and experiences with those of others.[13]

> A humane (*ren*) person loves others by wishing for others what they wish for themselves, and establishing others in the same way they establish themselves.

Confucius also stressed that a *ren* person would practise *shu* whole-heartedly, as captured by the value of *zhong* 忠 (doing one's best). Sharing about his own approach, Confucius pointed out that *shu* (empathy) and *zhong* (doing one's best) combine to form a 'single thread' that 'binds my way together' (吾道一以貫之 also see 15.3). *Zhong* refers to carrying out one's duties to the best of one's abilities. By linking *zhong* to empathy, Confucius brought home the idea of being committed to benefit others in the same way as one would benefit oneself (6.30). In summary, *shu*, complemented by *zhong*, inspires all human beings to help each other and develop *ren* in their thoughts, feelings, and actions mindfully, enthusiastically and consistently.

The example of Confucius

Confucius demonstrated and advanced the traits of *ren* (humanity) and *shu* (empathy) in his encounters with people. A representative example was how he showed great sensitivity and consideration to a blind musician, as detailed in the following passage:

> 15.42 師冕見。及階，子曰：「階也！」及席，子曰：「席也！」皆坐，子告之曰：「某在斯！某在斯！」師冕出，子張問曰：「與師言之道與？」子曰：「然，固相師之道也。」

> Mian, the Master Musician, called. When he came to the steps, the Master said, 'You have reached the steps', and when he came to the mat, the Master said, 'You have reached the mat.' When everyone was seated, the Master told him: 'This is So-and-so here and that is So-and-so over there.' After the Master Musician had gone, Zizhang asked: 'Is that the way to talk to a musician?' The Master said: 'Yes. That is the way to assist a musician.'

In the above passage, Zizhang was prompted to ask a question as he observed that Confucius had gone to great lengths to attend to the blind musician. Confucius demonstrated respectful mindfulness towards the blind musician, which is a manifestation of his *ren* (his love for the blind musician).¹⁴

> Whenever a friend died who had no kin to whom his body could be taken, Confucius said, 'Let him be given a funeral from my house' (*Analects* 10.17).

In another episode, when Confucius realized that Zilu, a disciple of his, was despised by other disciples, he made a special effort to praise Zilu in front of the other disciples (11.15). Confucius's action was driven by his empathy for Zilu and his desire to help the latter gain the acceptance of other disciples. Confucius also encouraged people around him to practise humanity. For example, he urged his steward, who had been given 900 measures of grain – a significant amount at that time – to share them with his neighbours (6.5). Confucius's empathic concern for others, especially the underprivileged, is illustrated in this passage: 'Whenever a friend died who had no kin to whom his body could be taken, he [Confucius] said, "Let him be given a funeral from my house"' (朋友死，無所歸，曰：「於我殯。」10.17).

Confucius's kindness and compassion extended to people whom he did not know personally. In an incident where Confucius learnt that the stables had caught fire, his immediate response was to ask if anyone had been injured (10.17). This shows his love and care for fellow human beings. Confucius also exemplified thoughtful consideration for people who were unpopular, as seen in the following passage:

> 7.29 互鄉難與言，童子見，門人惑。子曰：「與其進也，不與其退也，唯何甚？人潔己以進，與其潔也，不保其往也。」

> People of Hu Hsiang were difficult to talk to. A boy was received and the disciples were perplexed. The Master said: 'Approval of his coming does not mean approval of him when he is not here. Why should we be so exacting? When a man comes after having purified himself, we approve of his purification but we cannot vouch for his past.'

In the above passage, Confucius's action illustrates the two dimensions of empathy: not imposing on others what you yourself do not desire (15.24) and helping others to take their stand (6.30). First, Confucius was willing to receive the boy despite the reservations of his disciples. Confucius told his disciples to not be so judgemental and to welcome the boy instead. After all, the boy had already done what was required for the occasion in ancient China, which was to purify himself when asking a Master for teaching.[15] We see here that Confucius extended his goodwill to the young visitor by being willing to assist the boy to take a stand, that is, improve himself and behave normatively. Second, Confucius exercised empathy by refraining from being too exacting, as this was what he did not wish others to do to him too. He was effectively practising what he preached about 'not imposing on others what you yourself do not desire' (15.24).

Having analysed the Confucian concepts of *ren* (humanity) and *shu* (empathy), the next section elucidates how a mindful leader may serve others by being grounded in and motivated by these two ideals. Specifically, I shall explain how serving others is enacted through two Cs: (1) community-building and (2) coaching.

> The concept of a good life, for Confucius, is not pre-social, atomistic and individualistic. Rather, human flourishing presupposes a community of virtuous people united by harmony.

Community-building

Guided by humanity and empathy, an exemplary leader builds and sustains a *community of exemplary persons*. From a Confucian viewpoint, a person cannot be an exemplary person without support from like-minded people. The *Analects* states that an exemplary person 'looks to friends for support in *ren*' (以友輔仁 12.24). The concept of a good life, for Confucius, is not pre-social, atomistic and individualistic. Rather, human flourishing presupposes a community of virtuous people united by *he* (harmony 和). Described as the 'most valuable' (為貴) and 'most beautiful' (斯為美), harmony is 'followed alike in matters great and small' (小大由之) by the Former Kings (1.12). The Former Kings were the sage-kings in ancient times, such as Yao and the rulers from the Xia, Shang and Zhou dynasties. They were commended for making possible a peaceful and cohesive state of affairs in days of old.

Confucius focused attention on the need for human beings to coexist peacefully, purposefully and joyfully as a body.[16] Pointing out that 'virtue never stands alone; it is bound to have neighbours' (德不孤，必有鄰 4.25), Confucius celebrated the joy of having virtuous friends (1.1, 12.5, 16.4). The goal of a leader, it follows, is to establish a community of exemplary persons (*junzi*) who serve one another, and collectively practise, model and foster humanity and empathy. The picture of harmony and community is portrayed in Photo 5.1 that shows a group of learners practising Chinese calligraphy mindfully, looking at each other's writing and learning from one other.

It is important to note that harmony is not about homogeneity.[17] Confucius rejected uniformity by claiming that 'the exemplary person seeks harmony, not sameness' (君子和而不同13.23). Returning to Photo 5.1, all the learners may write the same Chinese characters in calligraphy but the stylized artistic writing each learner produced is unique. Confucian harmony is about collaboration by harnessing each individual's unique strengths so as to achieve a common objective. The etymology of *he* (harmony) is music, where different chords are perfectly combined to form a majestic composition.[18] Confucius explained the link between music and harmony:

3.23   子語魯大師樂，曰：「樂其可知也：始作，翕如也；從之，純如也，皦如也，繹如也，以成。」

Photo 5.1 A community of learners in ancient China.

The Master talked of music to the Grand Musician of Lu, saying, 'This much can be known about music. It begins with playing in unison. When it gets into full swing, it is harmonious, clear and unbroken. In this way it reaches the conclusion.'

In a performance, musicians who 'play in unison' may not necessarily be playing the same musical instruments or identical musical notes. Instead, they specialize in playing different instruments and are responsible for specific sections of the score. It is precisely because of their differentiation that they can come together to produce stirring music through harmonization. Continuing with the analogy of music, a harmonious community is likened to singing in unison. The *Analects* records Confucius who, upon hearing someone sing, asked to hear it again before joining in the singing (7.32). He also showed the powerful influence of the community when commenting on the outstanding character of a person from the state of Lu:

5.3 君子哉若人！魯無君子者，斯焉取斯？

What an exemplary person this man [Zijian] is! If there were no exemplary person in Lu, where could he have acquired his qualities?

Zijian was a governor of Shan Fu from the state of Lu, a place known for its righteous people. Confucius's argument was that Zijian's model behaviour was, to a large extent, due to the excellent example set by his peers in Lu. Besides influencing each other through moral conduct, exemplary persons also support one another through team work, for instance, when a group completes a project by capitalizing on its members' strengths.[19] Confucius gave this example: 'In composing the text of a treaty, P'i Ch'en would write the draft, Shih Shu would make comments, Tzu-yu, the master of protocol, would touch it up and Tzu-ch'an of Tung Li would make embellishments' (為命：裨諶草創之，世叔討論之，行人子羽修飾之，東里子產潤色之 14.8).[20]

How then does an exemplary leader establish and nurture a community of like-minded people? This is attained through three main ways: (1) role-modelling, (2) promoting self-reflection and (3) advancing mutual learning. These three aspects are elaborated on in the next section.

> Besides influencing each other through moral conduct, exemplary persons also support one another through team work, for instance, when a group completes a project by capitalizing on its members' strengths.

Role-modelling

First, a leader builds a community of exemplary persons by role-modelling virtuous conduct. The idea of role-modelling has already been covered in the previous chapter. Serving others is premised on a leader acting as a paragon of morality. Such a leader treats others with kindness (2.20), values the abilities of their followers (1.6, 16.5), helps others realize what is good in them (12.16), does not show favouritism (15.22, 20.1), sets strict standards for themselves (15.15), makes allowances for others (15.15) and employs people at the right time (1.5).

Role-modelling is underpinned by respectful mindfulness towards others. It is not possible to treat another person with kindness if one is not attentive to and appreciative of that person in the first place. Confucius reinforced the importance of mindful observing, seeing, listening and acting in his advice to a disciple who was seeking a career as an official:

2.18　多聞闕疑，慎言其餘，則寡尤。多見闕殆，慎行其餘，則寡悔。言寡尤，行寡悔，祿在其中矣。

Listen widely but leave out what is doubtful; repeat the rest with caution and you will make few mistakes. Use your eyes widely and leave out what is hazardous; put the rest into practice with caution and you will have few regrets. When in your speech you make few mistakes and in your action you have few regrets, an official career will follow as a matter of course.

To serve as a desirable model also entails not jumping to conclusions when making decisions. An exceptional leader should rely on observation and evidence in arriving at judgements about people and events. A leader's assessment, particularly of one's followers, should be based on facts, and not hearsay, guesswork or prejudice. Confucius shared the following test that guided his evaluation of a person:

15.25　吾之於人也，誰毀誰譽？如有所譽者，其有所試矣。

Whom have I ever praised or condemned? If there is anyone I praised, you may be sure that that person had been put to the test.

> An exceptional leader should rely on observation and evidence in arriving at judgements about people and events.

The 'test' Confucius referred to in 15.25 comprises all the situations and problems human beings experience in life. The moral deliberation, decisions, judgement and responses of a person attest to that person's ethical code, cultivation and conduct. Restating the usefulness of the test, Confucius shared: 'Now having listened to a person's words I go on to observe that person's deeds' (聽其言而觀其行 5.10, also see 1.9, 2.10, 15.23). It is particularly critical for leaders not to judge a person based on a popularity vote: how much that person is liked or disliked by others. What is needed, instead, is to 'go carefully into the case of the person who is disliked by the multitude' or 'liked by the multitude' (眾惡之，必察焉；眾好之，必察焉 15.28). The same yardstick applies to the appraisal of things and events. The insufficient historical documentation on the states of Qi and Song explains why Confucius admitted that he could not support what he said with evidence regarding these two states (3.9).

Promoting self-reflection

Second, the promotion of self-reflection is vital for community-building. Self-reflection involves regularly examining one's thoughts, feelings and actions, correcting one's shortcomings and observing *li* (normative behaviours) more faithfully. Doing so facilitates community-building by ensuring that each member of the community maintains respectful mindfulness towards each other, and collectively sustains a moral community. A disciple of Confucius instantiated self-reflection in the questions he asked himself (also see 19.6):

> 1.4 曾子曰：「吾日三省吾身—為人謀而不忠乎？與朋友交而不信乎？傳不習乎？」
>
> Master Zeng said: 'Every day I examine myself on three counts. In what I have undertaken on another's behalf, have I failed to do my best? In my dealings with my friends, have I failed to be trustworthy in what I say? Have I passed on to others anything that I have not tried out myself?'

Exemplary persons engage in self-examination to ensure that they are blameless in their treatment of others. As Confucius put it, 'If, on examining oneself, a person finds nothing to reproach oneself for, what worries and fears can such a person have?' (內省不疚，夫何憂何懼？ 12.4). The process of reflection necessarily involves the heart-mind (心 *xin*) where cognition and emotion are integrated. This means, for example, that a person not only thinks highly of another person because of the latter's achievements (cognition) but also experiences admiration for that person (emotion). Self-reflection also enhances community living by prompting all members to love learning, improve themselves and demonstrate *ren* (humanity) (17.8). Underscoring the primacy of having a teachable and humble spirit, Confucius exhorted:

4.17 見賢思齊焉；見不賢而內自省也。

When you meet someone better than yourself, turn your thoughts to becoming that person's equal. When you meet someone not as good as you are, look within and examine your own self.

Confucius himself endorsed mutual learning by expecting his disciples to give their own views, and even to disagree with him if the need arose.

Advocating mutual learning

Besides self-reflection, mutual learning is also encouraged by an exemplary leader. Confucius maintained that leaders should be deferential and modest enough to learn from their followers. An example is sage-king Wen, who was admired by Confucius for being 'quick and eager to learn: he was not ashamed to seek the advice of those who were beneath him in station' (敏而好學，不恥下問 5.15).

Confucius himself endorsed mutual learning by expecting his disciples to draw their own conclusions and debate ideas with him. This is why Confucius praised two disciples, Zixia and Zigong, for their insights into the Book of Odes (3.8, 11.4). For the same reason, Confucius expressed his disappointment with another disciple, Yan Hui, for agreeing with everything he said (11.4). Confucius also demonstrated mutual learning when he readily admitted his mistake when he was corrected by a disciple, and told the others: 'My friends, what Ziyou says is right. My remark a moment ago was only made in jest' (二三子！偃之言是也；前言戲之耳！17.4). Another instance is a historical episode where Confucius changed his mind and took the advice of his disciple:

A noble in league with Yang Hu rebelled against Duke Zhao of Lu, and when their rebellion failed, the two escaped to nearby Qi. When the noble asked Kongzi [Confucius] to come see him, Kongzi's eager reaction was entirely inappropriate. He was ready to go at a moment's notice to work for a traitor on behalf of his old nemesis, Yang Hu . . . Kongzi's most outspoken disciple, Zilu, chastised him for such delusions of grandeur, and in the end Kongzi could come up with no further rationalization for serving the rebels. He reluctantly declined the offer and stayed in Lu.[21]

The foregoing has described the first 'C' for leaders serving others, which is community-building. It has been noted that an exemplary leader establishes and fortifies a community of like-minded people through role modelling, promoting self-reflection and mutual learning.

Coaching

The next 'C' for an exemplary leader to serve others is through coaching or mentoring, where a leader develops the staff through influence, guidance and other kinds of support. Coaching and mentoring are closely related and I have used both terms interchangeably in this book. Nevertheless, this does not mean that they are equivalent terms. It is beyond the scope of this book to give a detailed discussion of the similarities and differences between coaching and mentoring. It suffices to note that coaching, as used in this book, is not limited to a person's performance in some areas of work or life. Coaching, like mentoring, also includes other developmental aspects such as introducing the coachees/mentees to the culture of the profession, equipping them with life skills and sharing one's personal experiences with them.[22]

> Confucius modelled coaching by being zealous in teaching, guiding and moulding others. He declared that he was willing to teach anyone who was prepared to learn, regardless of the person's social status and family background.

Although Confucius did not use the terms 'coaching' or 'mentoring', he championed and modelled these practices. He asked rhetorically: 'Can you do your best for anyone without educating that person?' (忠焉，能勿誨乎 14.7). The Chinese word used by Confucius for 'educating' in this passage is 誨 (*hui*), which is to teach 'by way of imparting light' or 'throwing light'.[23] The word *hui* implies coaching (and mentoring) as it is about teaching through enlightening the learner using a variety of strategies, and not through didactic instruction, rote-memorization and regurgitation. Confucius averred that a good leader 'helps others to realize what is good in them' (成人之美 12.16); the goal of bringing out the best in others is essentially what coaching is about. Coaching is all-important if a political leader desires to raise up talented and upright people to office (2.19, 13.2). Confucius praised Gongshu Wenzi for grooming and supporting his household steward Zhuan to take up high public office, so that the latter could serve alongside him (14.18).[24] By the same logic, Confucius reproved Zang Wenshong for selfishly refusing to promote his own subordinate Liu Xiahui, despite knowing the latter's worthiness (15.14).

Confucius modelled coaching by being zealous in teaching, guiding and motivating others. He declared that he was willing to teach anyone who was prepared to learn, regardless of the person's social status and family background (7.7, 15.39). His teaching philosophy was that everyone had the potential to learn well, improve themselves, attain *ren* (humanity) and become a *junzi* (exemplary person). The determining factor for success is nurture, not nature, as Confucius asserted:

17.2 性相近也，習相遠也。

Human beings are close to one another by nature. They diverge as a result of repeated practice.

Confucius's provision of mass education, although commonplace today, was revolutionary in ancient China. During his time, education was available only to aristocrats and their children. Importantly, Confucius's own disciples came from a variety of backgrounds, ranging from the wealthy and learned to the poor and down-trodden (5.1, 6.6).[25]

Confucius gave personalized and one-to-one attention to his disciples, mentoring them to become exemplary persons. Specifically, Confucius adopted three coaching approaches that are instructive for leaders who wish to do likewise. They are (1) the use of dialogue and questions, (2) systematic guidance and customization and (3) the encouragement of independent thinking in his disciples. These three approaches are expanded on in the next segment.

Dialogue and questions

Confucius primarily used dialogue and questions to build understanding in his disciples. An example is the following conversation between Confucius and Zizhang. This is a lengthy passage that is worth reproducing in full, to give readers a more complete idea of Confucius's teaching method:

12.20 子張問士：「何如斯可謂之達矣？」

子曰：「何哉？爾所謂達者！」

子張對曰：「在邦必聞，在家必聞。」

子曰：「是聞也，非達也。夫達也者：質直而好義，察言而觀色，慮以下人；在邦必達，在家必達。夫聞也者：色取仁而行違，居之不疑；在邦必聞，在家必聞。」

Zizhang asked: 'What must an exemplary person be like before one can be said to have gotten through?'

The Master said: 'What do you mean by getting through?'

Zizhang answered: 'What I have in mind is a person who is sure to be known, whether one serves in a state or in a noble family.'

The Master said: 'That is being known, not getting through. Now the term "getting through" describes a person who is straight by nature and fond of what is right, sensitive to other people's words and observant of the expression on their faces, and always mindful of being modest. Such a person is bound to get through whether one serves in a state or in a noble family. On the other hand, the term "being known" describes a person who has no misgivings about one's own claim to *ren* when all one is doing is putting up a facade of *ren* which is belied by one's deeds. Such a person is sure to be known, whether one serves in a state or in a noble family.'

Confucius began by responding to Zizhang's question with a question. Confucius' objective was to clarify what Zizhang meant by 'getting through' (達 *da*), an expression that is ambiguous. True enough, Zizhang's reply revealed that he had conflated 'getting through' with 'being known' (聞 *wen*). Confucius then took the time to explain the difference between the two terms. He also capitalized on the occasion to encourage Zizhang to focus on the more noble aspiration of 'getting through', rather than the more self-serving goal of 'being known'.

> Confucius coached his disciples through discussions and reflections on everyday issues, problems and controversies.

The above passage is an instance of how Confucius coached his disciples through discussions and reflections on everyday issues, problems and controversies.[26] The *Analects* contains many accounts of Confucius's conversations with his disciples, rulers and other people. Notably, the *Analects* is so-named because *Lunyu* 论语 literally means 'compiled discourses'; it narrates how Confucius instructed, shared, exhorted and corrected others and learned alongside them.

Systematic guidance and customization

Confucius also taught his disciples in a systematic manner; he customized the learning pace and content according to the background, learning ability and needs of each student. A disciple, Yan Hui, testified that Confucius was 'good at leading one on step by step' (循循然善誘人 9.11). He meant that Confucius gradually broadened his (Yan Hui's) knowledge with culture and deepened his application with *li* (normative behaviours).

The coaching approach used by Confucius was not one-size-fits-all; it was tailored to suit the personalities and circumstances of each student. Confucius underscored the need to be mindful of when and what to speak, when one was with another person (15.8). A case in point is Confucius's calibrated responses to the same question asked by two disciples:

> 11.22 子路問：「聞斯行諸？」
>
> 子曰：「有父兄在，如之何其聞斯行之！」
>
> 冉有問：「聞斯行諸？」
>
> 子曰：「聞斯行之！」
>
> 公西華曰：「由也問『聞斯行諸？』，
>
> 子曰：『有父兄在』；求也問，『聞斯行諸？』
>
> 子曰：『聞斯行之』。赤也惑，敢問？」
>
> 子曰：「求也退，故進之；由也兼人，故退之。」
>
> Zilu asked: 'Should one immediately put into practice what one has heard?'
>
> The Master said: 'As your father and elder brothers are still alive, you are hardly in a position immediately to put into practice what you have heard.'
>
> Ranyou asked: 'Should one immediately put into practice what one has heard?'
>
> The Master said: 'Yes. One should.'
>
> Gongxi Hua said: 'When Zilu asked whether one should immediately put into practice what one had heard, you pointed out that his father and elder brothers were alive. Yet when Ranyou asked whether one should immediately put into practice what one had heard, you answered that one should. I am puzzled. May I be enlightened?'
>
> The Master said: 'Ranyou holds himself back. It is for this reason that I tried to urge him on. Zilu has the energy of two men. It is for this reason that I tried to hold him back.'

> The coaching approach used by Confucius was not one-size-fits-all; it was tailored to suit the personalities and circumstances of each student.

In the above passage, Confucius responded to the same query with diametrically opposing answers.[27] His goal was to mentor his disciples appropriately, in accordance with their individual personalities and developmental needs. In another exchange that further reveals Confucius' sensitive awareness of Zilu's impulsiveness, Zilu asked Confucius: 'If you were leading the Three Armies whom would you take with you?' (子行三軍，則誰與？ 7.11) Confucius replied,

> 7.11 暴虎馮河，死而不悔者，吾不與也。必也臨事而懼，好謀而成者也。
>
> I would not take with me anyone who would try to fight a tiger with his bare hands or to walk across the River and die in the process without regrets. If I took anyone it would have to be a man who, when faced with a task, was fearful of failure and who, while fond of making plans, was capable of successful execution.

Confucius had Zilu in mind when he referred to a person who 'would try to fight a tiger with his bare hands or to walk across the River and die in the process without regrets'. Confucius's objective was to counsel Zilu that the latter's idea of bravery – the courage to wrestle a tiger with his bare hands and walk across a river because there was no boat – was foolhardiness. What Zilu really needed was to take the time to think through and carry out the plan with caution (for another example with Zilu, see 14.12).[28] Confucius employed the same customized approach for another disciple, Sima Niu, who was known to be brash. When Sima Niu asked Confucius what *ren* was, the latter deliberately replied that a *ren* person was one who was slow to speak (12.3). Confucius's aim was to draw Sima Niu's attention to his quick-temper, and coached him to be less impulsive in speaking.

On the whole, Confucius was conscious of tailoring his mentoring based on the strengths and weaknesses of each disciple (11.3, 11.18). This principle of customized teaching (因材施教 *yincai shijiao*) requires a teacher who is mindfully respectful of the profile of each student, and adjusts one's coaching accordingly.

Confucius was unequivocal that his disciples should not learn mindlessly or passively, and should instead think critically and creatively.

Encouragement of independent thinking and knowledge application

The third coaching method employed by Confucius was to encourage independent thinking and knowledge application in his disciples. Confucius was unequivocal that his disciples should not learn mindlessly or passively, and should instead think critically and creatively. He elaborated:

> 7.8 不憤不啟，不悱不發。舉一隅不以三隅反，則不復也。
>
> I never enlighten anyone who has not been driven to distraction by trying to understand a difficulty or who has not gotten into a frenzy trying to put one's ideas into words. When I have pointed out one corner of a square to anyone and such a person does not come back with the other three, I will not point it out to that person a second time.

I have already explained the above passage in Chapter 2, so I shall not rehearse the points here. What is accentuated here is inferential thinking, where a learner draws out what is not stated in a source by interpreting the given information, combining ideas and arriving at the conclusion.

Lest we think that Confucius was only interested in cognitive development, he also emphasized knowledge application: 'If a person who knows the three hundred Odes by heart fails when given administrative responsibilities and proves incapable of exercising one's initiative when sent to foreign states, then what use are the Odes to that person, however many one may have learned?' (誦詩三百；授之以政，不達；使於四方，不能專對；雖多，亦奚以為 13.5). Confucius added that it was not enough for a person to be 'fond of making plans' (好謀). Such a person should, at the same time, be 'capable of successful execution' (成 7.11), a point that was mentioned earlier in our discussion of Zilu. It is therefore imperative for the coach to observe, monitor and provide timely feedback to one's coach so that the latter can progress through practice. Confucius underlined the need for teachers to scrutinize and assess the student's conduct in both the public and private spheres:

> 2.10 視其所以，觀其所由，察其所安。人焉廋哉？人焉廋哉？

> Look at the means a person employs, observe the path one takes and examine where one feels at home. In what way is a person's true character hidden from view? In what way is a person's true character hidden from view?

An instance of timely feedback was when Ranyou told Confucius that he did not have the strength to follow the way of Confucius. Confucius responded succinctly: 'In your case you set the limits beforehand' (今女畫 6.12). Confucius identified the root problem of Ranyou's lack of success: a lack of determination, which hindered Ranyou's progress in learning. A good coach, therefore, is one who is able to diagnose the coachees' weaknesses and identify areas for their improvement.[29]

An integral part of giving guidance is for the coach to model for the student the right way of doing things. An example is Confucius's demonstration, in the presence of his disciple Zizhang, of how to treat a blind musician appropriately. The passage 15.42, which has been expounded in an earlier section of this chapter, describes in detail how Confucius patiently guided the musician on where to walk and sit, so as to make him feel at home. After the musician left, Zizhang, having observed what Confucius did, curiously asked, 'Is that the way to talk to a musician?', and received an affirmative reply from Confucius. After witnessing how Confucius showed empathic concern to the blind musician – not just learning about it from textbooks – Zizhang was well-prepared and inspired to do likewise.

Implications for mindfulness and mindful leadership

Confucius's priority on expressing love by serving others is instructive for mindfulness and mindful leadership. Two major implications are discussed here: (1) an accent on the social and interpersonal dimensions of mindfulness and mindful leadership and (2) the central place of empathy in mindful leadership.

An accent on the social and interpersonal dimensions of mindfulness and mindful leadership

First, Confucius's notion of *ren* (humanity) rejects the individualistic approach in favour of the social and interpersonal aspects of mindfulness and mindful leadership. As noted in earlier chapters, the current mindfulness movement accepts and presupposes an individualistic orientation.[30] The pivot on individualism, though arguably part and parcel of self-improvement programmes and 'accountability' reforms against a backdrop of neoliberalism, unfortunately jettisons the relational or interpersonal dimension of mindfulness.[31]

> It is essential for mindfulness to transcend the individual level to arrive at the interpersonal and systemic levels.

Researchers have accordingly advocated a more contextualized and community-based approach to mindfulness.[32] It is necessary for mindfulness to transcend the individual level to arrive at the interpersonal and systemic levels.[33] Confucius's spotlight on humanity, which entails co-humanity, requires leaders to build community and coach followers whole-heartedly. Nestled within a congregation of like-minded and exemplary educators, teachers are empowered to be mindful and thankful towards others in the course of their work. A teacher who attended a mindfulness programme that encouraged participants to engage in gratitude and caring practices towards each other articulated it thus:

> It definitely made me think, okay well, if this person said they were gracious towards me, that made me feel so good and it was so simple. So it made me want to do that more for my students and their parents too, in emails from students to parents and just say, you know, 'Your son or daughter is doing a really awesome job and is excelling'[34]

Confucius's requirement for school leaders to be exemplars and to nurture an environment of care and harmony contributes to relational trust.[35] Role modelling, which is stressed by Confucius, is critical for a culture of trust. Leadership qualities such as trustworthiness, mutual respect and support between leaders and followers have a direct impact on the collective mindfulness of the organization.[36] Confucius's dialogic method of coaching, as part of mindful leadership, is also salient; leaders should create a safe and empathetic community for staff to speak freely without fear of repercussions.[37]

Coaching helps novice teachers succeed, which enhances retention outcomes in the long term.[38] It is a significant point that the Teaching and Learning International Survey (TALIS) 2018 reported that although school principals viewed mentoring as critical for teachers' work and students' performance, only 22 per cent of novice teachers were mentored on average across Organization for Economic Co-operation and Development (OECD) countries and economies in TALIS.[39] Coaching (and mentoring) removes impediments to change by building self-confidence and self-esteem – the coach directs, manages and instructs the protégé to support them through difficult transitions.[40]

Teachers can serve one another through *educative mentoring*, where novice teachers learn as they work with experienced teachers in co-thinking relationships.[41] There are three core tenets of educative mentoring: cultivating a disposition of inquiry, focusing on student thinking and comprehension, and fostering disciplined talk about problems of practice.[42] These three facets are observable in Confucius's coaching approach – he embraced learner exploration, independent thinking and discourses on applied learning in real-world settings.

> Confucius's requirement for school leaders to be exemplars and nurture an environment of care and harmony contributes to relational trust.

The central place of empathy in mindful leadership

The second implication concerns Confucius's teachings on *shu* (empathy) as a manifestation of one's humanity. His focus on loving others and reciprocal concern resonates with research on the importance of care and empathy for a mindful leader. Scientific research using brain imaging (Functional magnetic resonance imaging or fMRI) has reported that the insula becomes energized through mindfulness meditation, which contributes to increased empathy.[43] Confucian empathy is therefore pertinent for mindful leadership and the sustenance of a mindful school.

A recommendation is the enactment of *teacher empathy* through mindfulness.[44] It involves a sensitive awareness of students' personal and social circumstances and the corresponding show of care towards them.[45] An empathic teacher relies on *empathic pedagogy* by facilitating the sharing of thinking and feeling states in students, to enhance students' moral growth at the personal and societal levels.[46] An example of empathic pedagogy is to help students and staff develop their respectful mindfulness of others, enabling them to build connectedness with others and show love towards all. Another suggestion is loving-kindness meditation where one consciously and sincerely sends well-wishes to others.[47] A teacher who practised loving-kindness meditation testified as follows:

> Oh, the loving-kindness thing that we did, that was so helpful. Actually, that student that I was talking about who's challenging – I've consistently done my

loving-kindness meditation about that student, and it has helped me so much to be able to have this different relationship with him.[48]

Confucius's notion of empathy also promotes empathic mindfulness that allows school principals and administrators to feel into, feel with and feel for others.[49] A school leader of a middle school west of Boston illustrated this empathy through mindful listening and responding:

I found myself slowing down internally – being aware of how I listened and responded, and consciously working to slow down my thinking and how I responded to people. I tried to really listen, without coming up with solutions on the spot. I was more attentive and calmer. I walked more slowly, made more eye contact with students and adults, and really tried to smile a lot. I worked on my breathing, sometimes closing the door to my office when things got really stressful. Then I took a minute or two to focus on my breath.[50]

> Confucius's notion of empathy promotes empathic mindfulness that allows school principals and administrators to feel into, feel with and feel for others.

When adopting Confucius's idea of respectful mindfulness, leaders should be mindful of their own responses – as shown by the school leader from Boston – as well as express constant, whole-hearted appreciation to people around them. In addition, school leaders should not only 'really listen', as articulated by the school leader in the above quotation, but 'listen *respectfully*', and not only '[work] on [their] breathing' but also cultivate themselves morally to become *junzi* (exemplary persons).

Turning to teaching, children's empathic abilities can be developed early in life through formative communicative experiences.[51] Cultivating empathy throughout a child's education journey enables them to acquire the habit of reflecting on and caring for the effects of their actions on others.[52] Empathy can be effectively nurtured in students through strategies such as sharing personal stories, reading relevant literature, cooperative learning, cross-age and peer tutoring and role-playing. Books, paintings, music and films can similarly promote empathy.[53] Teachers could use language-mediated sources such as anecdotes or novels to help students intersubjectively connect with another's experience through the retelling of emotional events.[54] The teacher could ask the students to practise role-taking, which can be self-focused or other-focused.[55]

Self-focused role-taking requires students to analogously imagine themselves in a similar situation; *other-focused* role-taking directs the students to consider what the other is experiencing.

Role-taking activities also engender interpersonal and social empathy in the students. *Interpersonal* empathy is inculcated when the teacher encourages students to imagine the feeling and thinking states of another person and respond with sensitive care.[56] *Social* empathy, on the other hand, is achieved when students reflect on the systemic disparities and social injustice faced by others.[57] In alignment with Confucius's value of role modelling, school leaders and teachers should take the lead in helping the needy and disadvantaged in the community. Examples are school principals who distributed food to families, gave free digital devices to students and kept in touch with them through various means such as email messages during the pandemic.[58]

Conclusion

This chapter has delineated how a Confucian mindful leader serves others, based on the Confucian value of *ren* (humanity) that includes *shu* (empathy). *Ren* as love is the basis for a leader's service of others. Confucian humanity is intimately tied to mindfulness as a frame of heart-mind as well as an intentional state. Empathy for Confucius is more accurately described as empathic concern; more than perspective-taking, it also involves a motivation to care for the welfare of others. Serving others is enacted through two Cs: community-building and coaching. To build a community of virtuous people, an exemplary leader brings harmony to fruition. An exemplary leader also establishes and nurtures a community of like-minded people through role-modelling, furthering self-reflection and advancing mutual learning. Confucius's teaching approach is a form of coaching as he gave personalized and one-to-one attention to his disciples; he engaged in dialogue with them to guide them to become exemplary persons. Having elucidated the component of serving others, the next chapter discusses the last component of R|E|S|T.

6

Transforming Society

Human beings are capable of broadening the Way (dao) 人能弘道
(Confucius, Analects, 15.29)

The previous three chapters have analyzed the first three components of R|E|S|T, namely **R**espectful mindfulness, **E**xemplary living and **S**erving others. This chapter discusses the last component: **T**ransforming society (see Figure 6.1).

I shall explain how a Confucian mindful leader seeks to *transform society* as an exemplification of what Confucius termed 'broadening the Way'.[1] The first part of the chapter explicates the notion of *dao*, its relationship with transforming society, and the mandate for everyone, especially leaders, to broaden *dao*. Next, the chapter outlines ways for a mindful leader to transform society, using the endeavours of Confucius himself. The last part of the chapter draws out the key implications for mindfulness and mindful leadership.

What is *Dao* (Way)?

> The ancient Chinese believed that *dao* is the Way of Heaven (天 *tian*) that provides the guiding discourse or prescriptive tradition for human beings – it is a vision of human excellence.

The word *dao* (literally way or path) is widely used and embedded in Chinese cultures. To illustrate, the Chinese expression for 'I know' literally means 'I know *dao*' (我知道 *wo zhi dao*). Photo 6.1 illustrates the utmost importance of achieving *dao*; the sign on a building reads, 'The hall of respecting the Way.'

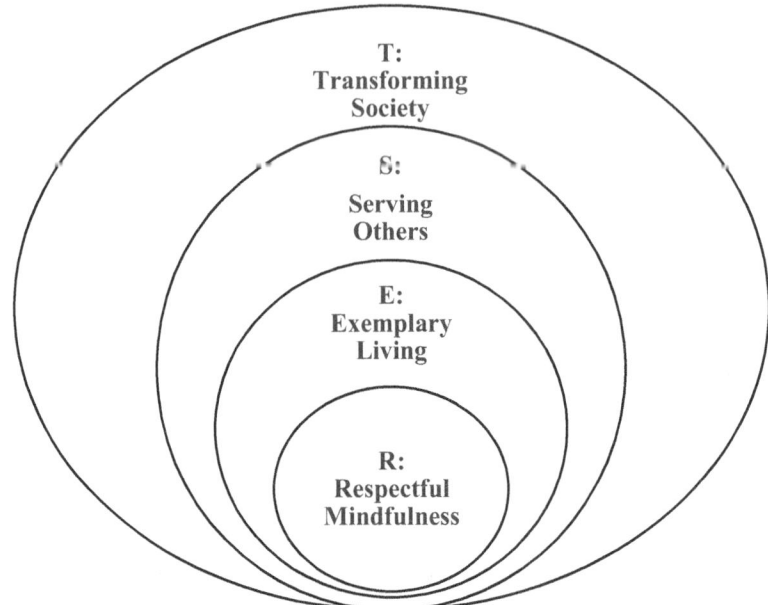

Figure 6.1 Transforming society.

Confucius had much to say about *dao*. He averred that we should all 'abide to the death in the good Way' (守死善道 8.13); in his view, a person 'who is told of and walks in *dao* has not lived in vain' (朝聞道，夕死可矣 4.8). Confucius also urged all to believe in, set one's sight on, and find delight in *dao* (1.15, 4.9, 7.6, 19.2).

The ancient Chinese believed that *dao* is the Way of Heaven (天 *tian*) that provides the guiding discourse or prescriptive tradition for human beings – it is a vision of human excellence.[2] From a Confucian perspective, *dao* is found in and preserved through the traditional texts, social institutions, cultural resources and virtuous conduct of sage-kings. In particular, Confucius admired the Zhou dynasty for embodying *dao* through its morally excellent leaders, knowledge base, values, beliefs and practices.[3] The attainment of *dao* is a distinguishing feature of an exemplary person 君子 (*junzi*). Such a person 'devotes one's heart-mind to attaining *dao*' (謀道 15.32), 'worries about *dao*' (憂道 15.32) and is drawn to people who 'realize *dao*' (有道 1.14).[4] Confucius himself had 'set his heart-mind on *dao*' (志於道 7.6), and prized it more than material gain:

> 4.5 富與貴，是人之所欲也；不以其道得之，不處也。貧與賤，是人之惡也；不以其道得之，不去也。

Photo 6.1 A sign on a building that reads 'The hall of respecting the Way' (*zun dao ting*).

Wealth and high station are what humans desire but unless I got them according to *dao* I would not remain in them. Poverty and low station are what humans dislike, but even if I did not get them by staying in *dao*, I would not try to escape from them.

During Confucius's time, *dao* was not prevalent. An official noted: 'The Empire has long been without *dao*' (天下之無道也久矣) (3.24). As mentioned in an earlier chapter, Confucius lived during a perilous period of political disintegration and social discord. Although *dao* did not flourish, it was not completely lost in Confucius's day. As articulated by a disciple of Confucius, 'The *dao* of King Wen and King Wu has not yet fallen to ground but is still to be found in human beings' (文武之道，未墜於地，在人 19.22). Confucius called upon all to restore and advance *dao*:

> 15.29 人能弘道，非道弘人。
> It is human beings who are capable of broadening *dao*. It is not *dao* that broadens human beings.

The word 'broaden' (弘 *hong*) refers to the act of realizing, perpetuating and promoting *dao* on earth for future generations.[5] Confucius's message to broaden *dao* indicates that *dao* is not pre-determined and unchanging, and can – and should – be (re)made through the conscious and collective efforts of humans.[6] As such, Confucius praised the sage-kings for holding fast to and expanding *dao* for the benefit of all human beings (15.25). Confucius believed human potential and capability were the prerequisites for societal transformation, which builds upon the other three features of R|E|S|T (respectful mindfulness, exemplary living and serving others).[7]

> Broadening *dao* (Way) refers to the act of realizing, perpetuating and promoting a vision of human excellence for future generations.

How to broaden the Way?

According to Confucius, broadening *dao* (Way) involves two main approaches: (1) critique and (2) change. These are closely related and mutually strengthening, and shall be elaborated on in the subsequent segment.

Critique

For Confucius, a critique comprises two elements: (1) it points out how leaders, officials and the governing system have deviated from the Way and (2) it expresses critical thinking that is underpinned by respectful mindfulness.

To point out how the leaders, officials and the governing system have deviated from the Way

First, exemplary persons promote the Way by pointing out how those in power as well as the administrative structure have violated the Way. The egoism of the rulers and other office-bearers, coupled with the political strife and moral degradation, was testament to the disrepair of the Way at that time. As observed by a disciple of Confucius, 'those in authority have lost the Way' (上失其道 19.19). Confucius thereby admonished the political leaders and adjured them to serve the masses rather than enrich themselves. When asked by Duke Ding what would ruin the state, Confucius replied that it was when no one dared to speak out when the leader had done wrong (also see 14.22):

> 13.15 如其善而莫之違也，不亦善乎？如不善而莫之違也，不幾乎一言而喪邦乎？
>
> If what one says is good and no one goes against that person, good. But if what one says is not good and no one goes against that person, then is this not almost a case of a saying leading the state to ruin?

Confucius was vocal about the bad example set by the political leaders, and was unafraid of rebuking them. When one ruler asked Confucius how to solve the prevalence of thieves in his state, Confucius replied in no uncertain terms that the ruler's own covetousness (欲 *yu*) has influenced the masses and emboldened them to steal (12.18, also see 3.1, 3.2, 9.18). Confucius also reminded leaders that what determined their legacy was their moral character, and not wealth or fame. Confucius cited historical precedents:

> 16.12 齊景公有馬千駟，死之日，民無德而稱焉；伯夷、叔齊餓於首陽之下，民到于今稱之。
>
> Duke Jing of Qi had a thousand teams of four horses each, but on his death the common people were unable to find anything for which to praise him, whereas Po Yi and Shu Qi starved under Mount Shou Yang and yet to this day the common people still sing their praises.[8]

Duke Jing lived an extravagant and decadent life during his reign whereas Po Yi and Shu Qi, who were sons of Lord Guzhu, were known for their integrity (also see 5.23, 7.15, 18.8). Po Yi and Shu Qi did not have *de jure* legitimacy like Duke Jing, that is, they did not hold any official positions; however, they were admired and fondly remembered in posterity, not Duke Jing. Confucius was clear that the broadening of the Way needs to be initiated and modelled by the leader – something that was unfortunately non-existent during Confucius's time (16.2).

Confucius was not just dismayed by the immoral conduct of the political leaders. He was also critical of the *appointment holders* of his day. When asked about the 'people who are in public life in the present day' (今之從政者), Confucius replied that 'they are of such limited capacity that they hardly count' (斗筲之人，何足算也 13.20). Confucius was not referring to their professional abilities when he mentioned 'limited capacity', but rather their moral character. When a disciple asked about the qualities of a *shi* 士, a scholar who held an office, Confucius responded that such a person should possess the following attributes: 'have a sense of shame in the way one conducts oneself and, when sent abroad, ... not disgrace the commission of one's lord' (行己有恥；使於四方，不辱君命), 'be praised for being a good son or daughter in one's clan and for being a respectful young person in the village' (宗族稱孝焉，鄉黨稱弟焉) and 'insist on keeping one's word and seeing one's actions through to the end' (言必信，行必果 13.20). All in all, virtuous officials were in short supply as the corrupt political leaders did not set a good example for their subordinates. The flagrant violation of *li* (normative behaviours) and disregard for *dao* as the guiding discourse inadvertently instigated the officials and the populace to be self-serving and greedy, like their lords.

> Confucius opposed the political and social structures during his time, which were characterized by harsh punishment, warfare and litigation among the people.

The contemptible conduct of the leaders also explained why the *prevailing governing system* was oppressive and toxic. The predominant principle for government privileged by power-hungry rulers was 'leading by edicts' (道之以政) where punitive measures were implemented to compel compliance in one's followers (2.3). The neglect of *dao*, resulting in widespread chaos and wickedness, fuelled Confucius's passion to transform society by reviving this normative tradition. In his words, 'If *dao* is found in the Empire, I will not need to change anything' (天下有道，丘不與易也) (18.6).⁹ Confucius opposed the political and social structures during his time, which were characterized by harsh punishment, warfare and litigation among the people. Aware of the prevalence of public grievances and court cases, Confucius stated: 'I try to get the parties not to resort to litigation in the first place' (使無訟乎 12.13).

Aiming to be a change agent, Confucius sought office to introduce humane governance and influence the political rulers to become exemplary persons. His noble goal, however, was met with lukewarm responses and even resistance from rulers who were conceited megalomaniacs. That said, Confucius's altruistic aspiration was noted and appreciated by a small minority. For instance, a border official of Yi told Confucius's disciples, 'Heaven is about to use your Master as the wooden tongue for a bell' (天將以夫子為木鐸 4.24), that is, to proclaim and spread *dao* to all and sundry.

To express critical thinking that is underpinned by respectful mindfulness

Second, critique presupposes critical thinking, understood here as a form of judgement that is based on the standard of *dao* (Way). Confucius used the prescriptive tradition derived from the Way, which was typified by the sage-kings, to judge leaders. He saw being 'critical' (切切 13.28) as an essential attribute of an exemplary person, but critical thinking was not about being uncharitable, overly judgemental, confrontational or violent. Consistent with the moral character of Confucian mindful leaders, critical thinking is underpinned by and expressed through respectful mindfulness. We have already noted in an earlier chapter that respectful mindfulness refers to the moment-by-moment, appreciative and whole-hearted attentiveness to oneself, people and events. Fundamental to respectful mindfulness is appreciation, that is, due regard for fellow human beings.

To communicate critical thinking with respectful mindfulness entails being mindful of when to speak and how to do so. A Confucian quality that captures this form practical wisdom is *yi* (義), which refers to 'appropriateness', 'righteousness' or 'rightness'. *Yi* is essentially about being sensitive to and doing what is fitting in certain situations through personal discernment and discretion.¹⁰ *Yi* is a distinguishing feature of an exemplary person, as Confucius described (also see 4.16, 17.23):¹¹

4.10 君子之於天下也，無適也，無莫也，義之於比。

> In one's dealings with the world the exemplary person is not invariably for or against anything. Such a person is on the side of what is *yi* (appropriate).

Confucius displayed *yi* when he stated that he 'practises what is *yi* (appropriate) in order to realize my Way' (行義以達其道 16.11). He also shared that he was flexible with 'no preconceptions about the permissible and the impermissible' (無可無不可 18.8, also see 14.32).[12] To exalt virtue, according to Confucius, was to 'move yourself to where *yi* is' (徙義 12.10).[13] The *Analects* gives numerous instances of *yi* in everyday life, such as dialoguing with someone (10.2, 10.15), receiving gifts (10.23), travelling (10.26) and social interactions (10.3, 10.4). *Yi* ensures that a person does not behave in an auto-pilot manner and instead makes sense of and responds to specific circumstances mindfully.

Yi is particularly needful in tricky situations such as correcting one's lord. Exercising critical thinking with respectful mindfulness means that one responds with *yi*, that is, one is conscious of when and how to remonstrate with one's leaders. Confucius cautioned against three errors when serving one's lord: 'To speak before being spoken to by the exemplary person is rash; not to speak when spoken to by that person is to be evasive; to speak without observing the expression on one's face is to be blind' (言未及之而言，謂之『躁』；言及之而不言，謂之『隱』；未見顏色而言，謂之『瞽』 16.6).[14]

> *Yi* (appropriateness) ensures that a person does not behave in an auto-pilot manner, and instead makes sense of and responds to specific circumstances mindfully.

Change

To transform society, it is not enough to identify what is problematic, undesirable and harmful; it is also necessary to suggest what is constructive, desirable and beneficial. In other words, transforming an organization, system or society requires detailing the changes that are needed. There are three broad areas of change: (1) The type of leaders, (2) choice of officials and (3) the governing system. These shall be amplified accordingly.

Type of leaders

First, the leadership of exemplary persons (*junzi*) is required to broaden the Way. The earlier chapters have clarified how good leaders, from a Confucian worldview, are role models with outstanding character who influence their followers to follow suit. Confucius compared the exemplary leader to the wind and petty people to grass: 'Let the wind blow over the grass and it is sure to bend' (草上之風必偃 12.19). His thesis was that the commendable traits of leaders will naturally reform the immoral conduct of others who come into contact with the leader. Using another analogy, the *Analects* teaches that leaders should be like the sun and moon that are seen by all and give light to everyone (19.24).

An exemplary person broadens the Way by setting one's heart-mind 'to help others stand and they will stand, to guide them and they will walk, to bring peace to them and they will turn to such a leader, to set them tasks and they will work in harmony' (立之斯立，道之期行，綏之期來，動之斯和 19.25). The mission of exemplary persons to extend the Way is the reason why they are keen to take up official positions – only if doing so advances the Way. Confucius made this point when he praised Qu Bo-yu for being 'prepared to hold an office only when the Way prevailed in a state' (邦有道，則仕 15.7). To revitalize and perpetuate the Way, an exemplary leader demonstrates and champions *ren* (humanity). Recall that an exemplary person, according to Confucius, 'never deserts *ren*, not even for the time it takes to eat a meal' (無終食之間違仁 4.5). This begs the question of how *ren*, the Way and the exemplary person are related. The following passage addresses this question:

> 1.2 君子務本，本立而道生。孝弟也者，其為仁之本與！
>
> The exemplary person devotes one's efforts to the roots, for once the roots are established, the Way will grow therefrom. Being good as a son or daughter, and obedient as a young person is, perhaps, the root of *ren* (humanity).[15]

The 'root of *ren*', as taught by Confucius, is filial piety, where one shows respectful mindfulness towards one's parents at home. I have already explained, in earlier chapters, how respect is one of the manifestations of *ren*. The analogy of a tree, as indicated by the word 'root', informs us that everyone should 'grow' by extending their respectful mindfulness to everyone in society, thereby broadening the Way of *ren*.

Confucius exhorted leaders to adhere to and propagate the principle of *zhengming* (正名), so as to transform society. *Zhengming* means 'rectification of names' or the proper use of names. When asked by a political leader about good government, Confucius replied: 'Let the ruler be a ruler, the subject a subject, the father a father, the son a son' (君，君；臣，臣；父，父；子，子 12.11). He expanded this idea:

13.3 名不正，則言不順；言不順，則事不成；事不成，則禮樂不興；禮樂不興，則刑罰不中；刑罰不中，則民無所措手足。

When names are not correct, what is said will not sound reasonable; when what is said does not sound reasonable, affairs will not culminate in success; when affairs do not culminate in success, *li* and music will not flourish; when *li* and music do not flourish, punishments will not fit the crimes; when punishments do not fit the crimes, the common people will not know where to put hand and foot.

> According to Confucius, one's name or social role is not just descriptive but also embedded with normative force. A ruler has a 'correct name' when they are desirable models who exhibit *ren* (humanity).

The expression 'names are not correct' denotes a failure to live up to the expectations associated with one's 'name' – specifically, one's social role, such as a ruler, subject, father or daughter. According to Confucius, one's name or social role is not just descriptive but also embedded with normative force.[16] A ruler has a 'correct name' when they are desirable models who exhibit *ren*. The policies of a benevolent ruler will accomplish their goals because their words 'sound reasonable' (13.3), that is, it is persuasive to the followers who see for themselves that the leader practises what they preach. Such a ruler, as a *junzi*, wins the hearts of the multitude by embodying and passing on the virtues of respectful mindfulness, tolerance, trustworthiness, diligence and generosity (17.6).

To further appreciate the contribution of virtuous leaders, it is useful to compare an exemplary person with a 'petty person' (*xiaoren*). We have already discussed these two contrasting terms in an earlier chapter. Relating these two types of people to leadership, Confucius observed (also see 14.1, 14.3):

13.25 君子易事而難說也：說之不以道，不說也；及其使人也，器之。小人難事而易說也；說之雖不以道，說也；及其使人也，求備焉。

The exemplary person is easy to serve but difficult to please. Such a person will not be pleased unless you try to please that person by following the Way, but when it comes to employing the services of others, such a person does so within the limits of their capacity. The petty person is difficult to serve but easy to please. Such a person will be pleased even though you try to please that person by not following the Way, but when it comes to employing the services of others, that person demands all-round perfection.

In the above passage, Confucius separated leaders into two main types: the exemplary person and the petty person. The former upholds the Way and puts in place the proper job scope, requirements and outcomes that are consistent with the Way. This means ensuring that the mechanisms, measures and decisions of a state reflect and perpetuate the guiding discourse inherited from the sage-kings. An official who, for example, aims to get into the good books of their lord, who is an exemplary person, by collecting exorbitant taxes from the masses will not be pleasing to their lord. The reason is obvious: unreasonably high taxation violates social justice and contradicts the values and actions of the sage-kings.

> The appointed officials are expected, and can be trusted, to live up to their names through their unsurpassed service.

An exemplary ruler bears no resemblance to a petty person – one who is self-centred, demanding and dismissive of the Way. Confucius reminded a disciple in 6.13 to be 'a counsellor who is an exemplary person (*junzi*), not a counsellor who is a petty person' (君子儒！無為小人儒). To Confucius, being erudite or powerful in itself does not mean that that person is doing what is morally right. In short, an exemplary ruler, as opposed to a petty person, is understanding and wise, and delegates work to the officials based on their respective talents and aptitude.

Choice of officials

Besides role modelling virtue, leaders transform society by appointing officials who are fellow *junzi* (exemplary persons) who follow the Way. Leaders, in choosing officials, need to ensure that they are virtuous persons who tread the same path. Confucius cautioned: 'There is no point in people taking counsel together who follow different ways (*dao*)' (道不同，不相為謀 15.40). Such an appointment follows naturally from the principle of *zhengming* (rectification of names) for both the ruler and officials, which was discussed earlier. An exemplary leader, in living up to their name, promotes morally excellent officials and keeps evil persons at bay (12.22). The appointed officials are expected, and can be trusted, to live up to their names through their unsurpassed service. These officials are deserving ministers, not officials with 'limited capacity' (斗筲 13.20).

In addition, Confucius distinguished between a 'great minister' (大臣) and a 'useful minister' (具臣) by pointing out that the former manifests virtue by 'serving their lord according to the Way' (以道事君 11.24). Confucius gave the example of one such 'great minister' – Guanzhong, the prime minister to Duke Huan of Qi in the seventh century BCE.[17]

14.17 微管仲，吾其被髮左衽矣！豈若匹夫匹婦之為諒也，自經於溝瀆，而莫之知也！

Guanzhong helped Duke Huan to become the leader of the feudal lords and save the Empire from collapse. To this day, the common people still enjoy the benefit of his acts. Had it not been for Guanzhong, we might well be wearing our hair down and folding our robes to the left.

The expression 'wearing our hair down and folding our robes to the left' refers to the lifestyle of barbarians. Guanzhong helped his lord, Duke Huan unite the feudal lords and defeat the invading foreigners; he contributed to the transformation of society by preventing its collapse and restoring order.[18]

To conclude this segment, exemplary leaders do not just appoint righteous people to office; these leaders also ensure that these people perform their jobs according to the Way. What is of essence, apart from professional competency, is moral character – a key consideration when hiring, assigning work to, appraising and rewarding employees.

The governing system

The third way to transform society is to reform the governing system so that it conforms to the Way. Leaders need to endorse systems thinking by introducing structures, institutions, mechanisms and policies that accord with *li* (normative behaviours). To do so, leaders need to go beyond day-to-day needs and demands, and attend to long-term considerations and achievements. To quote Confucius, it is to focus on 'great tasks' (大事) rather than 'petty gains' (小利 13.17, also see 15.12). Confucius reminded all: 'A person who gives no thought to difficulties in the future is sure to be beset by worries much closer at hand' (人無遠慮，必有近憂 15.12). The priority here is to re-envision the society they desire for themselves, their people and future generations.

The ideal society, according to Confucius, is one that thrives because its rulers lead by virtue rather than by edicts. During Confucius's time, the leaders were more fixated with and reliant on, oppressive rule through punitive measures. In a meeting between Confucius and Duke Ling of Wei, the latter was more concerned with questions about military formations. Confucius responded diplomatically: 'I have, indeed, heard something about the use of sacrificial vessels, but I have never studied the matter of commanding troops' (俎豆之

事，則嘗聞之矣；軍旅之事，未之學也 15.1). The *Analects* records that Confucius left the state the next day. The reference to 'the matter of commanding troops' signals the Duke's intention to use brute force to bring about a fearsome and powerful government. Confucius implied that a state did not need battalions of weapons to prosper as much as 'the use of sacrificial vessels'. Sacrificial vessels were items used in religious ceremonies – events that required respectful mindfulness.

Confucius's message was that the Duke needed to, first and foremost, be a mindful leader who manifested and role-modelled virtues, particularly that of respect towards all. The obsession with the army, warfare and killing was the opposite of respect; it indicated a disregard of human life and the welfare of the common people.

> The ideal society, according to Confucius, is one that thrives because its rulers lead by virtue rather than by edicts.

Following 15.1 cited above, to institute the rule by virtue is to observe, display and propound respectful mindfulness throughout the state. Etymologically linked to religious sacrifices, *li* (normative behaviours) was redefined by Confucius to encompass the values, attitudes and actions of the sage-kings who modelled themselves after the Way (12.1). An earlier chapter has shown that respectful mindfulness needs to be enacted through *li*. By referring to sacrificial vessels (15.1), Confucius was also reminding the Duke to behave morally in accordance with *li*. All human beings, especially leaders, must adhere to *li* by internalizing and demonstrating *ren* (humanity). The coupling of *li* and *ren* was underlined by Confucius: 'What can a person do with the *li* who is not *ren*?' (人而不仁，如禮何? 3.3). It follows that rulers need to install and sustain a governing system that conforms to *li* by subscribing to and celebrating the virtues of *ren* and its related qualities such as filial piety, empathy, wisdom, courage and harmony.

Although Confucius advocated leading by virtue by following the example of the sage-kings, he was not recommending a wholesale and unthinking acceptance of the practices of the sage-kings.[19] Such a blind allegiance reflects *mindlessness*, where the person clings to the past and exhibits a rigid and dogmatic mindset. Instead, exemplary rulers should exercise *yi* (appropriateness) by choosing what is the most suitable for their contexts, people and challenges. Confucius illustrated this in his advice on governing a state:

> 15.11 行夏之時，乘殷之輅。服周之冕。樂則韶舞。放鄭聲，遠佞人；鄭聲淫，佞人殆。
>
> Follow the calendar of the Xia, ride in the carriage of the Yin, and wear the ceremonial cap of the Zhou, but, as for music, adopt the *shao* and the *wu*. Banish the tunes of Zheng and keep glib people at a distance. The tunes of Zheng are wanton and glib people are dangerous.[20]

The above passage shows that Confucius did not assume that all traditional practices and resources were desirable. He recognized that certain resources and practices from the past should be avoided, such as the music produced by people from Zheng. Confucius recommended judicious selection by calling attention to the additions and omissions made by the Zhou dynasty, which Confucius regarded as the 'Golden Age': 'The Zhou built on the *li* of the Yin; what was added and what was omitted can be known' (周因於殷禮，所損益，可知也2.23).

Confucius also advised leaders to exercise their own judgement by making mindful changes; he shared his personal experience:

> 9.3 麻冕，禮也。今也，純儉，吾從眾。拜下，禮也。今拜乎上，泰也，雖違眾，吾從下。
>
> A ceremonial cap of linen is what is prescribed by *li*. Today black silk is used instead. This is more frugal and I follow the majority. To prostrate oneself before ascending the steps is what is prescribed by *li*. Today one does so after having ascended them. This is too casual and, though going against the majority, I follow the practice of doing so before ascending.[21]

Confucius agreed with the substitution of the material used for the ceremonial cap, from linen to silk, but did not follow the majority in changing the traditional practice of prostrating oneself before entering the hall. In both cases, Confucius's decision was not arbitrary but guided by moral considerations – the virtue of frugality in the first case, and the virtue of respect in the second.

Altogether, exemplary leaders and fellow estimable officials should mindfully enact and maintain a system that broadens the Way through ruling by virtue. By following the laudable examples of the sage-kings, while making necessary adjustments, exemplary leaders will succeed in transforming society.

> Confucius called into question the adequacy of mindfulness approaches that centre on self-improvement, personal healing and non-judgement.

Implications and conclusions

There are two major implications arising from Confucius's arguments on transforming society: (1) his approach to broaden the Way is a form of transformational, ethical mindfulness and (2) his orientation of critical thinking is not adversarial and contemptuous, but grounded in respectful mindfulness. These two implications are elaborated in order.

Transformational, ethical mindfulness

First, Confucius's call to broaden the Way reflects *transformational, ethical mindfulness that is carried out and modelled by exemplary leaders*. Confucius's notion of transforming society is in concert with a form of mindfulness that goes beyond individual, psychologized and non-moral approaches and practices. I have noted in Chapter 1 that the established mindfulness programmes and activities tend to be decontextualized and devoid of larger social, political and economic issues.[22] Confucius called into question the adequacy of mindfulness approaches that centre on self-improvement, personal healing and non-judgement. A version of mindfulness that is purely localized and therapeutic may unwittingly instil a passive acceptance of oppressive structures and practices. Social and economic inequalities faced by ethnic minorities or children from disadvantaged home backgrounds are likely to be overlooked and even perpetuated despite the proliferation of mindfulness programmes in schools.

> Confucius's recommendation of transforming society supports the goal of critical scholars to attend to the widespread problematic systems and leadership practices.

Another approach to mindfulness is therefore urgently needed – one that considers and redresses the sufferings, injustices and vexing problems in the world. Fortunately, some researchers, particularly critical scholars, have already begun work in this area, introducing terms such as radical mindfulness, integral mindfulness, socially transformative mindfulness, socially responsible mindfulness, civic mindfulness and critical mindfulness.[23] Confucius's recommendation of transforming society supports the goal of critical scholars to attend to the widespread problematic systems and leadership practices. Rather than preserving the status quo, Confucius championed

Way-making – the continuous process of realizing, extending and defending a vision of human excellence on earth for future generations. It follows from Confucius's transformational, ethical mindfulness that educators need to critique and change the existing systems, structures and values systems that contribute to social injustice.[24]

To transform society, exemplary leaders should focus on *social justice in education*. Social justice, in simple terms, is about respectful mindfulness – acknowledging the equal worth of all citizens, opportunities and life chances, for the elimination or reduction of unjust inequalities.[25] Social justice entails introducing social arrangements for everyone to participate fully and equitably in society. Some readers may question the relevance of social justice to Confucius; they may see social justice as necessarily or primarily linked to Western liberal presuppositions, such as individualism, democracy and autonomy. Although the term 'social justice' originates from Western histories and developments, there is no reason to define social justice in a culturally specific way by tethering it to Western traditions. Social justice is a broad and contested term, with numerous competing definitions and understandings. It is, by and large, understood as the promotion and enactment of social arrangements for everyone to participate fully and equally in society. Based on this interpretation, it is tenable that Confucius supported social justice by advocating societal transformation.

In the school setting, social justice is about abolishing unfair systems and practices through the implementation of ethical educational structures, policies and practices, as well as enabling the total participation of educational stakeholders.[26] A socially just education revolves around challenging neoliberal ideas, logics and strategies that condone or ignore exploitation, marginalization, powerlessness, cultural imperialism and violence.[27] Besides dismantling oppressive attitudes and practices, transformational school leaders should also enact educational structures, policies and practices that foster inclusion and equity, high expectations, reciprocal community relationships, a system-wide approach and direct social justice intervention.[28]

The above-mentioned reform goals in schools and communities would help chart a new path (*dao*) of educational equality for all students. Norms of equity and justice under the banner of Leadership for Social Justice or Culturally Responsive Leadership are essential for a caring and mindful school.[29] Schools, therefore, need to engage with the wider society through establishing strong bonds with community leaders and networking with other organizations and individuals.[30] Successful school leaders exercise their judgements (*yi* appropriateness) in making decisions based on the history, staff profile and prevailing needs of the school.[31] All things considered, transformational leaders need to go beyond the status quo to put in place *dao*-directed governing structures and target change at the systemic level.[32]

Although Confucius encouraged exemplary leaders to transform society, the changes he had in mind were not revolutionary but *evolutionary*. Recall that the modifications of *li* made by the Zhou dynasty and welcomed by Confucius were not radical actions that abolished traditional norms and practices. Rather, they were necessary changes implemented as part of a progressive broadening of the Way. Confucius supported the preservation and not the jettisoning of the old. He said: 'I transmit but do not innovate; I am truthful in what I say and devoted to antiquity' (述而不作，信而好古 7.1). He also claimed: 'I am for the Zhou' (吾從周 3.14, also see 8. 20, 17.5). The before-mentioned passages do not mean that Confucius was a traditionalist or merely a transmitter of the Zhou dynasty. Rather, he believed that any changes made, or anything novel, must be based on a prior knowledge base. As he put it, we need to 'know what is new by keeping fresh in one's mind what one is already familiar with' (溫故而知新 2.11). The Chinese word *zhi* 知 in 2.11, translated here as 'know', does not refer to only intellectual knowledge, but also and more importantly, experiential knowledge.

Concluding this section, Confucius envisaged the realization of a shared vision of human excellence through a socially just educational system that mirrors transformational, ethical mindfulness.

> A Confucian Way-seeker aims to bring about transformation in the self and in the world by not just asking 'what it is' but also 'where should we go'.

Critical thinking and respectful mindfulness

The second significant implication is that Confucius's approach to critique and critical thinking was not confrontational, disrespectful or violent. As much as an exemplary person should promote the Way and remonstrate with one's leader who has strayed from the Way, they should do so through respectful mindfulness. Confucius valued showing respect to everyone, and eschewed the adversarial and contemptuous treatment of others. Exemplary persons always carry themselves in accordance with *ren*-based *li* (normative behaviours). As mentioned earlier, *ren* (humanity) is comprised of a plurality of virtues, including the value of respect (*jing*). Pointing out the flaws of someone does not give the critical thinker the license to abuse or despise that person. Instead, the critical thinker needs to continue to observe *li* by expressing benevolence and empathy towards people and the surroundings.

It is instructive that Confucius's reading of critical thinking is distinct from the dominant orientations in Anglophone contexts. In the West, a typical critical thinker is chiefly perceived as a 'truth-seeker' – an autonomous, rational and atomistic individual who has mastered the universal processes of logic and adversarial argumentation.[33] However, such a portrayal of a critical thinker is foreign to the Confucian tradition. Confucius's idea of critical thinker is more accurately described as a 'Way-seeker' – one who is action-oriented, ethical and interdependent. Unlike a 'truth-seeker', a Confucian critical thinker aims at actions that advance respectful mindfulness, exemplary living and serving others.[34] A Confucian Way-seeker aspires to bring about transformation in the self and in the world by not just asking 'what it is' but also 'where should we go'.[35]

As an extension of Way-seeking, the transformed society Confucius had in mind was inherently *ethical* in nature. Any social changes, from a Confucian standpoint, must be premised on moral self-cultivation. Through respectful mindfulness and a lifelong effort to learn and practise virtues, everyone is invited to partake in a creative process of the transformation of self and society.[36] *Ren* must be the focal point of all observances of *li*. *Ren*-centred critical thinking, therefore, is put forward. This form of critical thinking enables human beings to incrementally expand the Way that connects the past to the present and future. The desired outcome of the transformation of society is made possible by exemplary persons coming together to critique, reflect on, appropriate and adapt traditional beliefs and practices, as well as apply them to their own unique circumstances.[37]

By combining the old and the new, Confucius offered new insights into familiar concepts and challenged the traditional thinking and conduct of the Chinese in antiquity. Alluding to Confucius's idea of building the new upon the old, research has shown that Easterners, in contrast with Westerners, tend to relate the new to the old that is undergirded by social and moral values. In general, Easterners interpret transformation of society as building upon and extending from prior traditions and practices. In contrast, unprecedented and disruptive changes are more observable and acceptable in the West.[38]

Confucius's conception of critical thinking shows that thinking, as well as rationality and judgement, is not context-free, and is instead circumscribed by local cultures. Critical thinking occurs in specific sociocultural contexts in response to particular situations. Standards of rationality, evidence and logic are necessarily dependent on historically concrete languages and practices. There is no 'view from nowhere'; all reasoning and conclusions arise from and are conditioned by particular historical, political, economic and social conditions.[39]

> Easterners, in contrast with Westerners, tend to relate the new to the old that is undergirded by social and moral values.

Conclusion

This chapter has outlined the last component of R|E|S|T for a Confucian mindful leader, namely Transforming society – furthering social justice mindfully by broadening the Way. The major changes in society can take place at different levels, across various professions and in diverse ways. Although it may seem a mammoth task for school leaders to transform society at the macro level, they can begin with their own schools. After all, a school is a microcosm of a society and a site of enculturation for children and youth. Educational leaders exercise an immense sphere of influence in their own schools. They can start by bringing the staff and other stakeholders together to question the universal trends, habits and taken-for-granted assumptions. They could then enact changes in different areas such as the management system, curriculum, teaching, assessment or professional development of teachers. Beyond the school context, school leaders can also impact society through home-school partnerships or community outreach. Whichever the initiative is, the targeted outcome of the school leader is to be mindful to contribute to the well-being of everyone.

It needs to be reiterated that although R|E|S|T (Respectful mindfulness, Exemplary living, Serving others and Transforming society) ends with transforming society, Confucian Mindful Leadership (CML) does not need to be developed in this order. As explained in previous chapters, the four circles in R|E|S|T do not indicate a linear progression and instead represent the conceptual relationships between and expanding social influence of the four components. In practice, a fluid and evolving combination of the components of R|E|S|T is cultivated and demonstrated by different practitioners in their daily interactions with people. What is vital is that a Confucian mindful leader demonstrates respectful mindfulness and exemplary living, and is engaged in serving others and transforming society. Having covered all the four dimensions of R|E|S|T for CML, the next chapter will draw the discussions in this book to a close.

7

Conclusions

Confucius lived during a period that was not that different from ours – he was confronted with and distressed by social instability, human strife and an uncertain future. For us, modern technologies have made our lives more comfortable, but sadly, no less troubling and stressful than that of Confucius. Whether we live in antiquity or in the present time, we need to extricate ourselves from daily pressures and multitasking, and take time to keep silent, as shown in Photo 7.1. Living in a post-pandemic world, where school closures and disrupted learning have become commonplace, Confucian Mindful Leadership (CML) is urgently needed in schools. This book has proposed a novel interpretation to mindful leadership by combining ancient wisdom and modern educational research.[1] The various chapters have explained the concept of CML, highlighting respect as the starting point of mindfulness, virtue as the defining character of the leader, and doing good to others and improving society as evidences of excellent leadership.

This concluding chapter sums up the contents and contributions of CML by returning to the research gaps mentioned in the preface. The first section gives details on how CML through R|E|S|T responds to questions that have not been adequately answered in the existing literature. The next segment brings attention to the significant contributions of CML to the research on mindfulness and mindful leadership, as well as the key critiques of this approach.

Contributions of CML

Confucian Mindful Leadership (CML) clarifies and justifies the concept of mindful leadership by answering this central question: *How is mindful leadership an integral part of a good life?*

Photo 7.1 A sign in a Chinese garden that reads 'Keep silence' (*zhi yu*).

The preface has identified two major research gaps in the extant literature: a lack of clarity on the concept of mindful leadership, and the limited application of mindful leadership to schools. CML responds to these two under-explored areas as follows: (1) it clarifies and justifies the idea of mindful leadership and (2) it illuminates the application of mindful leadership to schools. These two points are explained in this section.

The first research gap: A lack of clarity on the concept of mindful leadership

CML addresses the ambiguity surrounding the notion of mindful leadership. As noted in the preface, there is insufficient provision of a theoretical framework and ethical basis for mindfulness in general, and mindful leadership in particular. A shared assumption by writers and practitioners is that mindful leadership is 'good' and 'right'. What is less clear is what mindful leadership is, and why this form of leadership is recommended in the first place. Although some researchers and mindful leaders have articulated what they believe are the salient elements of mindful leadership, a more coherent and convincing account of mindful leadership is still required.

CML clarifies and justifies the concept of mindful leadership by answering this central question: *How is mindful leadership an integral part of a good life?* To appreciate Confucius's contribution to mindful leadership, it is helpful to distinguish between the 'thin' and 'thick' conceptions of human good or perfection.[2]

Thin and thick conceptions of human good

A *thin* conception of human good refers to ideas such as what is 'good' and 'right' but does not stipulate substantial, particular frameworks of belief and value for individuals and communities. Such a conception may require basic social morality from everyone, but maximizes the freedom of individuals to decide on their diverse private conceptions of the good. A *thick* conception of human good, on the other hand, is substantially descriptive, in the sense that it provides a comprehensive view of human life and how it should be lived.

Following a *thin conception of human good*, mindful leaders are assumed to be good leaders, but the specific beliefs and values that comprise goodness are not explained and left to individual leaders to determine. An advantage of this approach is that the notions of mindful leadership are free of explicit and pre-determined moral values and judgments. It gives leaders the autonomy to pursue their own ideas of the human good, including their personal and diverse understandings of 'good' leadership. Nonetheless, the appeal of a thin conception of human good for mindful leadership is also its weakness: there is an absence of evaluative and substantive descriptions of mindful leadership. We are still left with fundamental questions about mindful leadership such as the following:

- What exactly is mindful leadership?
- Why should leaders be mindful?
- What do we mean when we say that mindful leadership is 'good' or 'right' – is it for the leader, followers or the organization?
- Is 'good' mindful leadership equivalent to instrumental outcomes, such as helping the leader meet the organization's key performance indicators (KPIs)?
- In the specific context of schools, are the KPI primarily test scores and awards within a performative culture?
- If so, is mindful leadership really 'right' for the students and teachers? What about the holistic development and well-being of students, staff and other educational stakeholders?

> Is 'good' mindful leadership equivalent to instrumental outcomes, such as helping the leader meet the organization's key performance indicators (KPIs)?

Without spelling out the underlying beliefs and values of mindful leadership, this leadership approach is open to moral abuses.[3] This relates to the critique on the limited ethical justification for mindful leadership. It is entirely possible for a leader to use mindfulness strategies for morally questionable goals by ignoring underlying organizational or societal problems and injustices, and shifting the blame to the employees.

A case in point is the concepts of collective mindfulness, mindful organizing and organizational mindfulness, which were discussed in Chapter 1. Briefly, *collective mindfulness* is about the arrangements and habits of practice that motivate the staff to focus on and respond to specific situations in a timely manner. *Mindful organizing* spotlights operations and comprises five interrelated processes: attention to failure, refusal to simplify interpretations, scrupulous focus on operations, commitment to resilience, and flexible decision structures. Finally, *organizational mindfulness* is enacted by the organization's top administrators at the strategic level, with an emphasis on producing a culture of openness and agility, as well as enhancing employees' information processing and attentional resources.

It appears that collective mindfulness, mindful organizing and organizational mindfulness are largely result-oriented, and enable leaders to run the organization efficiently. Although these three concepts are useful for leaders, what is de-emphasized are the moral values that undergird and accompany mindful leadership, which go beyond technical rationality and productivity.[4] Without a moral vision, it is tempting for leaders to treat mindful leadership strategies as merely a means to an end.[5] This is essentially an instance of *McMindfulness* – nudging staff on to be more productive through mindfulness exercises, while neglecting the systemic problems and injustices that may exist at the workplace.

As such, it is vital for mindful leadership to be grounded in a *thick conception of human good*. Such a conception situates mindful leadership within a comprehensive account of human life and how it should be lived. Concepts and theories of mindful leadership are substantially descriptive; they guide leaders to think, feel, be predisposed towards and act in ways that constitute, justify and fortify the common good. What amounts to 'the common good', as well as associated ideas of 'human good' and 'the good life', are open to personal and collective reflections, discussions and dialogues. It needs to be clarified that what is not recommended here is an imposition or indoctrination of mindful leadership based on a thick conception of human good. What makes up the good life for a leader should not be something that is decided by the authorities and prescribed for individuals. Each person is free to – and should – take time to contemplate and craft their own conceptions of a flourishing life and the corresponding leadership practices that support their preferred conceptions.

A compelling formulation of mindful leadership – one that aims to persuade leaders to become and remain as mindful leaders – needs to go beyond vague terms such as 'good' and 'right' leadership, to identify, spell out and justify the substance of and moral principles for mindful leadership. The desired outcome is a plurality of thick conceptions of human good, negotiated between and accepted by the leader, followers and other social actors, who support and justify mindful leadership. Within an organization such as a school, it is critical for all the educational stakeholders to discuss and agree upon a shared *dao* (Way) – a vision of human excellence. This common purpose should transcend a thin conception of human good to a thick one, so as to make clear the *dao* of educating students.[6] Whatever the shared vision, it should not be limited to academic performance or prizes won by high-performing students but extended to the inclusive growth, total well-being and values inculcation of every child.

It is therefore crucial for researchers to delineate how mindful leadership (as well as mindfulness) is part and parcel of a thick conception of human good, and the moral values that underpin this form of leadership.

> A compelling formulation of mindful leadership – one that aims to persuade leaders to become and remain as mindful leaders – needs to go beyond vague terms such as 'good' and 'right' leadership, to identify, spell out and justify the substance of and moral principles for mindful leadership.

CML as an example of a thick conception of human good

In view of the problems associated with the thin conception of human good, this study has adopted the thick conception of human good, by drawing upon the educational ideas of Confucius. This book has put forward CML as a form of mindful leadership that is based on and guided by four cardinal Confucian qualities through R|E|S|T (see Figure 7.1).

CML is directed at respectful mindfulness, which refers to the moment-by-moment, appreciative and whole-hearted attentiveness to oneself, people, things and events. A mindful leader is a *junzi* – an exemplary person who seeks to broaden *dao* (Way), which is the normative discourse for human beings. A key characteristic of Confucian mindfulness is that it is a trait, state and practice. The R|E|S|T approach, as a *trait*, predisposes leaders to respectful mindfulness as a

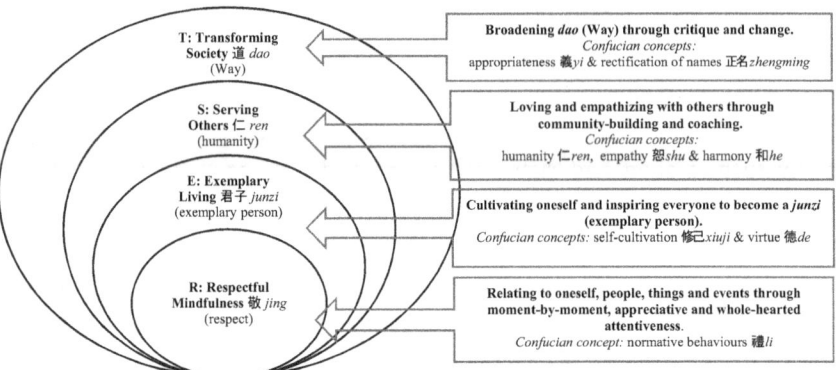

Figure 7.1 Confucian Mindful Leadership (CML) through R|E|S|T.

general condition of the heart-mind. All the four components of R|E|S|T are not simply discrete descriptions of occasional activities or outcomes; they describe a continuous and evolving process of leadership. As a *state*, a leader manifests respectful mindfulness to varying degrees and in different ways, depending on the object, time, place and circumstances. Finally, Confucian mindfulness is also a *practice* in the sense that a mindful leader needs to invest time and effort to cultivate oneself to become and remain, an exemplary leader for life. A Confucian mindful leader adheres to, demonstrates and role-models R|E|S|T naturally, thereby motivating others to do likewise. A mindful school, it follows, puts into practice collective mindfulness, mindful organizing and organizational mindfulness, not in an amoral manner that follows McMindfulness, but through respectful mindfulness, exemplary living, serving others and transforming society.[7]

A clarification about CML is that different individuals are likely to learn and develop the four components of R|E|S|T in diverse ways and to varying degrees of success. For example, a leader who is an excellent coach may be more proficient in the domain of serving others than in the aspect of transforming society that requires systems thinking. There could also be divergence between leaders within each component. Take for instance the component of serving others. One leader may be more adept at the sub-component of mentoring others, whereas another leader may be more competent in the sub-component of community-building. It follows that becoming a Confucian mindful leader is not an either-or state of affairs, and is always a work in progress. The key question is not whether a person is or is not a Confucian mindful leader, but in what ways and to what extent does the person exhibit the various components and sub-components of R|E|S|T.[8]

CML and the ethical justification for mindful leadership

The R|E|S|T framework of CML provides an *ethical justification* for mindful leadership by foregrounding the moral qualities of respect, exemplary personhood, humanity and *dao* (a vision of human excellence).[9] CML positions ethics as indispensable for good leadership; it helps to address a critique of the current mindfulness programmes as being largely therapeutic, amoral or non-moral, inward-looking, utilitarian and commercialized.[10] A mindful person, according to Confucius, is one who is necessarily respectful towards others. This means holding others in high regard by demonstrating deference towards them. Confucius's accent on respectful mindfulness inspires everyone to go beyond egoistic concerns and individualistic advancement to show humility, empathy and kind-heartedness towards others.

> A Confucian mindful leader displays executive virtues such as doing one's utmost, as well as substantive virtues such as respect and humanity.

CML also goes beyond the dichotomy of seeing leadership as either *doing* or *being*; it puts an emphasis on both. On the one hand, CML acknowledges the importance of doing for leaders. Confucius enjoined leaders to walk the talk by taking concrete measures to serve others and transform society. On the other hand, CML does not limit good leadership to the leader's actions or the consequences. Instead, CML, in line with the moral approach of *virtue ethics*, gives prominence to the leader's character as the basis from which the leader views, interacts with and impacts others. CML, through R|E|S|T, transcends doing; it is about the attitude and habit of mindfulness.

Consistent with virtue ethics, a Confucian mindful leader role-models both executive virtues and substantive virtues.[11] *Executive virtues* such as courage, patience and determination centre around a person's will power or self-mastery, which are influential to the achievement of one's plans. *Substantive virtues* include qualities such as kindness, compassion and loyalty, which motivate a person's actions. Confucius distinguishes between executive virtues such as courage that enable one to perform actions effectively, and substantive virtues such as respect that motivate one towards moral goodness. However, executive virtues, for Confucius, are not non-moral, and are in fact grounded in the moral principles of *ren* (humanity), *dao* (Way) and other virtues associated with a *junzi* (exemplary person).[12] A Confucian mindful leader displays executive virtues such as doing one's utmost as well as substantive virtues such as respect and *ren* (humanity). Both sets of virtues are important and mutually reinforcing: executive virtues without substantive virtues are directionless, whereas substantive virtues without executive virtues are inefficacious.[13] Harmonizing executive and substantive virtues, a Confucian mindful leader inspires and serves others through altruism, empathic concern, doing one's best and prudence.

In all, CML provides a moral foundation for mindful leadership by making the qualities of respect, virtue, co-humanity and moral transformation the basic constituents of good leadership.

The second research gap: Limited application of mindful leadership to schools

CML also addresses the literature gap on the *limited application of mindful leadership to schools*. I have noted in the preface that the bulk of the existing publications on mindful leadership pertain to non-schooling organizations, and do not discuss specific educational concerns such as student development and well-being.[14]

Applying CML to schools means that school leaders first need to model and advocate excellent character traits as the antecedent of being exemplary leaders. The target is not simply improving student outcomes or teacher capacity, but more fundamentally, demonstrating and furthering exemplary living for the school community. Research shows that effective school leaders possess a good mix of both executive and substantive virtues, such as mindfulness, clarity of vision and perseverance, with courage of conviction, fair-mindedness, justice and emotional intelligence.[15] Successful school leaders achieve their goals not only through judiciously selected policies and practices, but also through their personal values and conduct.[16] The following summarizes the research findings on the admirable attributes of outstanding school principals:

> There are many personal qualities, beliefs and values that help principals be successful leaders. Acumen, optimism, persistence, trust (behaving in a way that promotes the attribution of trust in the leader by others, and also displaying trust in others), tolerance, empathy, alertness (shown through high levels of physical and mental energy), curiosity, resilience, benevolence, honesty, openness, respectful and humbleness were some of the traits on display. They have a strong ethic of care, empathy for others, value individuality ... driven by the desire to

provide the best educational environment they can for all students . . . they have the courage to do what is right to help their students be the best they can.[17]

R|E|S|T enables school leaders to become genuine, moral and supportive leaders who foster teacher growth, student development and community involvement. School leaders should therefore infuse R|E|S|T into the school ethos and practices by creating and sustaining mindful classrooms. Table 7.1 gives an example of a lesson plan for a mindful classroom for a school year in Singapore. In a nutshell, CML empowers leaders to manage schools successfully by demonstrating four core sets of practices: determining the shared vision and direction, developing people and building relationships, reconceptualizing the school structures and policies, and enhancing the instructional programme.[18]

CML's contribution to mindfulness

Apart from addressing the existing research gaps on mindful leadership, CML also contributes to the extant research on mindfulness in two important ways: (1) CML illustrates a virtues-centric approach to mindfulness and (2) CML debunks an East-West dichotomy on mindfulness.

> Confucius's notions of mindfulness were not entirely Eastern – he did not teach meditation or non-judgemental awareness. Instead, his focus was on moral cultivation through normative behaviours and humanity.

First, CML adds to the existing scholarship by illustrating a *virtues-centric approach to mindfulness*. This point has been reiterated throughout this study. When we compare Confucius's formulation of mindfulness with the dominant understanding of the term in the current literature, we can identify both similarities and differences. In terms of convergence, Confucius's notion of respectful mindfulness is aligned with the prevailing interpretation of mindfulness as the capacities of attention, awareness, memory and discernment. Confucius's stress on being deferential, reflective and alert, dovetails with the emphasis in mindfulness on personal awareness, memory and acceptance of one's encounters, surroundings and relationships.

Nevertheless, Confucius's construal of mindfulness is not purely non-judgemental and focused on present-state awareness. Rather, *jing*, as respectful mindfulness, gives evidence to one's exemplary personhood and leadership.

Table 7.1 An Example of a Lesson Plan for a Mindful Classroom

Schedule for the School Year	Micro-mindfulness Moments and Big Red-Flag Provisions
January: Start of the term. Orientation programme for new students.	**Micro-Mindfulness Moments:** **(1) My signature greeting:** My signature greeting is to stand in the middle of the class, scan the classroom to look at everyone and say with a smile, 'Good morning/afternoon! Good to see everyone here. I am Mrs Lim and welcome to this class!' I will articulate the words with a smile that reveals my calm, approachable and gentle demeanour. Indeed, my students have given me feedback that I come across as calm and affable. I consciously smile not just with my lips but also my eyes. **(2) Routine events for micro-mindfulness moments for students**: (1) Mindful mornings where I greet every student with direct attention and a sense of care; (2) planning mindful moments where specific curriculum time is set aside for students to practise mindfulness; (3) creating a peace corner where students can choose to go to when they want some rest or alone-time; (4) using mindful language such as heartfulness, where students learn to send kind thoughts to one another and (5) making agreements by inviting students to create shared group agreements based on common values such as respect, safety and fun. **(3) My 'Caring Phrases':** To assure my students that I am present with them, care for them and that they are safe. • I am right here for you. • You are in a safe learning environment. • I care for you. **(4) Buddy system**: I will pair students up so that they support each other mindfully.
March: Semester test. Students will sit for their first test since their enrolment in the school.	**Big Red-Flag Provisions:** **Three Senses.** This exercise is useful in reducing stress and helps the students to focus as they prepare for their first test in high school.
May: Mid-year examination.	**Big Red-Flag Provision:** **(1) Mindfulness Relaxation Exercise** This complements the 'Three Senses' exercise and serves to help students cope with the stress and pressure as they prepare for their mid-year exam. By this time, my students would be quite familiar with the 'Three Senses'. This practice extends their mindfulness from their sense perceptions to their bodies.

Table 7.1 (continued)

Schedule for the School Year	Micro-mindfulness Moments and Big Red-Flag Provisions
June: One-month vacation.	**Big Red-Flag Provision:** (1) **Mindfulness project on climate change**: I will get students to be involved in a community involvement project on recycling during the vacation. **Micro-Mindfulness Moments:** (1) **Virtual gratitude wall:** I will get the students to post gratitude notes on Padlet during their June vacation. (2) **Smiling Mind app:** I will introduce this to students so that even though they will not be engaging in mindfulness practices in school, they can do it at home.
July: Start of second half of the school term.	**Micro-Mindfulness Moments:** I will continue with the mindfulness practices that I have adopted in the first half of the year. In addition, I will also introduce the following: (1) **Mindful listening through nature.** This helps students to appreciate nature around them. Besides getting them to watch the video clip, I may also take them out on an excursion to the parks and islands, so as to practise mindful walking. (2) **Loving-kindness exercise**: This helps them to appreciate others and extend their empathy to people around them, including those they find it hard to get along with. (3) **Confucian mindfulness lessons.** This will strengthen what my students already know about mindfulness and its practice by linking mindfulness to their Confucian cultural heritage. They will then better appreciate the relevance of mindfulness and channel what they have internalized to acquire a growth mindset and enjoy heartfulness.
September: Semester test.	**Big Red-Flag Provision:** A potential issue is to help students who are struggling with their studies, relationship problems and other personal issues. To do so, I will introduce this mindfulness practice for these students: **Relaxation to deal with anger practice.**
November: Final year exam.	**Big Red-Flag Provision:** **Three-minute Breathing Space Meditation** This is helpful for students who may not have time for the Mindfulness Relaxation Exercise and prefer a shorter practice. This exercise only takes three minutes and is something they can do in between their studying and exam preparation.

(continued)

Table 7.1 (continued)

Schedule for the School Year	Micro-mindfulness Moments and Big Red-Flag Provisions
December: One-month vacation.	**Big Red-Flag Provision:** (1) **Mindful Community Food Voucher Programme:** I will arrange for the students to partner with the community centre to launch a food voucher programme for low-income families. **Micro-Mindfulness Moments:** I will implement the same strategies as those for the June vacation: (1) **Virtual gratitude wall:** I will get the students to post gratitude notes on Padlet during their vacation. (2) **Smiling Mind app:** I will introduce this to students so that they can engage in mindfulness practices in school at home.

Instead of being values-neutral and individualistic, Confucius's vision of mindfulness is grounded in and motivated by *ren* (humanity), which requires one to love others.[19] CML thus remedies a prominent tendency to take on technical and amoral approaches to mindfulness in a neoliberal educational context.

The second major implication of CML is that it *debunks the East-West dichotomy of mindfulness*. Recall that Western approaches to mindfulness concentrate on the cognitive and social aspects of mindfulness, whereas Eastern perspectives of mindfulness feature meditation and personal growth. This division does not apply to CML, however, as it straddles both traditions. On the one hand, Confucius's ideas on mindfulness are aligned with the Western emphasis on the social and cognitive aspects of mindfulness. We have seen how Confucius rejected rote-learning and a blind acceptance of prevalent norms in favour of inferential thinking and context-sensitive responses.[20]

On the other hand, Confucius's notions of mindfulness were not entirely Eastern – he did not teach meditation in the form of mindfulness techniques or non-judgemental awareness. Instead, his focus was on moral cultivation through *li* (normative behaviours) and *ren* (humanity). Confucian mindfulness is not about self-therapy through mindfulness practice, or advancing one's interests as a leader. Rather, it is about locating oneself within a web of human interdependence, and striving to bring out the best in others. Confucian mindfulness is in tandem with a thick conception of human good, which accentuates the eudemonic, moral, social and engaged approaches to mindfulness. By challenging the simplistic East-West binary, CML supports the need for more research, discussions and debates on the multiple, alternative and competitive concepts and theories surrounding mindfulness and mindful leadership across contexts and cultures.

Critique of CML

The foregoing has elucidated how CML through R|E|S|T provides a substantive, reasoned and ethics-based formulation of mindful leadership that rests upon a thick conception of human good. CML addresses the limited application of mindful leadership to schools by enabling school leaders to become authentic, moral and supportive leaders who champion teacher growth, student development and community involvement. Nonetheless, the aforementioned strengths of CML do not mean that this leadership approach has no flaws; drawing insights from Confucius does not mean or imply that his teachings are perfect.

Hence this segment spells out three major critiques of CML that stem from Confucius's philosophy: (1) Confucius's extremely high expectations of leaders, (2) his faith in the power of leading by virtue and (3) the difficulty in implementing his ideas.

> Confucius was similar to Plato in placing his faith in the exemplary person or philosopher-king to shape the thinking, values and behaviour of the ruled majority through the leader's moral excellence.

Confucius's extremely high expectations of leaders

First, Confucius's belief in the irresistible influence of exemplary leaders places a huge responsibility on leaders. To be sure, Confucius was not the only thinker who favoured ethical leadership; neither is CML unique in bringing to the fore the moral character of the leader. The literature on authentic leadership, for example, also underscores the necessity for leaders to match their leadership behaviours with their espoused values and convictions; doing so helps them gain trust, respect and credibility in the eyes of their followers.[21]

However, CML is exceptional among the existing concepts of mindful leadership as it identifies moral character as a defining element of a mindful leader; this raises the bar for anyone who aspires to be a mindful leader. From a Confucian perspective, it is insufficient for a mindful leader to merely acquire the 'know-how' of mindfulness and leadership techniques, such as deep breathing techniques and empathic listening. What is more foundational and non-negotiable is for the leader to demonstrate and model respectful mindfulness – the spontaneous, sincere, positive attentiveness to self, people, things and events – as well as related virtues such as kindness, empathic concern, justice and wisdom.

CML therefore may be daunting to some aspiring leaders; it requires them to resolve to cultivate, manifest and role-model R|E|S|T, and persist in doing so. Such a leader displays and propagates respectful mindfulness and exemplary living, bringing to fruition a school culture and learning environment that is marked by humanity, mutual service and societal transformation. On the one hand, it is natural to expect school leaders, whose mission includes inculcating moral values in children and youth, to walk the talk. On the other hand, Confucius has placed an enormous burden on these leaders, who are fallible human beings like everyone else, to become *junzi* (exemplary persons). One may question whether Confucius's extremely high expectations of leaders as charismatic, ethical change-makers are reasonable.

Confucius's faith in the power of leading by virtue

The second critique of CML is Confucius's privileging of leading by virtue over leading by edicts. He was conditioned by the prevailing harsh laws and guided by his belief that everyone could become an exemplary, *ren* person. Unsurprisingly, he placed much attention on socialization and role-modelling while downplaying the positive effect of the law on human beings. In this sense, Confucius was similar to Plato in placing his faith in the exemplary person or philosopher-king to shape the thinking, values and behaviour of the ruled majority through the leader's moral excellence.[22]

A criticism is that Confucius was too optimistic about the transformative power of virtue in the real world. To remedy this weakness, it is essential to balance moral development and suasion with the necessary remedial and reformative measures in place. In the context of a school, this requires a school leader to complement the required disciplinary structures with R|E|S|T at the heart of the school mission. Although students still need to be corrected and counselled through appropriate punitive mechanisms, they should be treated with respectful mindfulness, and mentored by caring, empathic school leaders and teachers who model virtues.

Difficulty in implementation

> A significant challenge is that few schools today can afford to prioritize respectful mindfulness as a school goal, and (re)design their structures, curriculum, pedagogy and assessment along the lines of R|E|S|T.

The final critique is the difficulty in implementing CML due to practical constraints. Although CML provides a potentially thoughtful and rational schooling programme that supports the development of mindfulness in learners, this educational vision cannot be attained within a short time. Beyond ad hoc mindfulness intervention programmes and after-school activities, CML requires a school-wide and long-term approach, where respectful mindfulness is infused into and across the curriculum. Recall that there are two main approaches to promoting mindfulness in organizations, as discussed in Chapter 1. The first approach focuses narrowly on mindfulness training programmes and views mindfulness as an optional and piecemeal practice. The second approach, which is consistent with the orientation of CML, is more all-encompassing and sustainable. Confucian school leaders are energized to create and maintain mindful schools by integrating mindfulness values, dispositions and practices into the curriculum.

However, a significant challenge is that few schools today can afford to prioritize respectful mindfulness as a school goal and (re)design their structures, curriculum, pedagogy and assessment along the lines of R|E|S|T. Confucius's expectation of teachers as *junzi* (exemplary persons) in a community is also difficult to attain in reality. The school leaders may not have the time or capability to coach teachers; some leaders may also be reluctant to redistribute power to others. Teachers themselves are also hard-pressed for time, often rushing to complete the syllabus and meet performative yardsticks. Modern schooling is circumscribed by an audit culture that holds the teachers accountable for high test scores. The reality of a neoliberal educational environment for schools explains why McMindfulness, which is a quick-fix approach to mindfulness, is readily embraced by leaders and entrenched in the school culture. Notwithstanding the high standards expected of school leaders and the time-consuming and demanding process of enacting R|E|S|T, Confucius's conception of CML promises a *dao* of human excellence for educational administrators.

Conclusion

CML, embodied through R|E|S|T, provides a thick conception of human good for school leaders around the world. A Confucian explication of mindful leadership extends the existing literature on the theoretical and ethical foundations of mindfulness and mindful leadership for educational institutions.

I should add that this book does not present CML as the perfect approach to mindful leadership, nor is it assumed that CML is superior to the existing concepts of mindful leadership. As explained in the preface, this study is motivated by a dearth of literature on mindfulness and mindful leadership from non-Western traditions and perspectives, apart from that on Buddhism. Although originating from Eastern philosophies, mindful leadership theories, programmes and research are primarily undertaken by scholars, leaders and practitioners in the West, and then introduced to Eastern societies.[23] There is therefore a need for more research that is derived from resources from non-Western histories, worldview and presuppositions.[24] This book represents one such scholarly undertaking, by offering an interpretation of mindful leadership based on a textual analysis of the *Analects*.

It is hoped that the concept of CML will open a line of inquiry into, and initiate discussions and dialogues on, the noteworthy features and practices of mindful leadership across cultures.[25] In the final chapter of the *Analects*, Zigong who was a disciple of Confucius described the legacy of his master (italics added):

> 19.23 夫子之牆數仞，不得其門而入，不見宗廟之美，百官之富。
>
> The Master's walls are twenty or thirty feet high so that, unless one gains admittance through *the gate*, one cannot see the magnificence of the ancestral temples or the sumptuousness of the official buildings.

The teachings of Confucius are like a gate (see Photo 7.2), by which the eyes of human beings are opened to things that are magnificent and sumptuous. For Zigong and his peers, Confucius's thought was the only way ('the gate') to the vision of human excellence in ancient Chinese traditions. For people in the modern times, of course, Confucius is not the only channel. But as I have attempted to demonstrate in this book, Confucius's thought provides a gateway for us to rethink the current conceptions and developments on mindfulness and mindful leadership.[26] This book, by extracting the teachings of Confucius to formulate a new version of mindful leadership, envisions Confucius as a gate through which humanity may find inspiration and renewed hope in the contemporary world.

Photo 7.2 The entrance to Robert Black College of the University of Hong Kong.

Notes

Preface

1 Davenport and Beck (2002) coined the term *attention economy* to describe a situation where attention is a scarce resource in an information-flooded world.
2 The term *telepressure* is taken from Ehrlich (2017).
3 For details, see Buller (2019) and Rowland (2017).
4 The lack of clarity on mindful leadership is an offshoot of the prior ambiguity, contestation and confusion over the notion of *mindfulness*. Mindfulness is a 'floating signifier' (King & Badham, 2020, p. 166), denoting different things to different people and in diverse contexts.
5 I shall give more details of the existing research on mindful leadership in Chapter 1.
6 This is taken from Cissna and Schockman (2021, p. 551).
7 An example is the formulation of mindful leadership by Marques (2021); she stressed the importance of leaders being mindful, which is,

> [the] ability to be aware of all the factors that matter in the choice process. Mindfulness is our basic human ability to be fully present and not reactive or distracted by external occurrences . . . In making choices, especially those with high impact, there is no room for neglecting factors that could be critical for the outcome. We will therefore have to be attentive to details, but also to the bigger picture. (p. 116)

The above outlines an important axiom for leaders to function effectively. That said, the argument would be more persuasive if she had clarified the theoretical basis for mindful leadership. What, for example, is 'the bigger picture' – is it the organizational goals, shareholders' priorities, staff welfare or societal needs, among others?

8 This response also raises the question of why a person would choose *mindful* leadership, among other leadership theories, to fulfil one's aspiration of being a good leader. This harkens back to my earlier point on a lack of compelling theoretical foundations for mindful leadership. The key question is what sets mindful leadership apart from other equally popular leadership concepts, styles or practices, such as authentic, distributed and instructional leadership.
9 Long (2021) listed Aetna Insurance, Google, Mayo Clinic and the US Army as examples of organizations that have implemented mindfulness programmes or practices.

10 McMindfulness was coined by Purser and Loy (2013), who wrote: 'Rather than applying mindfulness as a means to awaken individuals and organizations from the unwholesome roots of greed, ill will and delusion, it is usually being refashioned into a banal, therapeutic, self-help technique that can actually reinforce those roots' (p. 1). Cautioning against McMindfulness, Forbes (2016) averred: 'Instead of letting go of the ego, McMindfulness aims to enhance it and promotes self-aggrandizement; its therapeutic function is to comfort, numb, adjust and advance the self within a neoliberal, corporatized, individualistic society based on private gain' (p. 357).
11 Hyland (2016) asserted that the ethical and educational elements in mindfulness-based interventions are neglected in the current mindfulness movement.
12 It is important to keep in mind that the etymology of *education* is not just 'drawing out' (*educere*), which entails training, knowledge transmission and skills-acquisition, but also 'cultivating' (*educare*) learners.
13 A review of the growing body of literature on mindful leadership for schools reveals the same concerns noted earlier regarding mindful leadership – an inadequate focus on the theoretical and moral basis of this leadership concept (Brown & Olson, 2015; Buller, 2019; Wells, 2015).
14 A clarification is needed on the use of the terms 'East(ern)' and 'West(ern)' in this book. The term 'East' refers to China and other Confucian Heritage Cultures societies, such as South Korea and Japan. I have followed Niu and Sternberg (2006) in defining 'the West' as 'the culture of Europe and the people who share the same root or have religious link to Europe. Geographically speaking, it includes most parts of Europe, North America, Australia and New Zealand' (p. 20). My references to 'East' and 'West' are not intended to essentialize and stereotype both cultures. Rather, the aim is to use them as useful conceptual tools to foreground the influential role of cultural traditions, while acknowledging the diversity within both categories.
15 This point is taken from Ie et al. (2014).
16 Commenting on the link between mindfulness and Buddhism, Komjathy (2018) described this phenomenon as 'Buddhist-neuroscientific hegemony' (p. 25). It needs to be clarified that the term 'Buddhist' in the Western academic discourse is not a monolithic or homogenous tradition. For example, the current mindfulness programmes and movement are drawn not just from Chan (Zen) Buddhism, but also Theravada and Vietnamese Mahayana Buddhism (Kirmayer, 2015). Stanley et al. (2018) observed:

> There are multiple viewpoints, diverse positions and profound conflicts and disagreements, with precious few points of consensus, within and outside of the 'Buddhist' traditions themselves, concerning basic questions of the meaning of mindfulness and ethics, whether 'Buddhism' is a singular or multiple phenomena, is itself a religion (or a psychology or philosophy or

universal dharma), whether the historical Buddha was himself a Buddhist, and the relative status of Buddhism to science when it comes to crucial and pressing debates about mindfulness and ethics. (p. 9)

17 See, for example, Moloney (2016), Samuel (2016) and Weintraub and Dust (2021). Ie et al. (2014) pointed out that the concept of mindfulness stems from not only ancient Buddhist traditions but also Chinese philosophies. However, they did not mention Confucianism in their writings.
18 A philosophical inquiry is beneficial to redress the overly positivist slant of the existing mindfulness research, comprising 'hypothetico-deductive studies aiming to predict and control human behaviour through psychometrics, experimentation and randomized clinical trials (RCTs)' (Stanley & Longden, 2016, p. 305).
19 See de Bary (1981) and Hwang (2013).
20 See Tan (2021a, 2021b, 2021c).
21 I shall use the terms 'disciple', 'protégé' and 'student' interchangeably to refer to the followers of Confucius. Brooks and Brooks (1998) claimed that Confucius's followers should be called 'protégés' instead of 'disciples' as the latter 'implies a relationship which arose only later, as the Confucian school became more organized' (p. 11). In using the term 'disciples', I do not assume that Confucianism had developed into a formal school system during Confucius's time.
22 This point is taken from Ames and Rosemont (1998). Given that the *Analects* came into existence a few centuries after the death of Confucius, it is not surprising that there are debates and questions about its authenticity. I have followed Confucian scholars who support the reliability of the classic. For example, Slingerland (2001) maintained that the *Analects* contains 'enough consistency in terminological use and philosophical and religious conceptualization to allow us to treat the text as a genuine representation of the state of the "School of Confucius" before the innovations of Mencius and Xunzi' (p. 98).

1 Mindfulness and Mindful Leadership

1 Hougaard et al. (2016) devised the expression *PAID reality*, denoting Pressured, Always-on, Information Overloaded and Distracted (p. 49). Becker (2013) added that modern-day stress is the *New Black Death*.
2 This is taken from Ehrlich (2017), who also reported that Microsoft managers needed more than thirty hours to resume their work for one third of the time.
3 This is taken from Ehrlich (2017).
4 Sethi (2009) highlighted a *leadership paradox*: 'To arrive at better answers they need to really think out of the box, but past success (and the hubris that comes with it) has imprisoned them in the box' (p. 10).

5 McGhee and Grant (2021) contended that mindfulness should no longer be considered a 'nice-to-have' but a 'must-have' to 'keep our brains healthy, to support self-regulation and effective decision-making capabilities and to protect ourselves from toxic stress (p. 219). Cissna and Schockman (2021) observed:

> The popular press has shown a growing interest in the topic of mindfulness in the workplace, with books like *The Power of Now* (Tolle, 2004), *The Mindful Leader* (Carroll, 2007), *Awake at Work* (Carroll, 2004), and *Resonant Leadership: Renewing yourself and connecting with others through mindfulness, hope, and compassion* (Boyatzis & McKee, 2005), *10% Happier* (Harris, 2014), *Waking Up* (Harris, 2014), and many more. Popular phone apps such as *Calm* and *Headspace* teach mindfulness and meditation techniques. This demonstrates a demand for leaders to understand and embrace mindfulness for leadership in the 21st century. (p. 550)

6 In 2007, Americans spent around US$4 billion on Mindfulness Based Stress Reduction (MBSR) and other mindfulness-related alternative medicine (Pickert, 2014). There are also conferences such as *Wisdom 2.0*, meditation apps such as *Headspace*, and educational programmes such as *Mindful Schools* that has trained educators in forty-three countries and reached at least 300,000 pupils (Pickert, 2014). A report titled *Mindful Nation UK* in 2015 advocated mindfulness for schools and other professional sites, and underlined the notion of 'mental capital' that refers to 'the cognitive and emotional resources that ensure resilience in the face of stress, and the flexibility of mind and learning skills to adapt to a fast-changing employment market and longer working lives' (cited in Levey & Levey, 2019, p. 2).

7 Mindfulness programmes have grown steadily in schools, promising to enable students to pay attention mindfully rather than live mindlessly. Weare (2014) noted: 'As an indicator of this growth of activity, a database of what is called in the US K-12 contemplative education programmes (i.e. those that are taught to children between the ages of 5 and 18 years) taught in the US and Canada has been compiled by the Garrison Institute (2012a) and, at the time of writing, lists 37 programmes, taught in a wide range of contexts' (p. 1037).

8 In the words of Rhys Davids (1910),

> Etymologically, Sati is memory. But as happened at the rise of Buddhism to so many other expressions in common use, a new connotation was then attached to the word, a connotation that gave a new meaning to it, and renders 'memory' a most inadequate and misleading translation. It became the memory, recollection, calling-to-mind, being aware of, certain specified facts. Of these the most important was the impermanence (the coming to be

as the result of a cause, and the passing away again) of all phenomena, bodily and mental. And it included the repeated application of this awareness, to each experience of life, from the ethical point of view. (p. 322, cited in King, 2016, p. 33)

9 I am using Buddhism synonymously with *Buddhadharma*. The reason is that some scholars in the West have questioned the appropriateness of the term 'Buddhism'. For example, Lewis and Rozelle (2016) wrote: 'We favour the term *Buddhadharma* over Buddhism whenever possible because the former is an ancient and indigenous Sanskrit word for the doctrines and practices based on the teachings of the Buddha (the Pali equivalent is *Buddhadhamma*), while *Buddhism* is a Westernised name dating to the 1830s, with no equivalent in Pali or Sanskrit' (p. 243). It is also pertinent, but somewhat puzzling, that Kabat-Zinn declared, 'The Buddha himself wasn't a Buddhist, and the term Buddhism is an invention of Europeans' (cited in Wallis, 2016, p. 502).

10 As taught by Thich Nhat Hanh (2011), mindfulness is about being aware of what is going on in our bodies, our feelings, our minds and the world, so that we consciously refrain from harming ourselves and others. He also introduced the Five Mindfulness Trainings that 'are a concrete expression of the Buddha's teachings on the Four Noble Truths and the Noble Eightfold Path, the path of right understanding and true love, leading to healing, transformation, and happiness for ourselves and for the world' (Thich, 2011, p. xx). Thich Nhat Hanh's formulation of mindfulness as having no craving and attaining *nirvana* (perfection) is different from Kabat-Zinn's; the latter's is more secular and individualistic. Kabat-Zinn (1990) described mindfulness as 'a way of looking deeply into oneself in the spirit of self-inquiry and self-understanding' (p. 12).

11 See Sethi (2009).

12 For a good discussion of mindfulness from a Hindu viewpoint, see Jagannathan and Rodhain (2016); for Daoist views on mindfulness, see Ambler (2007).

13 As Hadot (1995) put it, spiritual exercises are concerned with 'meditation, dialogue with oneself, examination of conscience, exercises of the imagination, such as the view from above on the cosmos or the earth, or in the order of action and of daily behaviour, like the mastery of oneself, indifference towards indifferent things, the fulfilment of the duties of social life in Stoicism, the discipline of desires in Epicureanism' (p. 31). Petranker (2016) commented:

> the Hellenistic thinkers of Greece and Rome presented philosophy as *therapeia* …: a therapy for the soul or simply for the condition of being human. In modern times, we place therapy in the realm of psychology, distinct from what we consider to be the abstract truths of philosophy. But the notion of philosophy as *therapeia* challenges this split. It suggests that if we see the world differently, that may be all the therapy we need. Such seeing

is not 'theoretical', at least in our modern sense. Instead, it involves activating a new vision. …Perhaps it is as *therapeia* in this sense that mindfulness [field-centred mindfulness] can extend the range of benefits that mindfulness [present-centred mindfulness] makes available. (p. 104)

14 Purser et al. (2016) noted that 'mindfulness in the West, under the claim that it is derived from Buddhism, has become severed from not only Buddhist ethical contexts, but also its roots in Buddhist philosophy and soteriology' (p. vii). Wongkom et al. (2019) from Thailand explained the key difference between Buddhist mindfulness and that which is prevalent in the West: 'In Buddhism, the goal of meditation is salvation, as Thai people are familiar with, but for the Western academics, meditation is used in management, individual's potential development, and organization development' (p. 135).

15 This is cited in Kabat-Zinn (2003, p. 145, italics added).

16 Below are two examples that follow or allude to Kabat-Zinn's focus on mindfulness as present-moment, non-judgemental awareness:

1. *Mindfulness* is simply noticing the way things are. It's not a technique, it's a skill – the skill of being aware without grasping or denying. Both grasping and denying are created states; they don't occur naturally. Therefore, mindfulness is the skill of being natural. It enables you to be aware of exactly who and what you are. (Gonzalez, 2012, p. 13, italics in original)

2. Mindfulness makes us aware of what is, as opposed to what needs to be done – to experience non-doing, or non-effort. In a state of mindfulness we self-consciously enable ourselves to suspend agendas, judgments, and common understanding. In being mindful, we are being several things all at once: passive, alert, open, curious, and exploratory. (Kets de Vries, 2014, p. 9)

17 Dreyfus (2011) highlighted another key difference between Kabat-Zinn's definition of mindfulness and Rhys Davids's by noting that the latter's 'is not the present-centred non-judgemental awareness of an object but the paying close attention to an object, leading to the retention of the data so as to make sense of the information delivered by our cognitive apparatus' (p. 47).

18 Tomassini (2016) noted that Langer's influential conception of mindfulness has been critiqued for being 'more concerned with awareness of external events than inner experiences (thoughts and emotions), and more concerned with goal-oriented cognitive tasks rather than nonjudgemental observation' (p. 217). I have described Langer's interpretation of mindfulness as *nonmoral* to mean that morality is not an issue in her formulation of mindfulness. I am not asserting that her conception of mindfulness is *amoral*, that is, lacking a concern about the rightness or wrongness of something.

19 This is taken from Langer (2000, p. 220).

20 The discussion on mindlessness, including the ideas of recurring actions and unitary exposure, is taken from Langer (1992, 2000). According to Langer (1992), mindlessness is 'a state of mind characterized by an overreliance on categories and distinctions drawn in the past and in which the individual is context-dependent and, as such, is oblivious to novel (or simply alternative) aspects of the situation' (p. 289). Also see Tan (2021b).
21 This is taken from Hopper (2010).
22 This is noted by Yadav (2021). Specifically, the works of Kabat-Zinn and Langer represent the Eastern and Western traditions of mindfulness, respectively. This will be elaborated on in a later section in the chapter.
23 The notion of mindfulness 'serves almost as a cipher into which one can read virtually anything we want' (Bodhi, 2011, p. 22). In the same vein, Van Dam et al. (2018) noted that mindfulness is 'an umbrella term used to characterize a large number of practices, processes and characteristics, largely defined in relation to the capacities of attention, awareness, memory/retention, and acceptance/discernment' (p. 37).
24 King and Badham (2020) explained that *individual-oriented* mindfulness concentrates on 'immediate personal experience, emphasizing awareness and attention to the present moment, stress reduction, emotion regulation, overcoming habitual thought and behaviour, etc.' while *collective-oriented* mindfulness centres on 'the reality of interdependence, group mind, relational mindfulness, and organizational support for cooperative and heedful thought and action' (p. 167).
25 King and Badham (2020) clarified the difference between instrumental and substantive mindfulness:

> Mindfulness perspectives are characterised in *instrumental* terms when they are focused on how individual performance and well-being might be improved through mindful thought and behaviour and how organizational sustainability and success might be enhanced. Mindfulness has a more strongly *substantive* focus when the viewpoint is mindful (re)consideration of purpose, the value of transcending self-centred concerns of individuals and organizations, and attending to the meaning of individual action and collective endeavours. (p. 167, italics added)

26 An example of mindfulness as a trait is Bodner and Langer's (2001) description of mindfulness as a 'personality trait' (p. 1) where one is predisposed to slight changes in setting and viewpoint about the observed subject. Attributes like the general tendency to take a challenging task, and socio-cultural factors such as shared habits and the intellectual climate are also trait mindfulness. It is relatively difficult to test or measure trait mindfulness and hence it can only be indirectly inferred (Yadav, 2021).

27 See Weintraub and Dust (2021, p. 31).
28 An example of a definition that follows state mindfulness is provided by King and Badham (2020), who defined mindfulness as 'a state or quality of mind that attends to experience by giving full and proper attention to presence, context and purpose' (p. 167). Likewise, Bill George interpreted mindfulness as 'a state of being fully present, aware of oneself and other people, and sensitive to one's reactions to stressful situations' (cited in Silverthorne, 2010, p. 1). State mindfulness is amenable to methodological and experimental manipulation; this form of mindfulness includes 'perceived demands and value of the task and the instructional procedures' (Yadav, 2021, p. 87).
29 This point is taken from Beck (2021).
30 This explanation is taken from Hanson et al. (2021), who wrote:

> Mindfulness as a construct can take on one of three different forms, including a state, a trait, or a practice . . . As a state, people's level of mindfulness is flexible and can change within person across time. As such, *state mindfulness* is defined as the extent to which one is currently 'attentive to and aware of what is taking place in the present' . . . Although people's state level of mindfulness can fluctuate across time, their overall trait level of mindfulness tends to remain rather stable. Indeed, *trait mindfulness* is defined as 'the tendency to be mindful' . . . Finally, as a practice, mindfulness is a skill that can be trained and honed. A *mindfulness practice* is a 'mechanism directed at enhancing one's state mindfulness and subsequently trait mindfulness, which can be cultivated through mindfulness-based interventions'. (p. 296, italics added)

31 The contents of the two approaches are taken from Kudesia and Lau (2021, p. 40).
32 Reina (2021) explained that the Western traditions focus on 'increased environmental sensitivity, openness to new information, the ability to create new categories to structure perception and increased awareness of multiple perspectives' (p. 55). Concurring with Reina is Pirson (2014), who observed that mindfulness from a Western-scientific tradition emphasizes novelty seeking, novelty producing and engagement, as represented by the works of Langer. Carmody (2014), while also differentiating Eastern and Western conceptions of mindfulness, referred specifically to 'Buddhist-derived conceptions of mindfulness as Eastern, and the psychological understandings as Western' (p. 49). By 'psychological understandings', Carmody had in mind Langer's theory on mindfulness that revolves around the creation of new distinctions coupled with the awareness and manipulation of new contextual cues. Ie et al. (2014) elaborated further:

> There currently exist two dominant mindfulness camps. The Western camp involves social psychological approaches to mindfulness, as exemplified

by the work of Ellen Langer. Langer's approach is sometimes referred to as 'mindfulness without meditation'. The nature of its practices is highly psychological, and very little to no emphasis is placed on meditation. The Western camp contrasts with more Eastern approaches to mindfulness, which are rooted in Buddhist philosophy and are more contemplative and based on meditation. A dominant branch of the Eastern camp is approaches to mindfulness that incorporate both psychological and meditative elements. These Eastern derived models borrow forms of meditation from the Eastern camp and empirically apply them in Western settings. The Western and Eastern models propose different and unique theoretical principles, but they also share significant similarities. Most important, both approaches aim to cultivate a present-oriented mind, thereby permitting individuals to increase health and well-being. (p. xxxiii)

33 This is noted by Pirson (2014). Carmody (2014) added that Eastern and Western traditions of mindfulness are differentiated by the following criterion:

The Eastern tradition emphasizes the necessity of the meditation practice characteristic of those programmes, and reductions in distress are indeed related to practice . . . And there is evidence that the learning results in a lasting increase in well-being . . . Just how much practice is required remains an open question. In contrast, the Western approach relies upon exercises that intellectually challenge existing categories or immersion in a structured environment that exposes them, and the derived benefits appear to be immediate. (p. 54; also see Ie et al., 2014)

34 Pirson et al. (2018) explained that the cognitive approach to mindfulness is

derived from Western-scientific literature, and is defined as cognitive flexibility, which allows individuals to actively construct novel categories and distinctions . . . This socio-cognitive approach to mindfulness differs from the meditative approach because it usually includes the external, material, and social context of individual participants . . . It pursues a learning agenda, can be very goal-oriented, and involves the use of mindfulness in enhancing problem solving and other cognitive exercises. (p. 169)

35 This is taken from Pirson et al. (2018).
36 This is taken from McGhee and Grant (2021) and Weare (2014). Arguing that mindfulness is 'what made Freud so effective', Kets de Vries (2014) posited that that Freud encouraged psychotherapists to employ 'evenly suspended attention' when working with clients (p. 8).
37 For details, see Rant and Mihelič (2021).

38 This is taken from Baelen et al. (2019) who reported: 'Mindfulness training programmes in the school setting are delivered in a variety of ways, from those that replace traditional classes or curricula (e.g. physical education or health class), to those that attempt a seamless integration with existing instructional time' (p. 15).
39 This is taken from Carmody (2014, p. 48).
40 For details, see King and Badham (2020).
41 See Lampe and Engleman-Lampe (2012).
42 The discussion on the two views and examples is taken from Lavelle (2016).
43 The information is taken from Reina (2021).
44 This is taken from Levey and Levey (2019). They stressed the importance of the VUCA index of leadership preparedness that consists of the following four domains (p. 4):

1. *Volatility*: how well do you anticipate and wisely respond to the volatile nature and speed of change?
2. *Uncertainty*: how wisely and decisively do you act when you lack certainty or a clear sense of direction?
3. *Complexity*: how wisely do you respond to complexity and confusion, and navigate the chaos present in the world around you?
4. *Ambiguity*: how well do you maintain your effectiveness when faced with a lack of dependable reference points or predictability?

45 Ashford and DeRue (2012) proposed that leadership is about 'influencing people and processes in service of accomplishing a collective aim or group goal' (p. 147). Ashford and DeRue (2012) also called for *exceptional leadership* during a 'new normal' so that all could 'see opportunities on the horizon, develop structures to motivate action and inspire people of all stripes to pursue opportunities with courage, passion and resilience' (p. 146).
46 This is cited in Brown and Olson (2015, p. 4). It is noteworthy that 'while an estimated $50 billion is invested in developing leaders around the globe each year, only a mere 37% of leaders rate their organization's leadership development programmes as effective' (Levey & Levey, 2019, p. 4).
47 There is a clear economic incentive for organizations to promote mindfulness. Levey and Levey (2019) reported: 'With large companies, such as insurance giant Aetna sharing data confirming that since rolling out their mindfulness programme, it has saved $2,000 per employee in healthcare costs, and gained $3,000 per employee in productivity, there is a growing recognition that the quantifiable return on investment helps explain why the mindfulness industry grew to nearly $1 billion in 2015' (p. 3).
48 Long (2021) reported:

> Some who have spoken about practising include: Goldman Sachs Group Inc. supervisory board member William George, who was also the past CEO of

Medtronic ...; Green Mountain Coffee Roasters Inc.'s founder Robert Stiller; Ramani Ayers, former Chairman and CEO of Hartford Financial Services Group, has engaged in practices for more than 25 years; along with Ray Dalio, CEO of the hedge fund Bridgewater Associates, who has practiced for more than 40 years. (p. 174). Also see Boyatzis and McKee (2005).

49 Wells (2015) identified the following sources for mindful leadership: (1) the synthesis of the attitudinal foundations of mindfulness with emotional intelligence, (2) social intelligence, (3) resonant leadership and (4) neuroscience. Also see Dickmann and Stanford-Blair (2008).
50 For example, Ritchie-Dunham (2014) followed Langer's ideas to describe a mindful leader as one who is open to and displays new perspectives, new categories and new information.
51 This is taken from Boyatzis and McKee (2005). Resonant leaders are mindful as they are 'fully aware of all that one experiences *inside the self* – body mind, heart, spirit – and ... pay full attention to what is happening *around us* – people, that natural world, our surroundings and events' (Boyatzis & McKee, 2005, p. 113; italics in the original). Wells (2015) applied the ideas of resonant leadership to schools, and posited that mindfulness for educational leaders 'serves the leader and the people in the schools through the practice of being fully present, with qualities of emotional and social intelligence such as listening, not judging self or others, while having compassion for self and others in the organization, constructs that are developed in mindfulness meditation' (p. 13).
52 Bill George argued that mindful leaders are more effective in understanding, relating to and motivating others toward a common vision. He linked mindfulness to authentic leadership:

> An essential aspect of effective leaders is authenticity; that is, being genuine and true to one's beliefs, values and principles that make up what we call someone's True North. Authenticity is developed by becoming more self-aware and having compassion for oneself, without which it is very difficult to feel genuine compassion for others. Self-awareness starts with understanding one's life story and the impact of one's crucibles, and reflecting on how these contribute to motivations and behaviours. ... Mindfulness is a logical step in this process of gaining self-awareness that should be combined with experiences in leading through challenging situations and gaining awareness through feedback and group support. (cited in Silverthorne, 2010, p. 1)

53 As explained by Saviano et al. (2018),

> The dimensions of mindfulness such as being fully present, aware, accepting and non-judgmental embody this way of being. As opposed to emphasis on an

act of *doing*, mindfulness allows for a sense of spaciousness that enacts patience, listening and compassion, all qualities important for leaders. Although classic leadership theory defines leaders by traits ..., Mindful Leadership offers a description of presence, a subtlety of describing how leaders enact these traits by *ways of being*. (p. 643, italics in the original; also see Wells, 2015)

54 This was noted by Rant and Mihelič (2021), who referred to the testimony of Harvard Business School professor Bill George.
55 This is taken from Cissna and Schockman (2021), and Mayer and Oosthuizen (2021). A mindful leader is also the one who embraces and models a growth mindset. As noted by Berger and Johnston (2015),

> Many leaders focus on important questions like, 'Who am I and what am I good at?' We'd like to expand those with different questions: 'Who have I been and who is the leader I want to be next?' These different questions come from the growth mindset and point us to our own emerging possibilities. This question and the growth mindset it encourages also make it more possible for each of us to learn from failure, which ... is key to living in complex, unpredictable spaces. (p. 177)

56 This is taken from Chaskalson et al. (2021).
57 Daniel Goleman introduced and popularized the term *emotional intelligence*. The information on emotionally intelligent leaders was taken from Salovey and Mayer (1990). Describing self-awareness as 'perhaps the most critical leadership competency', Sethi (2009) contended that mindful people are aware of their thoughts, feelings and emotions and thereby able to 'control any destructive emotions such as anger as they arise and make midcourse corrections in [their] behaviour' (p. 10).
58 These six areas are taken from Ehrlich (2017, p. 235).
59 This is taken from Sethi (2009). Ehrlich (2017) added that mindful leaders ask questions such as 'Beneath the words, what are that person's thoughts, feelings, and intentions? What are the nonverbal cues that suggest what he or she is going through?' (p. 238). Daft (2005) contrasted a mindless person with a mindful person; the former 'let[s] others do the thinking for them, but mindful leaders are always looking for new ideas and approaches' by 'continuously re-evaluating previously learned ways of doing things in the context of evolving information and shifting circumstances' (p. 132).
60 This is taken from Dunoon and Langer (2011). Jagannathan and Rodhain (2016) established the link between mindfulness and emotional intelligence:

> A mindful leader is always aware of the present moment and is able to observe it without judgment. In that given moment, he or she is therefore able

to clearly comprehend the emotions of the self as well as of others. This helps the mindful leader to manage one's emotions and those of others better and with empathy and compassion. Therefore a mindful leader has high emotional intelligence. (pp. 98–9)

61 This is taken from Ashford and DeRue (2012). Through a mindful engagement process, 'individuals can approach, engage in, and reflect on their lived experiences in ways that promote learning and increase the developmental punch of any experience' (Ashford & DeRue, 2012, p. 147).
62 For details, see Weick and Roberts (1993), and Weick and Sutcliffe (2006, 2008). Mortlock (2021) pointed out that mindfulness at social or collective levels directs the attention of all the staff to 'the (often unconscious) collective habits and routines that drive collective impulses', which is critical as 'our work environment and our decisions in work situations are less affected by the unconscious spontaneous impulses of individuals, but by the (often equally unconscious) behavioural tendencies, rituals, and *culture* of work communities' (p. 262, italics in the original).
63 Sutcliffe and Vogus (2014) explained that *collective mindfulness* refers to 'patterns of organizing that result in a quality of organizational attention that increases the likelihood that people will notice unique details of situations and act upon them' (p. 410).
64 Levey and Levey (2019) propagated a similar concept called *shared mindfulness*, which is 'an embodied and relational practice that encourages Presence, Attunement, Resonance, and Trust (P.A.R.T.) in people's work together' (p. 5).
65 See Weick and Roberts (1993) and Pirson (2014).
66 This is taken from Mortlock (2021, p. 261).
67 Sutcliffe and Vogus (2014) described *mindful organizing* as 'a function of a collective's (such as a subunit or work group) attention to context and capacities to act' and 'provides a basis for individuals to interact continuously as they develop, refine, and update shared understanding of the situations they face and their capabilities to act on that understanding' (p. 410).
68 This is taken from Sutcliffe and Vogus (2014). For further reading on mindful organizing, see Jordan and Johannessen (2014).
69 This is taken from Jayawardena-Willis et al. (2021).
70 This is taken from Hanson et al. (2021).
71 This is taken from Levey and Levey (2019).
72 As Levey and Levey (2019) put it, the *first approach* sees mindfulness as 'an optional, peripheral, personal practice that one might bring to their work-life rather than as an essential, pervasive, inclusive and integral element of a personal and organizational "operating system" and success strategy"' (Levey & Levey, 2019, p. 5). The *second approach* is more sustainable and inclusive, as explained by Levey and Levey (2019):

This approach involves introducing mindfulness as an essential life skill for developing the organizational operating system necessary to sustain a thriving healthy organizational culture populated by well, caring and wise people. In such organizations, virtually every moment, activity, interaction, procedure and encounter is encouraged to be imbued with the mindful, caring presence of all of the employees involved. Once established, such a mindful organization operating system approach has proven to be more far reaching in its beneficial impacts and more enduring and sustainable over time. (p. 5)

73 Weare (2014) reported: 'Mindfulness has been shown to impact on many of the complex and interrelated mental qualities which underlie wellbeing, such as the ability to accept experience, to manage difficult feelings, to be resilient, motivated, persistent and optimistic, to enjoy good relationships and experience a sense of meaning' (p. 13). Masood and Karajovic (2021) summarized the findings:

Consistent with general findings on the positive effects of the practice on employees, mindfulness was found to reduce a variety of negative outcomes (anxiety, depression and burnout) in leaders across all levels of an organization … mindfulness builds psychological capital (PsyCap) in leaders, thereby helping them cope more successfully with negative psychological outcomes. Psychological capital (a type of positive organizational behaviour) consists of the traits of resilience (coping with and recovering from adversity), optimism (maintaining a positive outlook), hope (persisting in goals), and efficacy (having confidence in self). (p. 272)

74 This was noted by Langer (2010). Pipe and Bortz (2009) summed up the benefits of mindfulness practice: 'it can enhance present-moment attention, decrease stress and anxiety, prevent depression relapse, and enhance immunosuppression, cardiovascular integrity, and positive affect' (p. 37).
75 This is taken from Dickmann and Stanford-Blair (2008).
76 This is taken from Pirson (2014).
77 Sethi (2009) extrapolated the benefits of mindfulness as openness to new ideas for an organization:

Mindfulness helps us get rid of the tendency to cling to our own ideas and makes us more open to new ideas. Disagreement and even conflict can now be brought into the open and addressed without defensiveness. This is so much better than shoving them under the carpet as often happens, especially in executive teams. This authentic team behaviour in turn encourages giving and receiving of candid but caring feedback. Teams can now look at the reality of the marketplace and competition as it truly exists, listen to what customers and employees have to say without rationalising, and develop sharper strategies and deliver more coordinated and precise execution. (p. 10)

78 See Adriansen and Krohn (2016) and Weick and Sutcliffe (2006).
79 See Bellinger et al. (2015).
80 This is taken from Van Dam et al. (2018); also see Jennings et al. (2019); Mortlock (2021); Weintraub and Dust (2021).
81 See Coronado-Montoya et al. (2016); Purser et al. (2016); Walsh (2016).
82 See Meredith (2022).
83 Baelen et al. (2019), based on a review of literature, reported that 'results from these studies were often inconsistent or nuanced' and that the evidence for mindfulness training in schools is 'still nascent and tentative, especially with regards to academic performance (e.g. report card grades and tests of academic skills)' (p. 44). Weare (2014) cautioned that 'the field of mindfulness with children and young people is at present underdeveloped and methodologically weak' (p. 1039).
84 This is taken from Bodhi (2016) who described the feeling of incompleteness as *existential unease*. Wallis (2016) critiqued the current mindfulness movement as 'American pop psychology, the 1960s human potential movement, Perennial Philosophy, positive-thinking spirituality, and apocalyptic New Age thought' (p. 499).
85 See Drougge (2016), Ng (2016), Purser and Loy (2013), Samuel (2016) and Walsh (2016).
86 This term originated from Purser and Loy (2013). Forbes (2016) extended the argument to the introduction of Social Emotional Learning (SEL) in schools:

> Mindfulness practices along with social emotional learning (SEL) programmes in schools share the same approach and play well into reinforcing conformity to the individualist, competitive, and marketing aspects of neoliberal culture. Left behind by mindfulness education programmes in the wake of the neoliberal wave is the cultural capital of many schools and communities of colour in urban areas. It is rare that mindfulness school programmes acknowledge these and work with and within them to discuss and employ shared skills, strengths, and interests. (p. 359)

87 Mayer and Oosthuizen (2021) noted that 'mindfulness interventions promise to deal with the discontent of employees without challenging the social and economic causes of discontent, and therefore is happily adopted by the managerial and leadership elite' (p. 509).
88 Purser and Loy (2013) rightly pointed out that mindfulness is not merely an 'ethically-neutral technique for reducing stress and improving concentration' but 'a distinct quality of attention that is dependent upon and influenced by many other factors: the nature of our thoughts, speech and actions; our way of making a living; and our efforts to avoid unwholesome and unskilful behaviours, while

developing those that are conducive to wise action, social harmony and compassion' (p. 2; also see Brazier, 2016; King, 2016; Purser et al., 2016). Purser (2018) asserted that mindfulness reflects 'pop capitalist spirituality' where the former is lauded as 'a panacea for all that ails us with no trade-offs whatsoever, whether it is money, power and well-being' (p. 105).

89 Stanley et al. (2018) described mindfulness as 'a *neoliberal* therapeutic self-technology – one which medicalizes, psychologizes and individualizes well-being and distress as being the sole responsibilities of autonomous individuals within consumer capitalism' (p. 6, italics added).

90 The danger when mindfulness is promoted in schools, as Flores (2016) put it, is that children may be discouraged to speak up when faced with wrongdoing and injustice; they are encouraged instead to 'become peaceful and passive in their acceptance of hardships, rather than questioning, or holding an oppositional stance to inequities of social class, race, or gender' (p. 444; also see Mitra & Greenberg, 2016; Stanley et al., 2018).

91 Repetti (2016) highlighted that 'the corporate use of mindfulness is suspected of anaesthetizing corporate executives, management and employees from any moral sense about their presumably ethically questionable actions by way of the detachment and non-judgement encouraged by some forms of the practice' (p. 476; also see Walsh, 2016).

92 For example, after explaining that mindfulness involves sharp focus and open awareness, Hougaard et al. (2016) posited: 'As we are developing greater self-awareness we are simultaneously cultivating the ability to have *greater empathy* for others. Once we can see and understand our own struggles and challenges, we have a greater ability to recognise those in people around us. Therefore, moving from a high degree of mindfulness of self towards mindfulness of others is a natural transition' (p. 55, italics added).

93 The distinction of moral and nonmoral virtues are taken from Pojman (1990), who defined virtues as 'excellences of character, trained behavioural dispositions that result in habitual acts' (p. 163).

94 To give an example, Marques (2021) listed some qualities needed by leaders: reflection, courage, intelligence and consideration. Courage is described by Marques (2021) as 'a leap in the dark that may require smart adjustments when complications arise that we had not foreseen' (p. 115) whereas consideration is 'the process of weighing all the options, just before making a decision' (p. 116). On the one hand, courage and consideration are desirable attributes. On the other hand, courage and consideration (as careful thought) are *nonmoral virtues* to help leaders succeed in the workplace. Nonmoral virtues, although necessary, are insufficient for altruistic school leaders who wish to advance the well-being of all their students and staff within a caring school community.

95 This critique has been raised about *transformational leaders* too (Zhang & Tan, 2021). A major criticism of transformational leadership is the potential for the abuse of power. As noted by Bass and Steidlmeier (1999), transformational leaders may manifest the following characteristics: 'narcissism, authoritarianism, Machiavellianism, flawed vision, a need for power coupled with lack of activity inhibition and promotion among followers of dependency, personal identification, and lack of internalization of values and beliefs' (p. 182). Yukl (2006) concurred, and cautioned against the 'dark side of charisma', where the leader lacks the requisite moral qualities and encourages follower dependency (p. 226).
96 For example, Magrì (2019) and Battaly (2011) claimed that empathy is not a moral value, and is merely a capacity that is necessary for ethical conduct. Taking the same position, Songhorian (2019) argued that empathy may be amoral, is not always necessary for moral judgement or action, and may even contribute to immoral behaviour.
97 This description of cognitive empathy is taken from Maibom (2009).
98 Decety and Yoder (2016) wrote that personal distress generates 'an egoistic motivation to reduce it [personal distress], by withdrawing from the stressor, for example, thereby decreasing the likelihood of prosocial behaviour' (p. 9).
99 The concept of *empathic concern* is credited to Decety and Yoder (2016). Kim and Kou (2014) explained that empathic concern engenders altruistically motivated behaviour because it generates shared feelings and consequently an intrinsic desire to alleviate the suffering of others.
100 This notion is proposed by Pipe and Bortz (2009).
101 For details, see Pipe and Bortz (2009).
102 This is taken from Pipe and Bortz (2009, p. 36).
103 To give another example, Buller (2019), in his formulation of mindful leadership, included compassion as one of the attributes that a mindful leader needs to cultivate. In the same vein, Magee (2016) defined mindfulness as 'a state of awareness with compassion' (p. 425). However, there is little elaboration on the theoretical foundation of compassion.

2 Confucius, Mindlessness and Mindfulness

1 He was also known as Zhongni (仲尼), which was his alternative Chinese name (also known as 'Chinese style name') given to adults in ancient China.
2 Nylan and Wilson (2010) observed that Confucius has been pictured variously as 'a fortune-cookie phrasemaker, a brilliant moral philosopher, a fusty antiquarian, a divine sage, an old man with a scraggly white beard fussing over some detail of ritual or a down-to-earth thinker with an honest assessment of the human propensity to falter' (p. 25).

3 The primary traditional sources on Confucius's life are the *Analects*, *Zuo Commentary* (左传 *Zuozhuan*), *Records of the Grand Historian* (史记 *Shiji*) and *the School Sayings of Confucius* (孔子家语 *Kongzi Jiayu*). I have also consulted secondary sources: works by Chin (2007), Clements (2004) and Nylan and Wilson (2010).
4 On Confucius burying his parents in a new graveside, Clements (2004) commented, 'Demonstrating innovative thinking, he "broke with tradition by erecting an earth mound over the double grave"' (p. 18).
5 Wilson (1995) explained that the Golden Age was a period 'in which the basic features of civilized human life were thought to have been discovered and instantiated in a perfect social, political and ethical order' (p. 270).
6 For details, see Clements (2004) and Nylan and Wilson (2010).
7 Confucius's inability to carve out a successful career as a minister is noted in the *Analects*: someone asked why Confucius did not participate in government (2.21), and another person commented that Confucius did not hold an official position (3.24).
8 There is a total of twenty books in the *Analects*. The reference '3.13' means Book 3, section 13. In some cases, I made minor changes to Lau's translation. This point was explained in the preface and will be reiterated in the second part of this chapter.
9 This explanation is taken from Chin (2007) who clarified this passage:

> The 'southwest corner' is the darkest spot in a room where there is no window or any source of light; it refers to Nanzi, who sits in the inner palace. The 'kitchen hearth' [kitchen stove] is an open space where people gather to have a meal or a chat; it refers to Wang Sunjia, who lives and works in the public arena. Wang implies that it is probably more effective for Confucius to go to him rather than to Nanzi if Confucius is looking for a place in Wei politics. Confucius's response is not unlike what he said to Zilu: If you have done something wrong – if you have offended Heaven – there is no god you can appeal to; if you have done no wrong, then you can swear an oath without the fear of Heaven's retribution. The principle applies to all, himself being no exception. (p. 91)

More will be said about *dao*, but at this juncture, it suffices to note that it encompasses the moral path or normative tradition inherited from one's cultural predecessors. Slingerland (2003) described *dao* as 'the unique moral path that should be walked by any true human being, endorsed by Heaven and revealed to the early sage-kings' (p. xxii).

10 For an interesting account of the relationship between Confucius and his disciples, see Shi (2010), who relied on the following sources: *Records of the Historian*,

Zuo Commentary, *Mencius* and *Xunzi*. For a detailed description of Confucius's disciples, see Fu (2011).

11 This is recorded in Clements (2004).
12 This is taken from Nylan and Wilson (2010, p. 19).
13 This is taken from Chin (2007, p. 122).
14 This is taken from Clements (2004, p. 16).
15 I translated *li* here as rites as this is the traditional, common understanding. *Li* has also been variously translated as 'ritual propriety', 'rules of propriety' and 'ceremony'. In a later chapter, I shall provide my definition of *li*. Despite the different translations, the bottom line, as agreed on by scholars, is that *li* refers to specific human behaviours that are regarded as 'proper', 'acceptable' and 'good' by people during Confucius's time.
16 It is unclear what the original meaning of *ren* was, but scholars believe that it probably refers to the attribute associated with an aristocratic clan or noble huntsmen. For details, see Shun (1993) and Yu (1998).
17 Li (2010) explained the historical meaning of *junzi* before Confucius's time:

> The original meaning of 'a gentleman' [*junzi*] is that he is a member of aristocratic society, which even includes female members. This society is composed on the basis of blood relations. Its members, as long as they have the same surname (it is another matter for aristocracy with different surnames), are all the offspring of the ruler; either they are the children of the deceased ruler, or they are the children of the current ruler, and that is why they are called gentlemen. In the upper reaches of noble society, there are emperors, dukes and marquises; below that are ministers and knights. Gentlemen is the general term for this type of people. (p. 56)

18 Women during Confucius's time were largely deprived of formal education, kept away from public view and segregated from men. The minority of women who received an education were from the aristocratic class and taught by private tutors at home.
19 Women in ancient China were known for their social roles as someone's daughter, wife or concubine; it was therefore impossible for women to learn from Confucius or assume any public office, even if they aspired to do so.
20 For further discussion, see Tan (2013, 2019a, 2020a, 2020c).
21 As far back as the 1980s, the American sinologist William Theodore de Bary already translated the Confucian virtue of *jing* as 'mindfulness' (de Bary, 1981). It needs to be clarified that de Bary's focus was on the works of neo-Confucian philosopher Zhu Xi rather than Confucius.
22 Throughout the book, I used 'Confucian mindfulness' synonymously with Confucius's mindfulness, for ease of expression. This usage is not to deny the

multiple formulations of Confucian mindfulness that are traced back and linked to different Confucian schools of thought. For example, Zhu Xi's conception of mindfulness is not identical to that of Confucius as the former includes neo-Confucian notions of *qi* (气 energy) and *li* (理 principle). On Zu Xi's concept of mindfulness, see Tan (2019b).

23. The description of mindlessness is taken from Langer (2000).
24. As mentioned in the preface and this chapter, I have changed all male pronouns used by Lau (1997) to gender-neutral ones when translating the *Analects* in this book. In this passage, I have replaced 'man' with 'person'.
25. The classics were treasured by the ancient Chinese as 'the direct words and teachings of the great sages of antiquity, men whose exemplary wisdom and virtue served as an eternal model for the ages' (Gardner, 2007, p. xv). There is a small collection of classics in the history of China. From the Han dynasty (206 BCE–220 CE) till the end of the Qing dynasty (1644 CE–1911 CE), scholars studied what is known as 'Four Books and Five Classics' (四書五經 *Sishu Wujing*) for the imperial examination. The 'Four Books' are the *Analects, Mencius* (孟子 *Mengzi*), *The Great Learning* (大學 *Daxue*) and *The Doctrine of the Mean* (中庸 *Zhongyong*). The 'Five Classics' are *The Book of History* (書 *Shu*), *The Book of Odes* (诗 *Shi*), *The Book of Rites* (禮 *Li*), *The Book of Changes* (易 *Yi*) and *The Book of the Spring and Autumn Annals* (春秋 *Chunqiu*).
26. This does not mean that memorization had no place in the Confucian tradition. Confucius expected his students to master the grammar rules, poems and historical facts when learning the 'six arts'. Memorization as a form of learning provides a firm foundation for reflection. According to Confucius, learning and reflection went hand in hand. Confucius's disciples needed to learn and memorise the Odes first before they could draw inferences from them and apply the Odes to their daily life.
27. Chin (2007) wrote:

    Keen discernment was what Confucius hoped his students would use when faced with a moment that shook their hearts. The best student, he felt, was someone who, on the strength of his clear judgement, could refuse to go along with his teacher should the teacher insist on a different point of view; and the right teacher would want his student to break away because he knew that this was all he could do for his student. (pp. 146–7)

28. Nylan and Wilson (2010) noted that Confucius 'judged a single act both from the point of view of the actors involved and from the standpoint of the larger consequences of the act' (p. 82).
29. Hagen (2010) explained: 'The fact remains that choosing which elements are to be conserved is necessarily an interpretive project and the resulting mix will always

be novel. These considerations militate against the idea that Confucius is trying to return to a particular way that existed in the past' (p. 9).
30 Sutcliffe and Vogus (2014) observed that 'a "chasm" exists between West and East perspectives [that] persists among some scholars, particularly those studying individual mindfulness' (p. 415)
31 Sutcliffe and Vogus (2014) summarized the two approaches:

> Mindfulness is seen as an antidote to mindlessness. In other words, organizing in a way that enables seeing similarities in things thought different and differences in things thought similar ... is privileged ... Through this 'Western' lens, perception and conception are in the foreground ... In contrast, Eastern perspectives on mindfulness more explicitly associate it with processes of attention and attending. For example, mindfulness is described as 'non-superficial awareness. It sees things deeply, down below the level of concepts and opinions ... it manifests itself primarily as a constant and unwavering attention that never flags and never turns away' ... From this 'Eastern' perspective, becoming alert and aware, and keeping present details in mind are in the foreground. (p. 416)

32 Confucius stressed 'personalization through reflecting on what we have learned and the application of this learning in an appropriate way to the business of the day' (Ames & Rosemont, 1998, p. 59).
33 This is taken from Clements (2004, pp. 94–5).
34 That mindfulness extends to how one moves is seen in this episode of Confucius's observation upon entering a civilized area:

> Confucius was impressed even with the way they walked, commenting to his driver that the boy carrying a pitcher seemed to have internalized many of the teachings of the sages' music. No extant classical Chinese song records the virtues of correct posture, but presumably Confucius was impressed either with the boy's mode of lifting, or simply a gait that reflected regular dancing exercise. (Clements, 2004, p. 31)

35 Langer and Moldoveanu (2000) explained why *non-judgement* is essential in Buddhism: 'Mindful individuals are able to clear their minds through meditation and through non-judgmental attention of their inner experience, which ultimately allows them to see the world as it really is, a concept known as veridical perception' (p. 55). Here, I do not mean that Buddhism teaches or support a form of mindfulness that is amoral. Buddhism, as a religion and worldview, certainly passes on its unique set of ethical perspectives. Scholars have rightly pointed out that the current mindfulness movement does not fully capture Buddhist teachings and ethics. Lewis and Rozelle (2016), drawing on their research on mindfulness-based

intervention, concluded that these programmes 'are not focused on the deepest level of *dukkha* [suffering] and therefore cannot be meaningfully considered Buddhadharma by Buddhadharma's own standards, across all traditions' (p. 253). Purser et al. (2016) noted how 'mindfulness in the West, under the claim that it is derived from Buddhism, has become severed from not only Buddhist ethical contexts, but also its roots in Buddhist philosophy and soteriology' (p. vii).

36 The two concepts are taken from Chan (2006), who elaborated:

> *An intentional state* is directed at specific objects, and the descriptions under which the objects are viewed are essential to the identification of the mental state. For example, fear is an intentional state. When one fears, there is a certain object at which one's fear is directed, such as death. But fear may cease when its object is re-described, though it remains the same object. Hence, one's fear of death may dissipate when death is understood as a passage to heaven instead of the termination of one's existence. In contrast, *a frame of mind* need not be directed at a specific object. It is a general condition of the mind where a pervasive attitude dominates. And when a person is in a certain frame of mind, the mind tends to project the dominant attitude toward any object it encounters and to tone other psychological states such as perceptions and judgments. For example, when someone's frame of mind is marked by anxiety, one seems to be nervous about everything. (p. 231, italics added)

> It should be added that the two categories, 'frame of mind' and 'an intentional state' are not mutually exclusive but are instead related and overlap in practice.

37 It follows that Confucian *mindfulness* is more accurately described as Confucian *heartfulness-mindfulness*.

38 See Tan (2013). Gier (2001) added: 'Reason and the passions are united in *xin*, so the dichotomy that has plagued European thought is simply nonexistent. Assuming a thoroughly somatic soul, the Confucius of the *Analects* does not even oppose heart-mind to the senses and appetites, although this dichotomy does appear later in Mencius and Xunzi' (p. 283). For further discussions on *xin*, see Tan (2018b, 2018c, 2020a).

39 Lau (1997) translated *xin* as 'heart', but I have followed Ames and Rosemont (1998) in rendering it as 'heart-mind'. Ames and Rosemont (1998) argued that

> to divorce the mind from the heart – the cognitive from the affective – is to re-enter the Western metaphysical realm again, most especially via the mind-body dichotomy, and embrace the notion of an ahistorical, a cultural seat of pure rationality. To avoid this reference, we render *xin* as 'heart-and-mind', …

> to remind the reader that there are no altogether disembodied thoughts for Confucius, nor any raw feelings altogether lacking (what in English would be called) 'cognitive content'. (p. 56)

Hall and Ames (1987) added: 'It is not that the Chinese thinkers were able to reconcile this dichotomy [mind/body problem]; rather, it never emerged as a problem. Because body and mind were not regarded as essentially different kinds of existence, they did not generate different sets of terminologies necessary to describe them' (p. 20).

40 Researchers have noted that mindfulness theories such as Langer's, centre on 'improving physical and psychological health [and] is guided by the perspective that the mind and body comprise a single system, and that every change in the human being is simultaneously a change at the level of the mind (e.g. cognitive changes) as well as the body (e.g. cellular, hormonal, neural changes' (Ie et al., 2014, p. 2). Notably, Langer (1992) alluded to Confucius's heart-mind when she asserted that 'a clear division between the psychological and the physiological is not tenable' and that 'the mind-body distinction may be one of the deepest premature cognitive commitments in Western culture' (p. 302).

41 This does not mean that Confucius believed that everyone will eventually become a *junzi* (exemplary person). The different outcomes of aspiring *junzi* depend on contingent factors such as different capabilities, motivations and unequal access to resources. Instead, Confucius was teaching that everyone, from the aristocrat to the common person, could and should strive to become *junzi*. It is worthy of note that Confucius himself did not belong to the aristocratic clan. I shall return to this point about the potential and actuality of one becoming a *junzi* in the concluding section of this chapter. For further discussions on the *junzi*, see Tan (2016b, 2016c).

42 In moral philosophy, the three main moral/ethical approaches are Consequentialism, Deontology and Virtue Ethics. Briefly, *consequentialism* posits that the goodness of one's moral action is determined by the consequences of one's actions, as guided by one or more moral rules. An example is *Utilitarianism* based on the writings of philosophers such as Jeremy Bentham and J. S. Mill. *Deontology* shifts the focus away from consequences to moral duty; the rightness of one's moral action is determined by absolute moral duties that are independent of the consequences. An example is *Kantianism*, named after philosopher Immanuel Kant.

43 This is taken from Burbules (1995).

44 Gier (2001) illuminated Confucius's thought as a form of virtue ethics:

> The imperatives of virtue ethics – be patient, be kind, be compassionate, be courageous – better equip an individual to negotiate the obstacles of the moral life. The virtue-ethics approach is not to follow a set of abstract rules, but to develop a unique ensemble of behaviours, dispositions and qualities

that lead to human excellence. Virtue ethics may not have pat answers to specific cases – no ethical theory could offer this – but it does prepare the moral agent for adaptation, innovation and flexibility. (p. 300)

For further readings on Confucianism and virtue ethics, see Yu (1998) and Slingerland (2001).

45 Confucius exclaimed: 'There is something hopeless about a group of men spending time together all day, not touching on the subject of morality in their conversations and wanting only to show off their little cleverness' (Chin, 2007, p. 64). On the importance of moral self-cultivation, see Tan (2017b).

46 Purser et al. (2016) wrote: 'Advocates of secular mindfulness have for the most part downplayed questions of ethics and what constitutes the good life' (p. vii). Arguing that mindfulness is not identical to bare attention, Tomasini (2016) posited that 'mindfulness cannot be seen as neutral: an ethical dimension is omnipresent as it continuously distinguishes between wholesome and unwholesome mental states' (p. 222).

47 Cua (1992) explained, 'The ideal of *jen* [*ren*] allows for diversity of individual life plans as well as styles of life so long as they pay heed to the common form of life within a moral community. It is, so to speak, an ideal of "congeniality of excellences" rather than a universally prescriptive norm for human life' (p. 55). For further discussions on *ren*, see Tan (2018a) and Tan and Ibrahim (2017).

48 A more accurate rendering of 'know' in Confucianism is 'realize'. This is why Ames and Rosemont (1998) translated *zhi* as 'realize'. They rendered 溫故而知新 (*wen gu er zhi xin*) in 2.11 as follows: 'Reviewing the old as a means of realising the new'.

49 Pertinently, some scholars take the view that Buddhism promotes individualism, which makes Buddhism distinct from Confucianism. For example, Payne (2016) wrote: 'One characteristic of self-improvement Buddhism is its emphasis on individualism, a characteristic that expresses the typically American valuing of the autonomous individual – to the extent that individualism as a form of subjectivity is often conflated with democracy as a political philosophy' (p. 125).

50 This analogy of four concentric circles is borrowed from Tu (1985).

51 My understanding of leadership is aligned with that of Spillane (2006), who defined leadership as referring to 'activities tied to the core work of the organization that are designed by organizational members to influence the motivation, knowledge, affect, or practices of other organizational members or that are understood by organizational members as intended to influence their motivation, knowledge, affect, or practices' (pp. 11–12).

52 This is taken from Gurr (2015).

53 This is cited in Nylan and Wilson (2010, p. 210).

3 Respectful Mindfulness

1. This is taken from Chan (2006).
2. The idea of whole-heartedness here is consistent with Dewey's (1933) idea of whole-heartedness that denotes the genuine enthusiasm to channel one's mental, emotional and physical resources to resolve a problem.
3. Hawkins (2017) related mindfulness to the Chinese character for 'mindfulness' (念), noting that the character is 'a pictogram portraying the "present moment" sheltering the symbol for "heart" (sometimes translated as "heartmind")' (p. 92).
4. This is noted by Chan (2006).
5. Such a person embodied what Lyddy and Good (2017) termed 'being while doing'; Weintraub and Dust (2021) explained: '"Being" is a state centred in the present, self-quieted, goalless, intentional, and focuses on direct experience, whereas "doing" is focused on the past and future, evaluation-based, self-centered, goal-directed, and automatic' (p. 32).
6. The Chinese word *gong* (恭) can also be translated as 'respectful'. Lau (1997) translated *gong* 恭 as 'respectful' and *jing* 敬 as 'deferential'; both terms refer to respect.
7. The translation 'dignified, and was good-natured and agreeable' is by Ames and Rosemont (1998) whereas the translation 'composed and yet fully at ease' is by Slingerland (2003).
8. Chan (2006) explained that 'the intentional state of *jing* highlights both the object-regarding aspect of the response (i.e. recognition of the worth of the object) and the subject-regarding aspect of the response (i.e. seriousness). *Jing* as a frame of mind, on the contrary, has the subject-regarding aspect of the responses at the forefront of one's consciousness, and the object-regarding aspect in the background' (p. 236). She added that an intentional state 'is directed at specific objects, and the descriptions under which the objects are viewed are essential to the identification of the mental state' (Chan, 2006, p. 231).
9. This is noted by Lau (1997).
10. This point is noted by Lau (1997) in his commentary for this passage.
11. As further evidence of Confucius's respect towards those who were mourning, the *Analects* records: 'When eating in the presence of one who had been bereaved, the Master never ate his fill' (子食於有喪者之側，未嘗飽也 7.9); and 'On a day he had wept, the Master did not sing' (子於是日哭，則不歌 7.10).
12. Another example of Confucius's respect is noted in this incident:

> The intentional state of *jing* involves something more than seriousness. It also includes recognizing/appreciating the worth of the objects of *jing* . . . [In the *Analects*,] Confucius said, 'What is You [also known as Zilu]'s lute doing inside my door?' The disciples ceased to *jing* Zilu. Confucius said,

'You may not have entered the inner room, but he has ascended the hall' (*Analects* 11:15). Here Zilu loses his fellows' *jing* after Confucius has scolded him. Confucius then seeks to restore that *jing* by affirming the worth of Zilu, praising him for having achieved a high level of self-cultivation: he has ascended the hall, even if he has not yet got to the inner room. This passage clearly demonstrates that the object of *jing* is seen as having worth. (Chan, 2006, p. 233)

13 Lau's (1997) translation of this passage is: 'Tzu-lu [Zilu] asked about the gentleman. The Master said, "He cultivates himself and thereby achieves reverence."' I have changed Lau's translation of 'junzi' from 'gentleman' to 'exemplary person', and all male pronouns to gender-neutral terms throughout the book. I have also changed Lau's (1997) rendering of *jing* as 'reverence' to 'respect' throughout the book as the latter is a more accurate translation. Also, I have followed Ames and Rosemont (1998) in rendering 以 (*yi*) as 'by' instead of 'and thereby', as *yi* refers to the employment of something. Hence, 修己以敬 (*xiu ji yi jing*) is translated as 'cultivate oneself by being respectful' instead of Lau's (1997) 'cultivate himself and thereby achieves reverence'. It is noteworthy that Ames and Rosemont (1998) interpreted *jing* as 'respect' and Slingerland (2003) similarly rendered it as 'respectfulness'.

14 This point is noted by Slingerland (2003) who wrote that the exemplary person, whom he translates as 'the gentleman', is 'understood here as the gentleman-as-ruler' (p. 172). More needs to be said about the Confucian notion of an exemplary person (君子 *junzi*). This will be discussed in detail in the next chapter when we examine the component of *Exemplary living*.

15 *Li* does not have the negative connotations that are often associated with the English word 'ritual', such as superficiality, formalism or irrationality (Hall & Ames, 1998). Comprising 'rites, ritual practice, roles and relationships' (Hall & Ames, 1998, p. 269), *li* enables us to 'understand, express, develop, and continue to interpret who and what we are, and that gives concrete shape to our forms of life' (Ivanhoe, 2013, p. 34). Chin (2007) described *li* as the 'dictates of decorum – rules that are not fixed like laws but expressed as a rightness whose authority lies in the integrity of one's action' (p. 54).

16 I have given a detailed exposition of *li* in Tan (2013, 2020a, 2020c, 2020e).

17 I have changed all the male references in Lau (1997) to gender-neutral ones (e.g. 'a person'). I have also changed *jing* 敬 from 'reverence' to 'respect' for consistency of usage.

18 Chin (2007) wrote:

Whether he is dealing with officials or the common people, this person should treat everyone with respect. '[R]espect (*jing*)', with Confucius as its articulator, is not an abstract idea. It is tactile. It fills a person and shows up in his limbs and countenance, and it moves him in such a manner that he looks as if he is 'receiving an honoured guest' or 'participating in a grand sacrifice'. Thus when Confucius told Yan Hui that benevolence was about 'restraining the self and returning to the rites', he had in mind someone who has an enlightened and a refined self. The person who is benevolent is aware of what he is capable of doing to others, and to act on this awareness, he relies on his knowledge of ritual experience to hold him to the right measure. He will not look if he is not guided by perspicacity, he will not listen if he is not guided by keenness, he will not speak if he is not guided by a clear voice, and he will not take action if he is not guided by a discerning mind. He conducts himself in a manner that only the rites can cultivate, so that he is not wanton when he is joyful or broken when he is in sorrow; so that he does not give too much when he is happy or take away too much when he is sore. The practice of benevolence, therefore, begins and ends with the self – a person in the act of finding what is humane. (p. 169)

19 I change the expression 'habit of mind' to 'habit of heart-mind' to reflect the Confucian synthesis of the cognitive and affective functions. The term 'habit of mind' refers to a disposition towards certain behaviour. Examples of habits of mind are critical thinking, creativity and open-mindedness.
20 Besides 'respectful in deed', the 'ideal' in this passage also includes being conscientious and trustworthy in word and being single-minded in deed.
21 Chin (2007) noted:

Confucius relied on his awareness of the people around him to get himself anchored in a community or at court, in a temple or on the street … he wanted to understand what was appropriate and right in human relationships … The agility of his conduct – knowing when to be silent and when to be fluent, how far to stoop to receive a gift and how far to extend himself to help a friend in need – is proof of his mastery of the rites. Yet his subtle moves and deft performance also betray a compassionate heart and a keen knowledge of the human lot. (p. 180)

22 Lau (1997) translated 孝弟也者，其為仁之本與 as 'Being good as a son and obedient as a young man is, perhaps, the root of a man's character'. I would, however, render it as 'Being good as a son or daughter, and obedient as a person is, perhaps, the root of one's exemplary character'. The reason is that the Chinese character is 仁 (ren), which means not just 'character' but a supreme moral quality, usually translated as benevolence, humaneness, humanity, etc. I shall elaborate on ren in the next chapter.
23 This is noted by Slingerland (2003).

24 In this regard, 'respect' here is similar to Cranor's (1975) 'pro-attitude, appraisal respect'. Chan (2006) explained:

> This notion of respect is akin to esteem and reverence ... I can have appraisal respect only for those whose achievements I appreciate and admire, but I can have recognition respect universally for everyone, including my foe. Also, appraisal respect must be categorical and not based on one's own interests and ends. For example, if I have a positive evaluation of a worker's diligence only from the perspective of an employer, this is not appraisal respect ... [it] is based on a belief about the merit of the object of respect ... [and] also includes behavioral components such as the disposition to trust or rely on the belief that the object of respect has the relevant merits, and to recognize the value of the object's having those merits. (p. 238)

25 King (2016) observed: 'In the West, the material and the mental worlds have often been treated as two distinctive domains' (p. 32). Brown and Grassi (2019) also concurred: 'For centuries Western education has prioritized cognitive learning and suppressed the wisdom of the body, manifested in its senses and emotions. This legacy has unnecessarily isolated teachers and learners from the foundational roots of knowing and caring' (p. 214). Also see Hawkins (2017), McCown (2018), Moloney (2016) and Orr (2018).

26 Moloney (2016) averred: 'In their promise to unite these mental and somatic domains, mindfulness-based therapies seem to beckon towards a new era of more successful treatments' (p. 284, also see Fuchs, 2013).

27 The expression *mind-body medicine* is from Stanley and Longden (2016). A similar idea is *embodied presencing* mentioned by Miller (2016). Hawkins (2017) pointed out that 'training in mindfulness awareness is often focused on the body – on consciously cultivating the connections between mind and body that can help us find greater balance in our everyday experiences and behaviours' (p. 16).

28 Kirmayer (2015) claimed that a conception of mindfulness that is deprived of its moral foundation 'runs the risk of simply becoming a tool of pursuing goals that in themselves are unhealthy' (p. 462).

29 Carmody (2014) explained how Buddhist mindfulness is not non-judgemental:

> The Eastern conception of mindfulness emerges out of the primarily introspective approaches to knowledge extant in India at the time of the Buddha that *had the goal of reducing mental suffering*. In this view, the root problem preventing mental peace is ignorance of the momentary construction of the sense of self and ownership in the mind, and the *associated craving and aversion*. The term mindfulness has come to be the accepted English translation of the Pali word 'sati' (sometimes translated as awareness), which is one of the mental qualities whose cultivation is considered important in a

larger systematic path to *dispel that ignorance and the development of mental peace*. (p. 50, italics added)

30 I have given a detailed analysis of Confucius's idea of Heaven in Tan (2021c).
31 Brown and Olson (2015) elaborated:

> Formal practice usually involves mindful breathing, a body scan, sitting meditation, loving-kindness meditation, and mindful movement. The informal practice of mindfulness involves bringing the many daily activities of life – making the bed, shaving, washing the dishes, walking the dog, making a cup of tea, applying mascara – into a kind of present-centred focus in which we simply observe and experience the qualities of each of these activities. (p. 21)

32 The meditative aspect of mindfulness is discernible in neo-Confucianism from the ninth to eleventh century in China, due to its assimilation of Buddhist teachings. The Neo-Confucian philosopher Zhu Xi, for example, wrote about quiet sitting, which was a Confucian form of meditation. For details, see Tan (2020a).
33 This is noted in Brown and Olson (2015).
34 Brown and Olson (2015) wrote:

> The emotional climate and mood of a leader have dramatic effects on his or her team. Sour moods have 'ripple effects', affecting everyone on the team, both explicitly and subtly, and even relatively subtle emotional cues like a sarcastic eye roll can have a long-lasting impact on an executive's authority. It can also rock her entire team. On the other hand, having a broad repertoire of emotional intelligence skills and expressing positive emotions tend to enhance the performance of the individual, the group, and the entire organization – sometimes in subtle ways that are difficult to detect. (p. 33; also see Melwani & Barsade, 2011)

35 Brazier (2013) put forward the view that 'the contemporary condition of Western thinking and culture, which is increasingly focused on finding technical solutions to utilitarian problems and also on seeking comfort and stress-reduction', has neglected fundamental questions regarding purposes and meanings (p. 117). O' Donnell (2015) added that mindfulness is increasingly tied to an 'evidence-based' and 'what works' agenda that 'risks instrumentalizing what is a rich existential and ethical practice and using inappropriate forms of evaluation' (p. 196).
36 This is taken from Drago-Severson and Blum-Destefano (2019, p. 101, italics in the original).
37 Weare (2014) suggested that schools promote mindfulness in the school ethos and culture through *authentic mindfulness*, defined as an approach that 'sets out to cultivate in the learner a set of specific attitudinal qualities that originate in the

ethical foundations of the ancient contemplative traditions from which mindfulness came: They include open-minded curiosity, kindliness, empathy, compassion, acceptance, trust, patience and nonstriving' (p. 1045).

38 Weare (2014) recommended the following mindfulness techniques for children:

> Children generally respond best to active methods and materials that are pacey and light-hearted, with a focus on fun and seeing mindfulness as in some ways a game, and with varied stimuli that reach out to all learning styles, such as images, film clips, music, poetry, sensory experience, and stories, to help them respond and remember. They need experience to be concrete, and so efforts being made by several programs to introduce striking objects into the classroom (e.g. glitterballs, shockballs, blindfolds, chocolate, chilli) and use vivid metaphors and images (e.g. the mind is like an animal, the attention is like a puppy, avalanches, rough seas, thoughts as passing traffic) can be helpful. Examples in class and suggestions for home practice need to be grounded in the children's daily lives – of getting on and falling out, school and peer pressures, school deadlines, complicated relationships, managing social media, and surviving dysfunctional families – all the challenges of growing up in the 21st century. (p. 1047)

39 Drago-Severson and Blum-Destefano (2019) alluded to this idea when they suggested that school leaders foster mindfulness in their staff by offering 'to support mindfulness as an expression of care (i.e. not as a critique or a need for improvement)' (p. 97).
40 This is taken from Roberts and David (2017).
41 This is taken from Brown and Olson (2015).

4 Exemplary Living

1 This information is taken from Slingerland (2003).
2 A sage-king is a sage 聖人 (*shengren*), which is more admirable than a *junzi*. As explained by Ames and Rosemont (1998), a sage 'has risen beyond the level of *junzi*' and 'confers benefits on, and assists everyone' (p. 63). Even Confucius did not consider himself to be a sage (7.34) and shared that he had not encountered one in his life (7.26).
3 Ames and Rosemont (1998) pointed out that Confucius gave connotations and denotations to terms such as *junzi* 'that shifted their sense and reference away from position, rank, birth, or function toward what we (not he) would term aesthetic, moral, and spiritual characteristics' (p. 61). Also see Tan (2013, 2020b).
4 Confucius was not asserting or assuming that everyone *will* succeed in becoming a *junzi*. Success depends on, among other factors, one's capability, motivation and

access to resources. It is also helpful to note that Confucius himself did not belong to the aristocratic clan but to the *shi* 士 class, as noted in an earlier chapter.
5 This point is noted by Li (2010, p. 56).
6 It is interesting to note that some translators of the *Analects* such as Lau (1997) and Slingerland (2003) used the male pronoun for *junzi*, whereas others such as Ames and Rosemont (1998) and Chong (1998) used gender-neutral expressions.
7 Role-modelling extends to the private sphere where parents need to be good examples to their children, as seen in this episode where a father sued his own son:

> Confucius consulted with his advisors, argued it out with a few former pupils, and then left both father and son in jail for three months. At the end of their incarceration, he planned to simply release them both. Seeing this for the compromise it was, the Decisive Duke demanded an explanation. 'You once said that in a state or in a family, filial duty was the first thing to be insisted on. What hinders you now from putting to death this unfilial son as an example to all the people?' Confucius's reply cut to the heart of his philosophy. 'There is no justice', he replied, 'if we execute underlings for the failings of their superiors. This father has not taught his son to be filial – listening to his charge would require the punishment of the blameless. The manners of this age have long been in a sad condition; we cannot expect the people not to be transgressing the laws'. For Confucius, 'duty' was a two-way street. Sons were obliged to be loyal to their fathers, and commoners to their lords, but the authority figures had duties of their own. It was the first occurrence of a doctrine that would later be known as *noblesse oblige* – the idea that privilege brought its own responsibilities. (Clements, 2004, pp. 76–7).

8 This point was noted by Lau (1997) who wrote: 'Besides being homophones, the two words in Chinese are cognate, thus showing that the concept of "governing" was felt to be related to that of "correcting"' (p. 167).
9 Lau (1997) translated 欲 (*yu*) as 'a man of desires' but I prefer the word 'covetous' as it captures the idea of Ji Kangzi being a greedy person and setting a bad example by stealing from the people.
10 Lau (1997) rendered this passage thus: 'The Master said to Tzu-hsia, "Be a gentleman *ju* [*ru*], not a petty *ju*."' I have followed Ames and Rosemont in translating *ru* as 'counsellor'. Lau explained that *ru* 'probably referred to men for whom the qualities of the scholar were more important than those of the warrior' (p. 78).
11 Lau (1997) translated 道 (*dao*) as 'guide', but I have followed Ames and Rosemont in rendering it as 'lead'; this is closer to the meaning of *dao* as a road for one to tread on.

12 Confucius advocated rulers to follow the standard set by the Duke of Zhou. Chin (2007) explained the significance:

> Here 'the standard set by the Duke of Zhou' refers to the *feng jian* system this counsellor instituted at the founding of the dynasty, wherein the relationship of a regional ruler and his subjects was based on mutual support, not on material transactions: people contributed to the ruler and the state through their work on the public land, while the ruler made sure that his people would never be deprived of their basic sustenance. In Confucius's view, that relationship was ideal because it demanded reciprocity in the form of moral obligation and public service. (p. 125)

13 Cua (1992) explained how Confucius was a pioneer in recognizing the importance of role-modelling: 'In moral instruction or training, paradigmatic individuals may quite properly play the role of models for imitation or emulation by providing standards of aspiration or examples of competence to be attained. In the inculcation of *jen* [*ren*] or moral concern, they serve as standards of inspiration by providing a point of orientation rather than specific targets of achievement' (p. 60). On Confucius's accent on role-modelling, see Tan (2013, 2020a).

14 A truly virtuous person is contrasted with 'the village worthy' (鄉原 17.13), who is 'the ruin of virtue' (德之賊 17.13). Chin (2007), citing Mencius, explained that Confucius thought that the 'village worthy' was 'the ruin of virtue' because

> if you want to censure him, you cannot find any evidence of his wrongdoing, and if you want to attack him, you cannot find a clear target. He is in tune with the prevalent custom and blends in with the sordid world. When in a state of repose, he appears to be conscientious and trustworthy. When actively engaged with the world, he appears to be principled and immaculate. People all like him, and he thinks he is in the right. (p. 155)

15 This translation of 中庸之為德也 (*zhong yong zhi wei de ye*) is taken from Ames and Rosemont (1998). In my view, 'hitting the mark' is a more accurate translation of 中庸 (*zhong yong*) than Lau's (1997) rendition of 'the Mean as a moral virtue'. Confucius's point was to do what is appropriate rather than stick to the middle ground and avoid extremes.

16 Lau (1997) translated 因民之所利而利之，斯不亦惠而不費乎 as 'If a man benefits the common people by taking advantage of the things around them that they find beneficial, is this not being generous without its costing him anything?' The word *li* (利) refers to benefits rather than the act of taking advantage of something. Hence, I have replaced 'taking advantage of the things around them' with 'giving them things'.

17 Clements (2004) provided this surviving account from the *Kong Family Master's Anthology*:

> When a minister arrived late for a meeting, he offered as an excuse the fact that he had been obliged to defend an accused man from persecution by a local dignitary. The Honoured Duke was impressed, and boasted to Confucius that his officers were virtuous men – for even the prosecutor had been prepared to listen to a case for the defence. Confucius, however … pointed out that a truly virtuous official would have hired decent employees from the start, thereby ensuring that he did not waste any time on unnecessary legal proceedings. (pp. 35–6)

18 Chin (2007) commented: 'Confucius had good reasons to be enraged. The Jisuns constituted the largest landowner in Lu, with more administrative districts under their control than all that the rival families had in total. This meant that the land tax they reinstituted in must have caused widespread hardship' (p. 126).

19 This is taken from Mitra and Greenberg (2016). As Sullivan and Arat (2018) put it, the corporate motto for mindfulness is 'Keep mindful and stay productive' (p. 339; also see Miller, 2016).

20 For details, see Cheung (2018), Hyland (2016), King (2016), Orr (2018), Purser et al. (2016), Tomassini (2016) and Walsh (2016). Brazier (2016) held that 'the contemporary utilitarian version should really be called mind emptiness rather than mindfulness' as it is stripped of 'the emotive, ethical and imaginative dimensions' of mindfulness (p. 64).

21 Also see Hyland (2016) and Repetti (2016). Forbes (2016) summed up the detrimental effects of McMindfulness:

> McMindfulness occurs when mindfulness is used, either with intention or unwittingly, for self-serving and ego-enhancing purposes that run counter to both Buddhist and Abrahamic prophetic teachings to let go of ego-attachment and enact skilful, universal compassion. Instead of letting go of the ego, McMindfulness aims to enhance it and promotes self-aggrandizement; its therapeutic function is to comfort, numb, adjust, and advance the self within a neoliberal, corporatized, individualistic society based on private gain. (p. 357)

22 See Cheung (2018), Eklof (2016), Hyland (2016) and Payne (2018). Some researchers take a different approach by arguing that there are implicit ethics in mindfulness practices. An example is the argument by McCown (2018): 'The element of non-judgement in the co-created definition of mindfulness can blossom into "an affectionate, compassionate quality … a sense of openhearted, friendly presence and interest" (Kabat-Zinn, 2003, p. 145). The quality might be dubbed friendliness or even friendship, as there is a regard of the group within the group'

(p. 150, also see Monteiro, 2016). This approach to ethical cultivation is the 'discovery' model that 'that assumes ethics are intrinsic to mindfulness and that bare-attention practice can bring out or help participants discover their own innate ethical tendencies' (Cheung, 2018, p. 307). Notwithstanding the fact that values such as affection, friendliness and compassion are found in mindfulness practice, the critique of McMindfulness still stands, that is, the aim of mindfulness practice is still for utilitarian and personal advancement without the consideration of larger ethical questions such as the idea of a good life and a just society.

23 It is interesting that mindfulness presupposes an ethical dimension in the Christian tradition too. Stanley et al. (2018) wrote:

> In offering his translation of *sati*, Rhys Davids was partly influenced by the use of the adjective 'mindful' in the King James Bible (1604–1611) (see Bible: King James Version, 2017):
>
> My son, be mindful of the Lord our God all thy days, and let not thy will be set to sin, or to transgress his commandments: do uprightly all thy life long, and follow not the ways of unrighteousness.
>
> For they were pricked, that they should remember thy words; and were quickly saved, that not falling into deep forgetfulness, they might be continually mindful of thy goodness.
>
> Perhaps this 'hidden' Christian influence on the translation of this key Pali Buddhist word partly explains how we have come to inherit the idea of being mindful as somehow morally good or righteous. (p. 11)

24 See Eisenbeiss and van Knippenberg (2015), and Yadav (2021). Jennings et al. (2019) propounded a form of mindfulness in schools where 'individuals experience a deeper and more caring sense of connection to themselves, others, and the world around them when they bring mindful awareness into their daily lives' (p. 4). Mitra and Greenberg (2016) added that 'mindfulness necessarily encompasses ethical speech and compassionate action as part of a complex set of interrelated processes, including discernment, discrimination, remembrance, and imagination' (p. 412).

25 Gurr (2015) wrote:

> A standout characteristic of the principals is *the degree to which they are respected and trusted by their school communities* ... Acting with integrity and being transparent about their values, beliefs and actions, modelling good practice, being careful to ensure fairness in how they deal with people, involving many in decision making, are qualities and practices that *engender respect and trust*. Because of this, the school communities rarely challenge the principals if sometimes they have to make important decisions with little consultation; the foundation of respect and trust meant that top-down decisions could be accepted. (p. 139, italics added)

26 Pointing out that mindfulness is not purely about 'bare attention', Hawkins (2017) underscored the need for school leaders to advance 'a kindly, focused awareness and by building our capacity to turn towards difficulties with equanimity we are laying the foundation for an empathetic and compassionate connectedness' (p. 93). Tomassini (2016) asserted that mindfulness should not be 'limited by the present-moment as it includes the dimensions of *recollection* and *non-forgetfulness*, and also includes a *retrospective* memory or past events which helps in *prospectively* remembering to do something in the future' (p. 222, italics in the original).

27 Day et al. (2020) proposed that school leaders need to 'educate their students by promoting positive values (integrity, compassion and fairness), love of lifelong learning and fostering citizenship and personal, economic and social capabilities' (p. 7).

28 Buller (2019) pointed out that *metta* in Pali means 'benevolence, kindness, loving-kindness, friendliness, amity, friendship, goodwill, and active interest in others' (p. 91). *Metta*-based leadership was introduced by Buller (2019), who explained that it

> shouldn't be confused with merely being a popular or convivial leader. In the same way, it's not the same thing as just letting people do whatever it is they want to do. . . Instead, what *metta* helps leaders do is see matters from the perspective of the various stakeholders they serve. It causes us to recognise that even those who end up doing something very wrong probably started out by doing something they thought was good. We can thus provide better guidance for our areas because we better understand how the people we work with and for see the world, what matters to them, and where their individual challenges and frustrations lie. (pp. 102–3)

29 This is taken from Lavelle (2016).

30 Although Confucius's stand on human nature was unclear, other Confucian philosophers who followed after were more explicit about this issue. Mencius (*Mengzi*) 孟子 (372–289 BCE) argued that human nature is good. He cited the example of a person who happened to see a young child about to fall into a well (2A.6). This person, according to Mencius, would naturally be moved with compassion towards the child. This example exemplifies the innate goodness of all human beings that is represented by Mencius's theory of the 'four seeds' 四端 (*siduan*, also translated as 'four beginnings'). Xunzi 荀子 (310–235 BCE) argued that human nature is bad; people's nature is such that they are born with a fondness for profit in them. If they follow along with this, then struggle and contention will arise, and yielding and deference will perish therein. Xunzi viewed anarchy as caused by an absence of an inborn moral compass and external social restraint.

For more on Mencius's philosophy, see Tan (2018a, 2020a); for more on Xunzi's philosophy, see Tan (2017b, 2020a).

31 According to Cheung (2018), the *discovery model* 'assumes ethics are intrinsic to mindfulness and that bare-attention practice can bring out or help participants discover their own innate ethical tendencies' whereas the *developmental model* 'assumes ethics are developed and are not innate' and 'qualities cultivated through mindfulness would depend on what is actively pursued' (p. 307, also see Klein, 1995; Lindahl, 2015).

32 In terms of the relation between mindfulness training and moral instruction, Confucius's conception of mindfulness and mindful leadership is consistent with the *integral approach*. Payne (2018) clarified that this approach sees mindfulness practices as a part of a Confucian tradition, and mindfulness practitioners need to imbibe Confucian values if they were to practise mindfulness effectively. Besides the integral approach, the other two approaches delineated by Payne (2018) are *inherent* and *modular*. He explained:

> The conception that morality is inherent within mindfulness claims that morality arises spontaneously as a result of mindfulness practice. In this conception no moral instruction is necessary to produce an increase in moral behaviour, nor does the kind of meditation involved effect this change in the meditator's being in the world. The second conception, integral, is that mindfulness practices are part of the Buddhist tradition and that to be effective requires the practitioner to adopt those values promoted within the tradition. Last, the modular conception sees mindfulness training and moral training as fully autonomous from one another, and like other modular relations, they can be conjoined in various ways. The modular conception in turn has two variant forms, an implicit and an explicit version. In the implicit version, the values of the training context, such as those of the institution and of the personnel involved in the training programme, are communicated to clients without being formulated as a programme of moral instruction. In the explicit version, training in mindfulness meditation can exist independently, but it is also possible to add a programme of moral instruction to the mindfulness training. Further, there is nothing about the relation that mandates a preference for any specific system of morality. (p. 328)

33 This is reported in Seigle et al. (2019).

34 As reported by Seigle et al. (2019),

> The entire school community engaged in approaches not only to recognize moments of gratitude, but to actively nourish it with a practice of changing one's perspective from negative to positive when encountering a challenging situation. . . . For students, this practice helped them to see that they have

a choice in how they view situations ... They would first look at a situation without gratitude glasses – for example, 'I got too many problems wrong on the math assessment.' With their gratitude glasses on, they were able to see it differently: 'I know what I need to learn next, and my teacher can help me.' ... Gratitude practices were shared with adults in the neighbourhood and beyond as well. (pp. 74–5)

35 The Australia Catholic University and Erebus International (2008, p. 27) elucidated the five components of SEL:
   1. *Self-awareness*: Accurately assessing one's own feelings, interests, values and strengths; understanding one's own thinking and learning processes and maintaining a well-grounded sense of self-confidence;
   2. *Self-management*: Regulating emotions to handle stress, control impulses and persevere in overcoming obstacles; setting and monitoring progress toward personal and academic goals and expressing emotions appropriately;
   3. *Social awareness*: Being able to take the perspective of others and empathize with them; recognizing and appreciating individual and group similarities and differences and recognizing and using family, school and community resources;
   4. *Relationship skills*: Establishing and maintaining healthy and rewarding relationships based on cooperation; resisting inappropriate social pressure; preventing, managing and resolving interpersonal conflict and seeking help when needed and
   5. *Responsible decision-making*: Making decisions based on consideration of ethical standards, safety concerns, appropriate social norms, respect for others and likely consequences of actions; applying decision-making skills to academic and social situations and contributing to the well-being of one's school and community.
36 This is taken from Mischenko and Jennings (2019). Rechtschaffen (2014) added: 'When mindfulness links the brain up in this way, the five competencies of self-management, self-awareness, social awareness, relationship skills and responsible decision making naturally arise' (p. 18).
37 Leithwood et al. (2019) also reported that school leadership 'improves teaching and learning, indirectly and most powerfully, by improving the status of significant key classroom and school conditions and by encouraging parent/child interactions in the home that further enhance student success at school' (p. 8).
38 This is taken from Leithwood et al. (2020). On the need to overcome the dominant distrust among the educational stakeholders, Senge et al. (2012) opined: 'In a school that learns, people who traditionally may have been suspicious of one another – parents and teachers, educators and local business people, administrators and union members, people inside and outside the school walls, students and adults – recognise their common stake in the future of the school system and the things they can learn from one another' (p. 5).

39 I have adapted the term *embodied mindfulness* from Taylor et al.'s (2019) *embodied teacher mindfulness*. An exemplary person manifests embodied mindfulness through 'underlying mindful skills and dispositions related to the regulation of attention and emotion and to prosocial dispositions towards others, particularly empathy, compassion, and forgiveness' (Hawkins, 2017, p. 110). An exemplary person also models 'heartfulness', which is 'a general kindness towards the inner, outer, and other realms of experience' (Hawkins, 2017, p. 111).

5 Serving Others

1 Shun (1993) pointed out that there are at least two different meanings of *ren*: 'According to one view, the character originally referred to the quality that makes someone a distinctive member of an aristocratic clan. According to another view, it originally had the meaning of love, especially the kindness of rulers to their subjects' (p. 457). Yu (1998) suggested a third possible meaning of *ren*: it was used in the *Book of Songs* (also known as the *Book of Odes*) to describe noble huntsmen (p. 323).

2 I have changed Lau's (1997) translation of 敏 (*min*) from 'quickness' to 'diligence', following Ames and Rosemont (1998) and Slingerland (2003). This is because the term is more than just doing things quickly; it also connotes the values of being careful and persistent.

3 Strictly speaking, the character possessed by a *ren* person is not just moral but also aesthetic and spiritual. For discussion on the aesthetical and spiritual characteristics of a *ren* and an exemplary person (*junzi*), see Tan (2013, 2020e) and Tan and Tan (2016).

4 The various translations are taken from the following sources: 'Using oneself as a measure to gauge the likes and dislikes of others' (Lau, 1997), 'putting oneself in the other's place' (Ames & Rosemont, 1998) and 'understanding' (Slingerland, 2003). Cua (1992) described the concept of *shu* thus:

> The insight of the Confucian notion of reciprocity (*shu*) may be reformulated in this way: 'how others feel about our actions towards them should be internally related to our feeling about those actions, and hence their feelings should penetrate our motives'. Differently put, human lives within a moral community are possible because there exists a reciprocity of individual wills oriented toward a common *telos*, implying an acknowledgment of a bond. The bond is, so to speak, the intersection of individual lives, an anchorage for both personal and cultural identity. It is this attitude that provides a sense of significance to personal lives. Respect for persons, especially in the light of *jen* [*ren*], is not just a Kantian respect for persons as ends in themselves, but a

respect for individual styles of life, deemed as polymorphous expressions of a common culture. (p. 54)

5. Mou (2004) regarded 6.28 as the 'seemingly similar counterpart of the positive version of this methodological principle [of *shu*]' (p. 222). In comparing *shu* with the Golden Rule mentioned in the Bible, he claimed that 'the two versions share the same core idea to the effect that one can use one's own desires as a guide to how to treat others' (p. 221).
6. *Shu* parallels *identification respect* noted by Carl Cranor, which emphasizes the respect one has for others on the basis of sympathy of identification with another person. As noted by Chan (2006),

    The sympathy account holds that to respect others requires one to have 'an active sympathy' or the motivation to promote their interests and not merely feel sympathy for their sufferings. The identification account claims that respect for others requires an identification with them in the sense of taking up their point of view in seeing a given situation. Common to these two is the idea that respect involves adopting a more participatory stance toward others' interests, rather than merely refraining from harming them or interfering with their freedom. (p. 238)

7. This is taken from Decety and Yoder (2016).
8. See Eisenberg and Strayer (1987), Songhorian (2019) and Tan (2022).
9. This is taken from Decety and Yoder (2016).
10. See Kim and Kou (2014). *Empathic concern* is essentially 'a fellow-feeling that arises when we consider another's plight' (Prinz, 2011, p. 230). For more information on empathic concern, see Decety and Yoder (2016). Nylan and Wilson (2010) observed that Confucius's own injunction was 'to be "mindful of the limitation of others" (*shu* 恕) – a mindfulness that he eventually termed the "one thread" running through his mature teachings' (p. 18). Empathy, for Confucius, is more accurately described as 'empathic concern' that goes beyond perspective-taking or affection to a motivation to care for the well-being of others. Hereinafter, I shall use 'empathy' to mean 'empathic concern' when referring to Confucius's *shu*.
11. Nylan and Wilson (2010) wrote: '"Taking one's own feelings as a guide" always suffices when deciding how to act in official and private matters' (p. 23).
12. Ivanhoe (1990) explained that empathy needs to be performed through *li* (normative behaviours): 'Without a firm commitment to *li* [normative behaviours], the "kindness" of *shu* can collapse into vague, formless sentimentality' (p. 28).
13. It is helpful to note that the English word 'empathy' was coined by Edward Titchener in 1909 based on the German word *Einfühlung* that means 'feeling into another's emotion and perceptions' (Horsthemke, 2015).

14 Slingerland (2003) posited that Confucius 'puts aside the normal ritual behaviour of a host in order to deftly and respectfully serve as a guide for the blind Music Master, without being overly fussy or condescending' (p. 190).
15 Slingerland (2003) commented that a supplicant in ancient China would purify oneself by fasting and abstinence when asking a Master for teaching. He wrote: 'Most commentators take the point of this passage to be that a sincere act of good will should be honoured, no matter what a person's reputation or past behaviour. Some also see here an optimism in people's ability to change for the better (cf. 17.13)' (p. 74).
16 Li (2006) held that harmony is by its very nature relational:

> It presupposes the coexistence of multiple parties; a single item does not harmonize. As far as harmony is concerned, these parties possess more or less equal significance. Therefore, harmony is always contextual; epistemologically it calls for a holistic approach. A mentality of harmony is a contextual mentality. In other words, persons of harmonious mentality see things, and make judgments on these things, in relation, in context, not in isolation or separation. (p. 589)

17 Ames and Rosemont (1998) described harmony as 'the art of bringing together with mutual benefit and enhancement *without losing their separate and particular identities*' (p. 56, italics added).
18 Ames and Rosemont (1998) pointed out that the word 'harmony' is etymologically related to cooking – the art of bringing together elements for mutual benefit and enhancement without losing their separate and particular identities (p. 56). Li (2006), on the other hand, traced the roots of harmony to music:

> Therefore, we may conclude that the original meaning of *he* as harmony comes from the rhythmic interplay of various sounds, either in nature or between human beings, that is musical to the human ear, and that the prototype of he is found in music. From the notion of *he* as the harmonious interplay of sounds, it is not difficult to see how this can be expanded, by analogous thinking, to mean harmony in other things and hence harmony in general. (p. 584)
>
> Be it in the metaphor of food or music, harmony essentially involves uniting different elements to form an integrated whole, without sacrificing the individuality of the diverse components.

19 The existence of a community of *junzi* and their salutary reputation were noted in ancient China. Chin (2007) described:

> Lu and Wei were brotherly in other ways. During the Spring and Autumn period, it was common knowledge that the two states were never short of

men with integrity and political talent. If a person with some position had acted ingloriously, say, in the state of Qi, he would be very reluctant to go to either Lu or Wei because he would not be able to face the counsellors in those places. Confucius himself boasted: 'With one great change, the state of Qi can resemble the state of Lu. With one great change, [the government of] Lu can embody the way [that is moral and good] … Dilu Zifang from the state of Qi is an example. He was the family retainer of a Qi minister. Even when his life was in danger, he refused the help of an enemy of his lord because at the time he was thinking about fleeing to Lu or Wei. He said to others, "If I were to have private ties with the enemy while I am in the service of my lord, I wouldn't be able to face the gentlemen of Lu and Wei [when I see them]."' (p. 88)

20 Through harmony, the self is expanded and deepened in an ever-expanding circle of human relatedness (Tu, 1985). Harmonious persons 'see things, and make judgments on these things, in relation, in context, not in isolation or separation' (Li, 2006, p. 589). The interdependence of human beings is illustrated in Hall and Ames's (1987) analogy of *focus-field*: a person is a 'focus' whereas family ties and sociopolitical orders are the 'field' or 'sphere of influence'. On a neo-Confucian idea of interdependence, see Tan (2020f).
21 This is taken from Nylan and Wilson (2010, pp. 14–15).
22 On the difference between coaching and mentoring, Clutterbuck (2008) wrote: '*coaching* in most applications addresses performance in some aspect of an individual's work or life; while *mentoring* is more often associated with much broader, holistic development and with career progress' (p. 9, italics added). A useful definition of mentoring is provided by Hobson et al. (2009): 'The one-to-one support of a novice or less experienced practitioner by a more experienced practitioner, designed primarily to assist the development of the mentee's expertise and to facilitate their introduction into the culture of the profession and into the specific local context' (p. 207). My definition of coaching in this book is not limited to specific performance, and is more aligned with Hobson et al.'s formulation of mentoring.
23 This point is taken from Chin (2007), who shed light on Confucius's teaching method:

Whenever Confucius talked in the first person about teaching – 'I teach without growing weary,' for instance – he always used the word *hui*. He could have used another word, *xun*. They both mean 'to teach'. A first-century dictionary defined *hui* and *xun* in this way: *hui* is to teach 'by way of imparting light' or 'throwing light' (*xiaojiao*); *xun* is to teach 'by means of giving a lesson or a lecture' (*shuojiao*). Since *xun* does not appear in the *Analects*, it is possible that Confucius was not disposed towards making long disquisitions or speaking in front of an audience. There is also *jiao*, a more general word meaning 'to teach'. The same dictionary explains *jiao* as 'to emulate', but only in the case of a subordinate emulating the example set by a superior ... *Jiao* implies an unequal relationship – one bestows and the other receives – and the teacher in this relationship could not have been a teacher of Confucius, for Confucius found his 'even when walking in the company of two men. (p. 147)

For more discussions on Confucian approaches to teaching, see Tan (2015a, 2015b, 2016a).

24 Chin (2007) commented:

In time of crisis, the people of Wei, like the people of Lu, had always relied on good counsellors to help them avert catastrophe ... Confucius was familiar with those counsellors ... The ones he cited by name possessed these qualities: one was 'straight as an arrow whether or not a moral way prevailed', another 'took office when the moral way prevailed and let himself be rolled up and hidden away when the moral way did not prevail', a third one was so generous in spirit that he 'recommended a retainer in his household to the position of a state counsellor', thus letting his subordinate 'serve side by side with him'. (p. 89)

25 Huang (2011) pointed out that 史記 *Shiji* [Records of the (grand) historian], 呂氏春秋 *Lü shi chunqiu* [Mister Lü's spring and autumn] and the *Analects* inform us that 'Zilu (子路) was originally "uncivilized" (野人 *ye ren*), Zigong (子貢) was engaged in commerce (an occupation looked down upon in Confucianism), Zhonggong's (仲弓) father was a "lowly person" (賤人 *jianren*), Zizhang (子張) was from a family of low status in the state of Lu (魯) and Yan Zhuju (顏涿聚) was a robber' (p. 142).

26 Chin (2007) described:

Zizhang was not only self-absorbed, he was unembarrassed to let his teacher know that he wanted to advance in the world and that he intended to put himself on a salary track ... in response Confucius always tried to lead Zizhang back to self-cultivation ... Confucius first established how Zizhang understood adroitness. In Confucius's view, what Zizhang described was mastering the art of being smooth and ready and of giving the appearance of having distinction. These skills cannot bring about the ease with which a person of 'gentlemanly adroitness' conducts his work. It was not difficult for a clever man like Zizhang to learn the skills of a glib man, but the art of adroitness was a different matter. According to Confucius, to master the art, 'a person must be partial to the concept of fairness; he must want it so much that he tries for it in all he does; and he must, at the same time, be aware of what other people say and how they respond to him lest he becomes unbearable in their eyes through believing that what he does is good for them'. (pp. 132–3)

27 Chin (2007) gave another example:

On the subject of making friends, Zixia said, 'You should make friends with those whose characters are acceptable and reject those whose characters are not.' Zizhang said, 'This is not what I have heard. The gentleman respects the worthy and is generous towards the common people. He speaks highly of the good and is compassionate towards those who have a hard time trying to be good. If indeed I am a man of great worth, whom would I not embrace? If I am a person of no worth, others will for sure reject me. If that is the case, how can I reject them?' Both men thought they were relaying what their teacher had taught them about how to make friends … In his own words, Confucius seems to maintain both positions. On one occasion, he said, 'Do not make friends with those who are not as good as you.' On another occasion, he said, 'Love all, but stay close to those who are truly humane.' In the first instance, Confucius was thinking pragmatically about education – only a person who is nobler and better will have something to teach you. In the second instance, he was speaking broadly about educating the young – teach them not to abandon a single person but to gravitate towards the morally superior when making friends. (p. 134)

28 Chin (2007) commented:

The early sources also stress that Zilu was from Bian, a district in Lu reputed to have produced the bravest man in the Spring and Autumn history . . . Zilu also came to be known among Confucius's disciples as the one who loved valour and who was most likely to get involved in acts of valour. And it was to him Confucius would emphasize that it was not enough just to be 'trusty', 'straightforward', 'brave' and 'unbending'. A person may have these attributes, which may seem honourable and worthy, but without a love of learning, Confucius says, problems will begin to emerge for the protagonist: he will keep his word 'for the wrong reason', or be so forthright that he 'becomes a menace', so brave that he 'foments anarchy' and so unbending that he 'is simply mad'. (p. 78)

29 Noting that mindfulness is closely related to coaching ability, Kets de Vries (2014) compared effective leadership coaches to gardeners who help others root out the weeds in their lives to prevent them from growing again.

30 See Barker (2014), Lavelle (2016), Moloney (2016), Payne (2016) and Purser (2015). For example, Lavelle (2016) posited: 'Despite the rhetoric of interdependence in MBSR, for example, the causes of suffering are squarely located within the individual's ways of perceiving or misperceiving the world, and the path of healing involves individuals changing the way they see and relate to the world' (p. 241).
31 See Cobb (2019) and Payne (2016). The result of mindfulness meditation is what Bazzano (2016) called 'solipsistic concentration and self-absorbed relaxation' (p. 296; also see Bazzano, 2013a, 2013b, 2013c).
32 This is noted by Magee (2016); also see Cannon (2016) and Sullivan and Arat (2018).
33 Magee (2016), for example, proposed *community-engaged mindfulness* that operates simultaneously on three levels – personal, interpersonal and systemic (p. 429) – and involves the following: 1. developing the personal dimension of our own capacity to work with and learn from our own experiences, including experiences of social suffering and learning about the structural nature of the suffering of others (the *personal* dimension); 2. offering and receiving supportive practices and collaborating across lines of real and perceived cultural, racial and other differences (the *interpersonal* dimension) and 3. working with others to relieve suffering at all levels, including the material and structural-institutional (the *systemic* dimension).
34 This is cited in Taylor et al. (2019) who reported: 'Engaging in gratitude and caring practices fostered positive feelings among participating teachers that some wanted to share with others in the community' (p. 128).
35 Relational trust is the 'connective tissue that binds these individuals together around advancing the education and welfare of children' (Seigle et al., 2019, p. 62; also see Bryk & Schneider, 2002; Tschannen-Moran, 2014).
36 This is taken from Yadav (2021). Sethi (2009) pointed out that scientific research on the mind has validated the phenomenon of role modelling where human beings automatically mimic the mind, moods and feelings of others. This finding on mirror neurons makes mindful leadership critical for any organization:

> The virtuous cycle of mindfulness can best be unleashed by an enlightened and evolved CEO who believes in and role-models the practice and the process. This CEO in turn will need to have the entire executive team own the process and each level needs to take ownership for cascading it to the next level. Mindfulness principles need to be incorporated within all the teams and across the organization by including them in leadership development programs and processes, evaluation and performance reviews, and feedback mechanisms. (p. 10)

37 This point is from Rowland (2017) who, in his book on how to lead mindful change, suggested that people 'speak out and say risky things and have the hard-to-have conversations through empathy and high quality dialogue skills' (p. 137).
38 This is noted in Wilkin (1992) and Washburn-Moses (2010).
39 This is taken from OECD (2019).
40 See Salleh and Tan (2013), Hairon and Tan (2017).
41 This is taken from Feiman-Nemser (2001).
42 This is taken from Feiman-Nemser (2001).
43 This is taken from Williams and Penman (2011). Jennings et al. (2019) noted the value of empathy and compassion that enhance human connection regardless of differences such as one's ethnicity, gender, national origin or religion.
44 This is taken from Meyers et al. (2019). Also see Tan (2022).
45 Related to teacher empathy is what Rodgers and Raider-Roth (2006) termed *teacher presence*, which is 'a state of alert awareness, receptivity and connectedness to the mental, emotional, and physical workings of both the individual and the group in the context of their learning environments and the ability to respond with a considered and compassionate next step' (p. 266, cited in Taylor et al., 2019, p. 109).
46 This is taken from Schertz (2007). *Empathic pedagogy* helps to develop interpersonal and social empathy in students where 'one person can come to know the internal state of another and can be motivated to respond with sensitive care' (Batson, 2009, p. 160).
47 As explained by Brown and Olson (2015),

> Loving-kindness meditations can help evoke compassion and friendliness towards oneself and others, and are central practices for those who wish to increase their capacity to feel love for tenderness, kindness, and a sense of generosity towards oneself and others. The loving-kindness meditation is about 'planting the seeds of loving wishes over and over in our hearts', as described by the acclaimed mindfulness teacher Jack Kornfield. This meditation often begins with an embrace of oneself, moving outward to imagining love and compassion for others and the world. (pp. 1–2; also see Taylor et al., 2019)

48 This is cited in Taylor et al. (2019, p. 121).
49 This is taken from Fagiano (2019).
50 This is cited in Seigle et al. (2019, p. 65).
51 This is taken from Schertz (2007); also see Huppert (2017).
52 This is taken from Slote (2007).
53 See Decety and Yoder (2016) and Horsthemke (2015).
54 This is taken from Schertz (2007). Participation in activities such as a Japanese tea ceremony is also salutary in engaging the students' senses as well as developing their

aesthetic skills and characteristic dispositions (Tong, 1997). To help participants learn and practise respectful mindfulness, the Japanese tea ceremony could be modified to include the participants serving tea to one another mindfully.

55 This is taken from Hoffman (2000).
56 This is noted by Batson (2009).
57 *Social empathy* refers to 'the ability to understand people by perceiving or experiencing their lived situations and as a result gain insight into structural inequalities and disparities' (Segal, 2011, pp. 276–7).
58 This is taken from Stone-Johnson and Weiner (2020).

6 Transforming Society

1 I have spelt *Way* with a capital letter throughout this book to distinguish it from the English word 'way', which means a path.
2 This is taken from Cua (1989), Hansen (1989), Tan (2020a) and Tan and Tan (2016). Specifically, the expression *a vision of human excellence* is taken from Cua (1989).
3 On the 'way of the sage-kings of old', Wilson (1995) pointed out that it 'refers to a Golden Age in which the basic features of civilized human life were thought to have been discovered and instantiated in a perfect social, political, and ethical order' (p. 270).
4 For the expression 'devotes one's heart-mind to attaining *dao*', I have changed Lau's (1997) translation from 'mind' to 'heart-mind'. I have made a similar change to the expression 'set his heart-mind on *dao*' in the next sentence in the text.
5 To broaden the Way is to 'make and remake appropriate ways of living: There is no predetermined, transcendental way of living for Confucius' (Kim, 2004, p. 123). To do so is 'to experience, to interpret, and to influence the world in such a way as to reinforce and extend the way of life inherited from one's cultural predecessors' (Ames & Rosemont, 1998, p. 45). In other words, *dao* comprises 'the process of generating an actual order in the world rather than an already fixed order' and 'human beings have to set boundaries for themselves and for other things as they move forward in the world' (Li, 2006, p. 594).
6 Confucius's faith in human beings' capability to broaden the Way exemplifies an ancient Chinese belief that 'truth' is not an objective fact but a way of being. Li (2006) gave details:

> The Chinese typically do not see truth as correspondence with an objective fact in the world; rather they understand truth more as a way of being, namely being a good person, a good father, or a good son. For them there is no objective truth carved in stone, and consequently there is not an

ultimate fixed order in the world according to which things must operate. The Confucian *Dao* consists of the process of generating an actual order in the world rather than an already fixed order. Without a predetermined truth, human beings have to set boundaries for themselves and for other things as they move forward in the world. (p. 594)

7 Rather than locating knowledge in a transcendental realm, Confucius emphasized the human world as the source of knowledge and reality. Hall and Ames (1987) observed: 'For Confucius, knowledge is grounded in the language, customs, and institutions that comprise culture. Culture is the given world. Thinking is cultural articulation that renders this givenness effective. There is no knowledge to be gained of a reality which precedes that of culture or transcends its determinations. The "world" is always a human world' (p. 67).

8 Slingerland (2003) explained that Bo Yi and Shu Qi chose to starve themselves to death, refusing even to eat the wild grass and herbs of the Zhou, to protest against a minister attacking his lord in Zhou.

9 Lau (1997) translated this sentence thus: 'While the Way is to be found in the Empire, I will not change places with him'. I have, however, followed Ames and Rosemont in interpreting this as Confucius stating that his mission was to achieve the Way, which had been lost in the Empire. The word 'change' (易 *yi*) refers to Confucius changing the state of affairs in the world, not swapping places with the person.

10 Slingerland (2001) explained the meaning of *yi*: 'This sort of situation-centred reasoning resembles Aristotelian *phronesis*, and ultimately "what is right" in the ethical realm corresponds to what the gentleman (that is, the good person) [*junzi*] would do' (p. 103). *Yi*, like *phronesis*, is a form of judgement. Dunne and Pendlebury (2003) noted: 'Aristotle's treatment of *phronesis* incorporates the interrelated elements identified above under the rubric of "judgement"' (p. 201).

11 The value of *yi* (appropriateness) is linked to the idea of *recognition respect*. Chan (2006) elaborated on this:

> According to Darwall, recognition respect consists of 'a disposition to weigh appropriately in one's deliberation some feature of the thing in question and to act accordingly'. While recognition respect can have various sorts of objects such as persons, laws and social roles, strictly speaking its real objects are facts about those persons, laws, and social roles. If I have a recognition respect for the legal speed limit, I take it into account when I decide how fast I should drive and see it as placing restrictions on my driving speed. In brief, to have recognition respect toward someone is to give due weight to the relevant facts about the person and even to see those facts as constraints on our actions when we deliberate about actions toward the person. Since respect implies

rendering appropriate treatment to the object of respect, the treatment can be either positive or negative. Hence, this account allows us to have respect for a formidable foe as well as a hero. (p. 239; also see Darwall, 1977)

12 Confucius demonstrated appropriateness in tricky situations, as seen in the following account:

> When the body of the Shining Duke was returned to Lu for burial, it was interred in the cemetery of the Duke's ancestors. However, certain members of the Jisun clan, unable to lay aside the enmity that had consumed them all their lives, ordered that the Duke's tomb be placed at a distance from the others. It was an insult literally beyond the grave, using the rules of *feng shui* to shun the Shining Duke, so that even in death he might not find peace. Confucius was in a quandary. As minister for Public Works, the interment was one of his duties, but, as a former servant of the Shining Duke, he could not bear to cause his late lord any undue suffering in the afterlife. Eventually, he found a compromise solution, and did as he was ordered. But once the grave was dug and the Shining Duke laid to rest, Confucius ordered the digging of a ditch to surround the entire cemetery. By delineating a boundary that incorporated both the original ancestral tombs and the isolated Duke, the ditch made them one unified whole again. The leader of the Jisun clan demanded to know Confucius's intent, and Confucius told him straight that it was his way of atoning for his own disloyalty to his former master. It was a tense moment, but Confucius somehow got away with it. He had successfully manipulated protocol to save his face and his own skin, and such a stand seems to have impressed even those who disliked him. (Clements, 2004, pp. 70–1)

13 Chin (2007) wrote:

> A good man, Confucius said, 'is not slavish to a path others have trodden'. This man is not even slavish to the path he himself has trodden, for experience would teach him that every occasion is different: the circumstances change, and they change even as the occasion unfolds. Thus, each time, he has to size up the situation and decide how to make his next move. He marks the line. (p. 166)

14 Confucius demonstrated this in the following encounter:

> The government of Chu took control of She, and its representatives encouraged the people of Cai, who had decided not to move east with their ruler, to come and settle in She and to recognise Chu as their new overlord. When Confucius arrived in She, the governor had just been assigned there,

his subjects were essentially a foreign people, and he was a long way from his own political base in Chu. In their first conversation, the administrator asked Confucius, 'What is considered good government?' Confucius replied, '[A government is good] when those who are near are pleased and those who are far away are drawn to it.' The advice was appropriate to the governor's circumstances at the time. Surely he was hoping to keep his new subjects content and to inspire more settlers to come. The *Zuo* writers say that the governor remained in his position for twelve years. (Chin, 2007, p. 110)

15 Lau (1997) translated 其為仁之本與 as 'the root of a man's character', relying on a particular manuscript of the *Analects* that mentions 人 *ren* instead of its homophone, 仁 *ren*. I have followed Ames and Rosemont (1998) and Slingerland (2003) in relying on the manuscript that contains 仁 *ren* instead of 人 *ren*. Hence, I have translated the expression as 'the root of *ren* (humanity)'.
16 Lai (1995) explained: 'Individuals have to live appropriately according to the titles and names, indicating their ranks and statuses within relationships, by which they are referred to' because these terms 'prescribe how values upholding the various roles are to be realized within the fundamental reality of the lived human world' (p. 252).
17 This information is taken from Slingerland (2003).
18 Although Confucius praised Guangzhong for his service to his lord in this passage and his *ren* (humanity) (14.9, 14.16), he had reservations about Guanzhong's lack of *li* (normative behaviours) (3.22).
19 As noted by Lai (1995), *li* 'can be modified and, indeed, are varied and variable and manifest differently as they pertain to each different situation and to each particular relationship, although they may provide general guidelines for each kind of relationship' (pp. 255–6).
20 Lau (1997) translated 佞人 (*ningren*) as 'plausible men'; it is thus puzzling why Confucius would advise anyone to stay away from people who are 'plausible'. The word '佞' refers to glib or eloquent. Given the context where this word is used derogatorily, I have translated it as 'glib people'.
21 I have added the word 'too' before 'casual' to capture Confucius's point that not prostrating oneself before ascending the steps was objectionable. The word 泰 (*tai*) denotes casual or relaxed, but in this context, it connotes inappropriate behaviour and a lack of respect.
22 See Caring-Lobel (2016), Drougge (2016), Goddard (2014), Lavelle (2016), Mitra and Greenberg (2016) and Ng (2016). Purser et al. (2016) cautioned: 'Individualistic, *laissez-faire* oriented mindfulness programmes, perhaps unwittingly, are preserving the status quo and maintaining institutional structures that contribute to social suffering' (p. viii, italics in the original).

23 This is taken from Cannon (2016); also see Bodhi (2016) and Titmuss (2016). In the specific context of schooling, Jennings et al. (2019) advocated the following:

> What we are calling for is a complete transformation of the educational system. While reforms attempt to improve the condition of an existing system, transformation involves changing the very nature of the system itself. We do not hold that mindfulness and compassion alone are enough to fully transform schools, nor do we claim to possess the blueprint for the transformation we are seeking. However, we do feel that mindfulness and compassion can serve as an essential vision and framework for the transformation we seek. (p. 6; also see Cobb, 2019)

24 See Davies (2015), Eklof (2016), Forbes (2016), King (2016), Loy (2016), Magee (2016), Purser and Milillo (2014), Samuel (2016) and Walsh (2016). Forbes (2016) highlighted, in particular, the neglect of the needs of certain groups of students in schools that promote mindfulness: 'Left behind by mindfulness education programmes in the wake of the neoliberal wave is the cultural capital of many schools and communities of colour in urban areas. It is rare that mindfulness school programmes acknowledge these and work with and within them to discuss and employ shared skills, strengths, and interests' (p. 359). Agreeing with Forbes (2016) was Cannon (2016), who claimed: 'Mindfulness alone will not help youth of colour experiencing the traumas of our criminal (in)justice system, police surveillance and repression, poverty, lack of access to jobs, gentrification, and housing dislocation – to name but a few examples of historical and institutional racism' (p. 401). The mindfulness Cannon had in mind was the type that centres on individual practice and excludes larger sociopolitical, economic and cultural factors.

25 This is taken from Commission on Social Justice (1994).

26 Stingl and Weiss (2014) urge educators to '*mindfully* disrupt the unsatisfactory present to enact a more socially just future' (italics in the original). They gave an example of asking questions mindfully:

> When discussing the shift towards increased medication of children with ADHD, we can become more *mindful* in the questions we ask. We should not just ask, -'Is it bad to treat a child with Ritalin to manage his ADHD?' We must first ask, 'What is this "ADHD," and why do we want to manage it?' We could also ask, "How did we deal with this type of behaviour before, or was it even considered undesirable in the past?' As we showed (Stingl & Weiss, 2013), a radical historization of this topic reveals important historical and institutional insights into not only the origins of the social norm of attention in children, but the larger sociopolitical context of industrialised labour driving ideologies about human development in the social ecology. What social developments were necessary to allow the measuring of attention

such that there could be a 'deficit' in a person? With significant shifts in health-care policy (such as the passage of the Affordable Care Act), how does legitimization of particular regimens – resulting in insurance coverage of certain treatments – affect parental considerations about response options? (Stingl & Weiss, 2014, p. 624, italics in the original)

27 Social justice education involves 'a wide range of pedagogies that seek to ameliorate social harm wrought through inequitable practices and structures' (Todd, 2003, p. 491). Also see Todd (2004).
28 This is taken from Carlisle et al. (2006). Such a form of education 'encourages students to take an active role in their own education and support teachers in creating empowering democratic, and critical educational environments (Hackman, 2005, p. 103).
29 Leithwood et al. (2019) noted that

> Equity, also called 'leadership for social justice' or 'culturally responsive leadership', has received increasing attention in recent years. Not only do professional guidelines and standards emphasise the importance of equity (as discussed above) but the body of evidence is growing that illustrates that principals can have a key role in increasing the equitability of an education system. A recent study has outlined that in order for school leaders to contribute to equity, all leadership decision[s] (defining a vision; hiring and placing staff; CPD, etc.) have to be made with the most vulnerable student groups in mind. (p. 38)

> Day et al. (2020) reported that successful school leaders focus on 'establishing a proactive, collaborative school mindset, supporting and enhancing staff, as well as student motivation, engagement and well-being, and the collective commitment needed to foster improvement and promote and sustain success for schools and classrooms which serve a range of advantaged and disadvantaged communities' (p. 6).

30 This is taken from Leithwood et al. (2019).
31 Day et al. (2020) posited that successful school leaders 'apply their judgements about the timing and nature of change and prioritize the change strategies in their schools in different ways, reflecting their school's history, staffing and context' (p. 42).
32 This is noted by Rowland (2017).
33 Hall and Ames (1998) described such a person as a 'truth-seeker' who is resolved 'finally to get to the bottom line, to establish facts, principles, theories that characterize the way things are' (p. 105). This does not mean that alternative and competing conceptions of critical thinking do not exist in the Anglo-American contexts. An example of a conception that is contrasted with the dominant

individualistic, adversarial and logicistic formulations of critical thinking is one that emphasizes community of inquiry, cooperation and dialogue. For further discussion on a Confucian notion of critical thinking, see Tan (2017a).
34 See Tu (1985); also see Hall and Ames (1998) and Li (1999).
35 This is taken from Lao (1989).
36 Relating the Confucian concept of creativity to moral self-cultivation, Hall and Ames (1998) maintained that

> Creativity is a notion that can only be characterized in terms of self-cultivation and articulation ... creativity requires that each participant in a relationship be continually in the process of creating the other. Community thus defined through the creativity of its members is programmatic – a goal that is constantly pursued rather than an immediate reality or fixed ideal. (p. 273)

37 Ames and Rosemont (1998) termed the changes advocated by Confucius as *creative personalization*.
38 For further discussions, see Tan (2016b, 2016c).
39 Smeyers and Marshall (1995) commented that the historical and social rootedness of human beings 'will determine the kind of questions which will be raised, the kind of answers that can be given, and the kind of solutions which will make particular questions disappear for us' (p. 223).

7 Conclusions

1 This synthesis of the ancient and modern is not new in Chinese philosophy. Hall and Ames (1987) observed that in Chinese philosophy, 'the mark of excellence is found in the manner in which the wisdom of the originating thinkers of the past is appropriated and made relevant by extension to one's own place and time' (pp. 23–4).
2 I have borrowed the distinction from McLaughlin (1992). He explained:

> What is needed for this purpose is a 'thin' conception of the good, free of significantly controversial assumptions and judgments, which maximize the freedom of citizens to pursue their diverse private conceptions of the good within a framework of justice. An example of an aspect of a 'thin' conception of the good is a commitment to the requirements of basic social morality. The label 'thin' here refers not to the insignificance of such values, but to their independence from substantial, particular, frameworks of belief and value. (p. 240)

Although McLaughlin's concern was on citizenship education, the two concepts are nonetheless applicable for our discussion on mindful leadership.

3. Titmuss (2016) observed the insufficient exploration of the nature of mindfulness and supportive conditions to eradicate corporate abuse and social problems. He wrote: 'Mindfulness in the West requires a new definition to replace the outdated one, namely "mindfulness is being in the present moment, non-judgementally"' (p. 194).

4. Some researchers have mentioned or alluded to moral values of mindful leaders, such as building trusting relationships, empathic listening and maintaining collegiality. These terms, however, are primarily valued for helping the leader to achieve their goals, and are not linked to a larger substantive framework on the beliefs and values that comprise human good.

5. Ehrlich's (2017) model of mindful leadership similarly highlights the need for mindful leadership to be underpinned by a thick conception of human good. It revolves around six factors: spirit, emotion, mind, body, connecting and inspiring, as follows (p. 235, italics in the original):

   1. spirit – knowing where you are going and why it gives you a compass;
   2. emotion – staying with your feelings, you access the information they contain and learn to have these feelings and not *be had by them*;
   3. mind – paying attention to your thinking, you get clear and make better decisions;
   4. body – attending to your physical self, you relax and can practice better self-care;
   5. connecting – focusing on others, you listen better and build stronger trusting relationships and
   6. inspiring – having a vision, you lead with passion and motivate others to join in.

   On the one hand, this model helps leaders to pay attention to their thoughts, feelings and relationships with others; thereby enabling them to better motivate their followers and establish trusting relationships with them. On the other hand, what is not adequately explicated are questions surrounding conceptions of human good, such as the following: What is the moral purpose of mindful leadership? Is mindfulness valued largely for its utilitarian worth?

6. Leithwood et al. (2019) reported that effective school leaders 'had a very strong and clear vision and set of values for their school, which heavily influenced their actions and the actions of others, and established a clear sense of direction and purpose for the school. These were shared widely, and clearly understood and supported by all staff' (p. 28).

7. That said, Confucius's work was not just about 'moral education' or the cultivation of 'moral values'. His teachings definitely included ethical values, but it is more accurate to describe his work as spiritual-ethical-aesthetic teachings that were concerned with the human existence, condition, and vision. That is why Confucius

did not just discuss ethically right and wrong behaviour, but extended his teachings to spiritual concepts such as *tian* (heaven), *dao* (Way) and *he* (harmony). Beyond 'moral education', Confucius's teachings have significant implications for all areas of human life, such as education, politics, family life and human relationships. I have not dwelt on the spiritual aspects of Confucian mindfulness in this book as the focus is more on mindful leadership for schools in secular contexts.

8 That the attainment of CML is not an 'all-or-nothing' state of affairs parallels the cultivation of *ren* (humanity). Tu (1968) cautioned against treating *ren* (humanity) as an objective entity that one either possesses or not at all: 'The problem is not "either-or," for Confucius upholds a varied degree of actualization of *jen* [*ren*]. Every human being embodies *jen* [*ren*] to a certain extent, but no one in the process of becoming a man who more fully embodies *jen* [*ren*] can reach the perfect stage' (p. 32).

9 Rant and Mihelič (2021) posited that mindfulness enhances a leader's capacity to lead and act as a role model. But it is unclear how mindfulness could help a leader to do so. That is why I propose CML as a leadership concept to guide leaders to develop themselves as moral exemplars.

10 Lavelle (2016) concluded this from a review of mindfulness programmes: 'Such a frame [in mindfulness programmes] assumes that individuals, as autonomous agents, have full control and agency over their health and well-being, thereby ignoring social, political, and economic factors that have contributed to or adversely affected their health (Purser, 2015). Moreover, this individualistic frame fails to account for ways in which suffering is also interpersonal and social' (p. 241).

11 The terms *executive virtues* and *substantive virtues*, as well as their descriptions, are taken from Kupfer (1994).

12 It should be added that 'principles' for Confucianism do not mean or imply universal laws or rules, such as Kant's categorical imperative or a Utilitarian maxim of seeking the greatest good for the greatest number of people.

13 This point is noted by Kupfer (1994). The distinction between executive and substantive virtues loosely corresponds to non-moral and moral virtues mentioned in the preface. As explained in the preface, only moral virtues such as kindness, integrity and benevolence are bound up with moral principles. Non-moral virtues such as courage, rationality and patience are not tethered to moral principles. I have chosen to refer to executive and substantive virtues instead of non-moral and moral virtues in this chapter as executive and substantive virtues are more salient for CML. From a Confucian viewpoint, it is confusing to talk about non-moral virtues since all virtues are – and should be – linked to the supreme quality of *ren* (humanity).

14 Recall the assertion made by Leithwood et al. (2019), which is cited in the preface: 'The next stage of scholarship on school leadership needs to extend what is

known to explore in greater depth *how* school leaders enact certain practices, what those practices are and their resulting impact' (p. 12, italics in the original).

15 This is taken from Gurr (2015), who noted that the work of these successful school leaders 'was informed and driven by strong, clearly articulated moral and ethical values that were shared by their colleagues' (p. 25).

16 Leithwood et al. (2019) reported that 'successful school leaders achieved improved performance, not only through the strategies they used but also through the core values and personal qualities they demonstrated in their daily interactions' (p. 28). A survey of the extant literature on ethical leadership reveals an emphasis on the moral character of the leader and the theory of virtue ethics. Knights and O'Leary (2006) noted that the 'literature on ethical leadership has a strong focus on character and therefore is driven by virtue ethics' (p. 131).

17 This is taken from Gurr (2015, p. 140).

18 This is taken from Day et al. (2020).

19 In this sense, CML is, to borrow the words of O'Donnell (2015), 'a holistic practice, an ethics and a philosophy' (p. 196).

20 This synthesis avoids the essentialist fallacies identified by Stingl and Weiss (2014). They wrote:

> When examining changes in practices and knowledges, it is easy to fall into one of two traps: first, to assume that 'newer is better' and that 'modern methods' are, by virtue of their novelty, more effective/efficient/scientific/ truthy; second, to wax nostalgic about 'classic' or 'traditional' methods that were more 'natural' or 'less artificial.' Both are mindless polemics that commit essentialist fallacies rather than engage mindfully with the nuanced and varied ethical layers of the issue. (p. 622)

21 Authentic leaders 'act in accordance with deep personal values and convictions, to build credibility and win the respect and trust of followers by encouraging diverse viewpoints and building networks of collaborative relationships with followers, and thereby lead in a manner that followers recognize as authentic' (Avolio et al. or is it Avolio et al., 2004, p. 806).

22 This point is noted by Lai (1995).

23 Stanley et al. (2018) observed:

> In a perhaps bizarre twist of fate, mindfulness-based programmes are now being exported from the United States and United Kingdom east not only to the social democratic countries of Western Europe but also back to the East Asia of China, Japan, and South Korea as well as Southeast Asian countries including Sri Lanka and Thailand – countries where these practices arguably originated and flourished, as part of liberal democratic development programmes promoting 'global mental health'. (p. 5)

24 Otherwise, there is a risk of mindfulness initiatives being stereotyped as 'orientalist discourses of recruiting "eastern wisdom" for modern times' (Stanley & Longden, 2016, p. 306). Samuel (2016) asked: 'If MBSR [Mindfulness-Based Stress Reduction] derives from one specific modernist Buddhist tradition, why not look at the wider range of forms of practice . . . within other Asian religious contexts, such as Hinduism or Daoism?' (p. 51). This book responds to Samuel's question by turning to Confucianism, which is a predominant Asian tradition.

25 This book represents my identification with the *New Confucian* – one who, while believing in 'Confucianism [as] the core belief' and 'dominant force underlying all of Chinese culture,' also accepts the need to 'absorb and amalgamate Western philosophies, so as to bring about the modernisation of Confucianism' (Nylan & Wilson, 2010, p. 214).

26 Nylan and Wilson (2010) noted that the name Confucius was a signifier 'for all the hopes, desires, and impulses of the Chinese throughout imperial times' (p. 97).

References

Adriansen, H. K., & Krohn, S. (2016). Mindfulness for group facilitation: An example of Eastern philosophy in Western organization. *Group Facilitation: A Research and Applications Journal, 13*, 1728.

Akhavan, N., Goree, J. M. & Walsh, N. (2021). The benefit of mindfulness professional development for elementary teachers: Considerations for district and school level leaders. *Journal of School Administration Research and Development, 6*(1), 24–42.

Albrecht, N. J. (2016). Connection of a different kind: Teachers teaching mindfulness with children. *Waikato Journal of Education, 21*(1), 133–48.

Ambler, G. (2007, July 18). The practice of mindfulness [Web log post]. Retrieved from http://407 www.thepracticeofleadership.net/2007/07/18/the-practice-of-mindfulness/.

Ames, R. T., & Rosemont, H. J. (1998). *The Analects of Confucius: A philosophical translation*. New York: Ballantine Books.

Arthurso, K. (2017). Mindfulness stripped bare: Some critical reflections from the mindfulness at school evaluation. In T. Ditrich, R. Wiles & B. Lovegrove (Eds.), *Mindfulness and education: Research and practice* (pp. 55–75). Cambridge: Cambridge Scholars Publishing.

Ashford, S. J., & DeRue, S. D. (2012). Developing as a leader: The power of mindful engagement. *Organizational Dynamics, 41*, 146–54.

Avolio, B. J., Luthans, F. & Walumbwa, F. O. (2004). *Authentic leadership: Theory building for veritable sustained performance*. Working paper, Gallup Leadership Institute, University of Nebraska, Nebraska.

Baelen, R. N., Eposito, M. V. & Galla, B. M. (2019). A selective review of mindfulness training programs for children and adolescents in school settings. In P. A. Jennings, A. A. DeMauro & P. P. Mischenko (Eds.), *The mindful school: Transforming school culture through mindfulness and compassion* (pp. 14–56). New York: Guilford Press.

Barker, K. K. (2014). Mindfulness meditation: Do-it-yourself medicalization of every moment. *Social Science and Medicine, 106*, 168–76. doi:10.1016/j.socscimed.2014.01.024.

Bass, B. M., & Steidlmeier, P. (1999). Ethics, character, and authentic transformational leadership behaviour. *Leadership Quarterly, 10*, 181–217.

Batson, C. D. (2009). These things called empathy: Eight related but distinct phenomena. In J. Decety & W. Ickes (Eds.), *The social neuroscience of empathy* (pp. 3–15). Cambridge: MIT Press.

Battaly, H. D. (2011). Is empathy a virtue? In A. Coplan & P. Goldie (Eds.), *Empathy: Philosophical and psychological perspectives* (pp. 277–301). Oxford: Oxford University Press.

Bazzano, M. (2013a). Back to the future: From behaviourism and cognitive psychology to motivation and emotion. *Self & Society: An International Journal of Humanistic Psychology, 40*, 42–6.

Bazzano, M. (2013b). Mindfulness and the good life. In M. Bazzano (Ed.), *After mindfulness: New perspectives on psychology and meditation* (pp. 61–78). Basingstoke: Palgrave Macmillan.

Bazzano, M. (2016). The fourth treasure: Psychotherapy's contribution to the dharma. In R. E. Purser, D. Forbes & A. Burke (Eds.), *Handbook of mindfulness: Culture, context, and social engagement* (pp. 293–304). Cham: Springer.

Beck, J. (2021). How mindfulness impacts the way leaders connect with and develop followers. In S. K. Dhiman (Ed.), *The Routledge companion to mindfulness at work* (pp. 142–69). Oxon: Routledge.

Becker, D. (2013). *One nation under stress: The trouble with stress as an idea.* New York: Oxford University Press

Bellinger, D. B., DeCaro, M. S. & Ralston, P. A. S. (2015). Mindfulness, anxiety, and high-stakes mathematics performance in the laboratory and classroom. *Consciousness and Cognition, 37*, 123–32.

Berger, J. G., & Johnston, K. (2015). *Simple habits for complex times: Powerful practices for leaders.* Stanford, CA: Stanford University Press.

Bodhi, B. (2011). What does mindfulness really mean? A canonical perspective. *Contemporary Buddhism, 12*(1), 19–39. doi:10.1080/14639947.2011.564813.

Bodhi, V. B. (2016). The transformations of mindfulness. In R. E. Purser, D. Forbes & A. Burke (Eds.), *Handbook of mindfulness: Culture, context, and social engagement* (pp. 3–14). Cham: Springer.

Bodner, T. E., & Langer, E. J. (2001, June). *Individual differences in mindfulness: The mindfulness/mindlessness scale.* Poster presented at the 13th annual American Psychological Society Convention, Toronto, Ontario, Canada.

Boyatzis, R., & McKee, A. (2005). *Resonant leadership.* Boston: Harvard Business School Press.

Brazier, D. (2016). Mindfulness: Traditional and utilitarian. In R. E. Purser, D. Forbes & A. Burke (Eds.), *Handbook of mindfulness: Culture, context, and social engagement* (pp. 63–74). Cham: Springer.

Britt, M., Pribesh, S., Hinton-Johnson, K. & Gupta, A. (2018). Effect of a mindful breathing intervention on community college students' writing apprehension and writing performance. *Community College Journal of Research and Practice, 42*(10), 693–707. doi:10.1080/10668926.2017.1352545.

Brooks, B. E., & Brooks, T. A. (1998). *The original Analects: Sayings of Confucius and his successors.* New York: Columbia University Press.

Brown, R. (2017). The perceived impact of mindfulness instruction on pre-service elementary teachers. *Childhood Education*, *93*(2), 136–46. doi:10.1080/00094056.2017.1300492.

Brown, R. C., & Grassi, E. (2019). Finding peace in chaos: Mindfully prepared public school teachers. In P. A. Jennings, A. A. DeMauro & P. P. Mischenko (Eds.), *The mindful school: Transforming school culture through mindfulness and compassion* (pp. 213–40). New York: Guilford Press.

Brown, V., & Olson, K. (2015). *The mindful school leader: Practices to transform your leadership and school*. Thousand Oaks, CA: Corwin.

Bryk, A. S., & Schneider, B. L. (2002). *Trust in schools: A core source for improvement*. New York: Russell Sage Foundation.

Buller, J. L. (2019). *Mindful leadership: An insight-based approach to college administration*. Washington, DC: Rowman & Littlefield.

Burbules, N. C. (1995). Reasonable doubt: Toward a postmodern defense of reason as an educational aim. In W. Kohli (Ed.), *Critical conversations in philosophy of education* (pp. 82–102). New York: Routledge.

Camfield, E., & Bayers, L. (2019). Mindful assessment in support of student learning. *Journal of Contemplative Inquiry*, *6*(1), 121–44. Retrieved from https://escholarship.org/uc/item/3k4162dk.

Cannon, J. (2016). Education as the practice of freedom: A social justice proposal for mindfulness educators. In R. E. Purser, D. Forbes & A. Burke (Eds.), *Handbook of mindfulness: Culture, context, and social engagement* (pp. 397–409). Cham: Springer.

Caring-Lobel, A. (2016). Corporate mindfulness and the pathologization of workplace stress. In R. E. Purser, D. Forbes & A. Burke (Eds.), *Handbook of mindfulness: Culture, context, and social engagement* (pp. 195–214). Cham: Springer.

Carlisle, L. R., Jackson, B. W. & George, A. (2006). Principles of social justice education: The social justice education in schools project. *Equity & Excellence in Education, 39*(1), 55–64.

Carmody, J. (2014). Eastern and western approaches to mindfulness: Similarities, differences, and clinical implications. In A. Ie., C. T. Ngnoumen & E. J. Langer (Eds.), *The Wiley Blackwell handbook of mindfulness* (pp. 48–57). West Sussex: John Wiley.

Chan, S. Y. (2006). The Confucian notion of *jing* 敬 (respect). *Philosophy East and West*, *56*(2), 229–52.

Chaskalson, M., Reitz, M., Walker, L. & Olivier, S. (2021). Mindful leadership. In S. K. Dhiman (Ed.), *The Routledge companion to mindfulness at work* (pp. 124–41). Oxon: Routledge.

Cheung, K. (2018). Implicit and explicit ethics in mindfulness-based programmes in a broad context. In S. Stanley, R. E. Purser & N. N. Singh (Eds.), *Handbook of ethical foundations of mindfulness* (pp. 305–21). Cham: Springer.

Chin, A. (2007). *The authentic Confucius: A life of thought and politics*. New York: Scribner.

Chong, K. C. (1998). The aesthetic moral personality: *Li, yi, wen* and *chih* in the *Analects*. *Monumenta Serica, 46,* 69–90.

Cissna, K., & Schockman, H. E. (2021). The role of mindfulness in leadership, followership, and organizations. In S. K. Dhiman (Ed.), *The Routledge companion to mindfulness at work* (pp. 546–65). Oxon: Routledge.

Clements, J. (2004). *Confucius: A biography.* Gloucestershire: Sutton Publishing.

Clutterbuck, D. (2008). What's happening in coaching and mentoring? And what is the difference between them? *Development and Learning in Organizations, 22*(4), 8–10.

Cobb, V. L. (2019). Being in school transformation: Towards equity and social justice. In P. A. Jennings, A. A. DeMauro & P. P. Mischenko (Eds.), *The mindful school: Transforming school culture through mindfulness and compassion* (pp. 241–60). New York: Guilford Press.

Commission on Social Justice. (1994). Social justice: Strategies for national renewal. *Report of the Commission on Social Justice.* London: Vintage.

Coronado-Montoya, S., Levis, A. W., Kwakkenbos, L., Steele, R. J., Turner, E. H. & Thombs, B. D. (2016). Reporting of positive results in randomized controlled trials of mindfulness-based mental health interventions. *PloS One, 11*(4), 1–18.

Cranor, C. (1975). Toward a theory of respect for persons. *American Philosophical Quarterly, 12*(4), 309–19.

Crowley, C., & Munk, D. (2017). An examination of the impact of a college level meditation course on college student well-being. *College Student Journal, 51*(1), 91–8.

Cua, A. S. (1989). The concept of *li* in Confucian moral theory. In R. E. Allison (Ed.), *Understanding the Chinese mind: The philosophical roots* (pp. 209–35). Hong Kong: Oxford University Press.

Cua, A. S. (1992). Competence, concern, and the role of paradigmatic individuals (Chün-tzu) in moral education. *Philosophy East and West, 42*(1), 49–68.

Daft, R. L. (2005). *Leadership.* New Delhi: Cengage Learning India.

Darwall, S. (1977). Two kinds of respect. *Ethics, 88,* 181–97.

Davenport, T. H., & Beck, J. C. (2002). *The attention economy: Understanding the new currency of business.* Boston: Harvard Business Press.

Davenport, C., & Pagnini, F. (2016). Mindful learning: A case study of Langerian mindfulness in schools. *Frontiers in Psychology, 7,* 1372. doi:10.3389/fpsyg.2016.01372.

Davies, W. (2015). *The happiness industry: How the government and big business sold us well-being.* London: Verso Books.

Day, D. V., & Gregory, J. L. (2017). Mindfulness as a prerequisite to effective leadership: Exploring the constructs that foster productive use of feedback for professional learning. *Interchange, 48*(4), 363–75. doi:10.1007/s10780-017-9307-0.

Day, C., Sammons, P. & Gorgen, K. (2020). *Successful school leadership.* Reading: Education Development Trust.

de Bary, W. T. (1981). *Neo-Confucian orthodoxy and the learning of the mind-and-heart*. New York: Columbia University Press.

De Bruin, E. I., Meppelink, R. & Bögels, S. M. (2015). Mindfulness in higher education: Awareness and attention in university students increase during and after participation in a mindfulness curriculum course. *Mindfulness*, 6(5), 1137–42.

Decety, J., & Yoder, K. J. (2016). Empathy and motivation for justice: Cognitive empathy and concern, but not emotional empathy, predict sensitivity to injustice for others. *Social Neuroscience*, 11(1), 1–14.

Denford-Wood, G. (2017). Meditating mindfully: Teachers go within to ensure their students do not go without. In T. Ditrich, R. Wiles & B. Lovegrove (Eds.), *Mindfulness and education: Research and practice* (pp. 125–48). Cambridge: Cambridge Scholars Publishing.

Dewey, J. (1933). *How we think: A restatement of the relation of reflective thinking to the educative process*. New York: D. C. Heath.

Dickmann, M. H., & Stanford-Blair, N. (2008). *Mindful leadership: A brain-based framework*. Thousand Oaks: SAGE Publications.

Doss, K. K., & Bloom, L. (2018). Mindfulness in the middle school classroom: Strategies to target social and emotional well-being of gifted students. *Gifted Education International*, 34(2), 181–92. doi:10.1177/0261429417716352.

Drago-Severson, E., & Blum-Destefano, J. (2019). Modelling mindfulness. In P. A. Jennings, A. A. DeMauro & P. P. Mischenko (Eds.), *The mindful school: Transforming school culture through mindfulness and compassion* (pp. 78–106). New York: Guilford Press.

Dreyfus, G. (2011). Is mindfulness present-centred and non-judgmental? A discussion of the cognitive dimensions of mindfulness. *Contemporary Buddhism*, 12(01), 41–54.

Drougge, P. (2016). Notes towards a coming backlash: Mindfulness as an opiate of the middle classes. In R. E. Purser, D. Forbes & A. Burke (Eds.), *Handbook of mindfulness: Culture, context, and social engagement* (pp. 167–79). Cham: Springer.

DuFon, M. A., & Christian, J. (2013). The formation and development of the mindful campus. *New Directions for Teaching and Learning*, 134, 65–72. doi:10.1002/tl.20055.

Dunne, J., & Pendlebury, S. (2003). Practical reason. In N. Blake, P. Smeyers, R. Smith & P. Standish (Eds.), *The Blackwell guide to the philosophy of education* (pp. 194–211). Malden: Blackwell Publishing.

Dunoon, D., & Langer, E. J. (2011). Mindfulness and leadership: Opening up to possibilities. *Integral Leadership Review*, 11(5), 1–15. Retrieved from http://integralleadershipreview.com/3729-mindfulness-and-leadership-opening-up-to-possibilities/.

Ehrlich, J. (2017). Mindful leadership. *Organizational Dynamics*, 46(4), 233–43.

Eisenbeiss, S. A., & van Knippenberg, D. (2015). On ethical leadership impact: The role of follower mindfulness and moral emotions. *Journal of Organizational Behavior*, 36(2), 182–95.

Eisenberg, N., & Strayer, J. (1987). *Empathy and its development*. Cambridge: Cambridge University Press.

Eklof, J. (2016). Saving the world: Personalized communication of mindfulness neuroscience. In R. E. Purser, D. Forbes & A. Burke (Eds.), *Handbook of mindfulness: Culture, context, and social engagement* (pp. 323-35). Cham: Springer.

Ergas, O., & Ragoonaden, K. (2020). Two perspectives on teaching mindfulness in teacher education: A self-study of two selves. In O. Ergas & J. K. Ritter (Eds.), *Exploring self toward expanding teaching, teacher education and practitioner research* (pp. 179-96). Bingley: Emerald Publishing. doi:10.1108/S1479-368720200000034011.

Fagiano, M. (2019). Relational empathy. *International Journal of Philosophical Studies*, *27*(2), 162-79.

Feiman-Nemser, S. (2001). Helping novices learn to teach: Lessons from an exemplary support teacher. *Journal of Teacher Education*, *52*(1), 17-30.

Flores, N. (2016). A critical and comprehensive review of mindfulness in the early years. In R. E. Purser, D. Forbes & A. Burke (Eds.), *Handbook of mindfulness: Culture, context, and social engagement* (pp. 441-6). Cham: Springer.

Forbes, D. (2016). Critical integral contemplative education. In R. E. Purser, D. Forbes & A. Burke (Eds.), *Handbook of mindfulness: Culture, context, and social engagement* (pp. 355-67). Cham: Springer.

Fuchs, T. (2013). Depression, intercorporeality, and interaffectivity. *Journal of Consciousness Studies*, *20*(7-8), 219-38.

Gardner, D. K. (2007). *The Four Books: The basic teachings of the later Confucian tradition*. Indianapolis: Hackett Publishing.

Gier, N. F. (2001). The dancing *ru*: A Confucian aesthetics of virtue. *Philosophy East and West*, *51*(2), 280-305.

Gilbert, B. (2019). Mindful leadership and high-reliability schools. In B. L. Johnson & S. D. Kruse (Eds.), *Educational leadership, organizational learning, and the ideas of Karl Weick: Perspectives on theory and practice* (pp. 136-61). New York: Routledge. doi:10.4324/9781315114095-7.

Goddard, M. (2014). Critical psychiatry, critical psychology, and the behaviourism of B. F. Skinner. *Review of General Psychology*, *18*(3), 208-15.

Gonzalez, M. (2012). *Mindful leadership: The 9 ways to self-awareness, transforming yourself, and inspiring others*. Mississauga: John Wiley.

Graham, A., & Truscott, J. (2020). Meditation in the classroom: Supporting both student and teacher well-being? *Education, 3-13*, *48*(7), 807-19. doi:10.1080/03004279.2019.1659385.

Grant, K. C. (2017). From teaching to being: The qualities of a mindful teacher. *Childhood Education*, *93*(2), 147-52. doi:10.1080/00094056.2017.1300493.

Griggs, T., & Tidwell, D. (2015). Learning to teach mindfully: Examining the self in the context of multicultural education. *Teacher Education Quarterly*, *42*(2), 87-104.

Gurr, D. (2015). A model of successful school leadership from the International Successful School Principalship project. In K. Leithwood, J. Sun & K. Pollock (Eds.), *How school leaders contribute to student success: The Four Paths framework* (pp. 15–29). Cham: Springer. doi:10.1007/978-3-319-50980-8_2.

Hackman, H. W. (2005). Five essential components for social justice education. *Equity & Excellence in Education, 38*(2), 103–9.

Hadar, L. L., & Ergas, O. (2018). Cultivating mindfulness through technology in higher education: A Buberian perspective. *AI & Society, 34*, 99–107.

Hadot, P. (1995). *Philosophy as a way of life: Spiritual exercises from Socrates to Foucault.* Oxford: Blackwell Publishers.

Hagen, K. (2010). The propriety of Confucius: A sense-of-ritual. *Asian Philosophy, 20*(1), 1–25.

Haines, S., Clark, K., Tinkler, A., Kotsiopoulos, A., Gerstl-Pepin, C., Shepherd, K. G. & Milhomens, M. (2017). 'Let's just stop and take a breath': A community-driven approach to mindfulness practice in a high poverty elementary school. *LEARNing Landscapes, 10*(2), 189–205.

Hairon, S., & Tan, C. (2017). Professional learning communities in Singapore and Shanghai: Implications for teacher collaboration. *Compare: A Journal of Comparative and International Education, 47*(1), 91–104.

Hall, D. L., & Ames, R. T. (1987). *Thinking though Confucius.* Albany: State University of New York.

Hall, D. L., & Ames, R. T. (1998). *Thinking from the Han: Self, truth, and transcendence in Chinese and Western culture.* Albany: State University of New York Press.

Hansen, C. (1989). Language in the heart-mind. In R. E. Allison (Ed.), *Understanding the Chinese mind: The philosophical roots* (pp. 75–124). Hong Kong: Oxford University Press.

Hanson, M. D., Randall, J. G., Danna, G. C. & Le, H. Q. (2021). Enhancing workplace learning through mindfulness. In S. K. Dhiman (Ed.), *The Routledge companion to mindfulness at work* (pp. 295–315). Oxon: Routledge.

Harris, A. (2004). Distributed leadership and school improvement. *Educational Management Administration and Leadership, 32*(1), 11–24.

Hawkins, K. (2017). *Mindful teacher, mindful school: Improving wellbeing in teaching and learning.* London: SAGE Publications.

Hoffman, M. L. (2000). *Empathy and moral development: Implications for caring and justice.* Cambridge: Cambridge University Press.

Hopper, L. (2010). Mindful leadership. *Georgia Library Quarterly, 47*(2). Retrieved from http://digitalcommons.kennesaw.edu/glq/vol47/iss2/6.

Horsthemke, K. (2015). Epistemic empathy in childrearing and education. *Ethics and Education, 10*(1), 61–72.

Hougaard, R., Carter, J. & Coutts, G. (2016). Mindful leadership: Achieving results by managing the mind. *Leader to Leader, 79*, 49–56. doi:10.1002/ltl.20218.

Hsieh, C. C. (2018). Developing meaningful schools: An exploration of principals' mindful leadership. *Journal of Education Research, 292,* 69–86. doi:10.3966/168063602018080292005.

Huang, Y. (2011). Can virtue be taught and how? Confucius on the paradox of moral education. *Journal of Moral Education, 40*(2), 141–59.

Hue, M., & Lau, N. (2015). Promoting well-being and preventing burnout in teacher education: A pilot study of a mindfulness-based programme for pre-service teachers in Hong Kong. *Teacher Development, 19*(3), 381–401. doi:10.1080/13664530.2015.1049748.

Hughes, C. (2020). COVID-19 and the opportunity to design a more mindful approach to learning. *Prospects: Quarterly Review of Comparative Education, 49*(1–2), 69–72. doi:10.1007/s11125-020-09492-z.

Huppert, F. A. (2017). Mindfulness and compassion as foundations for well-being. In M. A. White, G. R. Slemp & A. S. Murray (Eds.), *Future directions in well-being: Education, organizations and policy* (pp. 225–33). Cham: Springer.

Hwang, K. (2013). Educational modes of thinking in neo-Confucianism: A traditional lens for rethinking modern education. *Asia Pacific Education Review, 14,* 243–53.

Hyland, T. (2016). Through a glass darkly: The neglect of ethical and educational elements in mindfulness-based interventions. In R. E. Purser, D. Forbes & A. Burke (Eds.), *Handbook of mindfulness: Culture, context, and social engagement* (pp. 383–96). Cham: Springer.

Ie., A., Ngnoumen, C. T. & Langer, E. J. (2014). General introduction. In A. Ie., C. T. Ngnoumen & E. J. Langer (Eds.), *The Wiley Blackwell handbook of mindfulness* (p. xxxiii). West Sussex: John Wiley.

Ingram, C. M., Breen, A. V. & van Rhijn, T. (2019). Teaching for well-being? Introducing mindfulness in an undergraduate course. *Journal of Further and Higher Education, 43*(6), 814–25. doi:10.1080/0309877X.2017.1409343.

Ivanhoe, P. J. (1990). *Ethics in the Confucian tradition.* Indianapolis: Hackett Publishing.

Ivanhoe, P. J. (2013). *Confucian reflections: Ancient wisdom for modern times.* New York: Routledge.

Jagannathan, S., & Rodhain, F. (2016). What is mindful leadership? *Compendium on Integrating Spirituality & Organizational Leadership, 5,* 94–100.

Jayawardena-Willis, T. S., Pio, E. & McGhee, P. (2021). Why manage with insight? A Buddhist view that goes beyond mindfulness. In S. K. Dhiman (Ed.), *The Routledge companion to mindfulness at work* (pp. 280–92). Oxon: Routledge.

Jennings, P. A., Demauro, A. A. & Mischenko, P. P. (2019). Where are we now? Where are we going? Preparing our students for an uncertain future. In P. A. Jennings, A. A. DeMauro & P. P. Mischenko (Eds.), *The mindful school: Transforming school culture through mindfulness and compassion* (pp. 3–13). New York: Guilford Press.

Jordan, S., & Johannessen, I. A. (2014). Mindfulness and organizational defences: Exploring organizational and institutional challenges to mindfulness.

In A. Ie., C. T. Ngnoumen & E. J. Langer (Eds.), *The Wiley Blackwell handbook of mindfulness* (pp. 424–42). West Sussex: John Wiley.

Kabat-Zinn, J. (1990). *Full catastrophe living: Using the wisdom of your body and mind to face stress, pain, and illness*. New York: Dell Publishing.

Kabat-Zinn, J. (2003). Mindfulness-based interventions in context: Past, present, and future. *Clinical Psychology: Science and Practice, 10*(2), 144–56. doi:10.1093/clipsy.bpg016.

Kavia, S., & Murphy, M. S. (2021). Coming into mindfulness: A practice of relational presence to cultivate compassion in one rural school. *LEARNing Landscapes, 14*(1), 189–202.

Kearney, W. S., Kelsey, C. & Herrington, D. (2013). Mindful leaders in highly effective schools: A mixed-method application of Hoy's M-scale. *Educational Management Administration & Leadership, 41*(3), 316–35. doi:10.1177/1741143212474802.

Kets de Vries, M. F. R. (2014). *Mindful leadership coaching: Journeys into the interior*. New York: Palgrave Macmillan.

Khng, K. H. (2018). Mindfulness in education: The case of Singapore. *Learning: Research and Practice, 4*(1), 52–65. doi:10.1080/23735082.2018.1428120.

Kim, K. H. (2004). An attempt to elucidate notions of lifelong learning: *Analects*-based analysis of Confucius' ideas about learning. *Asia Pacific Education Review, 5*(2), 117–26.

Kim, S. J., & Kou, X. (2014). Not all empathy is equal: How dispositional empathy affects charitable giving. *Journal of Nonprofit & Public Sector Marketing, 26*(4), 312–34.

King, R. (2016). 'Paying attention' in a digital economy: Reflections on the role of analysis and judgement within contemporary discourses of mindfulness and comparisons with classical Buddhist accounts of *sati*. In R. E. Purser, D. Forbes & A. Burke (Eds.), *Handbook of mindfulness: Culture, context, and social engagement* (pp. 27–45). Cham: Springer.

King, E., & Badham, R. (2020). The Wheel of Mindfulness: A generative framework for second-generation mindful leadership. *Mindfulness, 11*(1), 166–76.

Kirmayer, L. J. (2015). Mindfulness in cultural context. *Transcultural Psychiatry, 52*(4), 447–69.

Klatt, M. D. (2017). A contemplative tool: An exposé of the performance of self. *Journal of Transformative Education, 15*(2), 122–36. doi:10.1177/1541344616683280.

Klein, A. C. (1995). *Meeting the great bliss queen: Buddhists, feminists, and the art of the self*. Boston: Beacon Press.

Komjathy, L. (2018). *Introducing Contemplative Studies*. Hoboken: Wiley-Blackwell.

Kudesia, R. S., & Lau, J. (2021). Metacognitive practice: Understanding mindfulness as repeated attempts to understand mindfulness. In S. K. Dhiman (Ed.), *The Routledge companion to mindfulness at work* (pp. 39–53). Oxon: Routledge.

Kumar, S. (2021). Mindfulness in a Moroccan university: Exploring students' transformational journey through an academic course in mindfulness. *Journal of Transformative Education*, *19*(3), 241–60. doi:10.1177/1541344620986218.

Kupfer, J. (1994). Education, indoctrination, and moral character. In T. Magnell (Ed.), *Values and education* (pp. xxx). Amsterdam: Rodopi.

Lai, K. L. (1995). Confucian moral thinking. *Philosophy East & West*, *45*(2), 249–72.

Lampe, M., & Engleman-Lampe, C. (2012). Mindfulness-based business ethics education. *Academy of Educational Leadership Journal*, *16*(3), 99–111.

Langer, E. J. (1992). Matters of mind: Mindfulness/mindlessness in perspective. *Consciousness and Cognition: An International Journal*, *1*(4), 289–305.

Langer, E. J. (2000). Mindful learning. *Current Directions in Psychological Sciences*, *9*(6), 220–3.

Langer, E. J. (2010). A call for mindful leadership. *Harvard Business Review*, *28*, 60.

Langer, E. J., & Moldoveanu, M. (2000). The construct of mindfulness. *Journal of Social Issues*, *56*(1), 1–9.

Lao S. K. (1989). On understanding Chinese philosophy: An inquiry and a proposal. In R. E. Allison (Ed.), *Understanding the Chinese mind: The philosophical roots* (pp. 265–93). Hong Kong: Oxford University Press.

Lau, D. C. (1997). *Confucius: The Analects*. Hong Kong: Chinese University Press.

Lavelle, B. D. (2016). Against one method: Contemplation in context. In R. E. Purser, D. Forbes & A. Burke (Eds.), *Handbook of mindfulness: Culture, context, and social engagement* (pp. 233–42). Cham: Springer.

Lavy, S., & Berkovich-Ohana, A. (2020). From teachers' mindfulness to students' thriving: The Mindful Self in School Relationships (MSSR) Model. *Mindfulness*, *11*, 2258–73.

Le, T. N., & Alefaio, D. (2019). Hawaii educators' experiences in a professional development course on mindfulness. *Professional Development in Education*, *45*(4), 627–41. doi:10.1080/19415257.2018.1474485.

Lee, D., & Ryu, J. (2015). Mindful learning in geography: Cultivating balanced attitudes toward regions. *Journal of Geography*, *114*(5), 197–210. doi:10.1080/00221341.2015.1046897.

Leithwood, K., Harris, A. & Hopkins, D. (2019). Seven strong claims about successful school leadership revisited. *School Leadership & Management*, *40*(4), 5–22. doi:10.1080/13632434.2019.1596077.

Leithwood, K., Sun, J. & Schumacker, R. (2020). How school leadership influences student learning: A test of 'The Four Paths Model'. *Educational Administration Quarterly*, *56*(4), 570–99.

Levey, J., & Levey, M. (2019). Mindful leadership for personal and organizational resilience. *Clinical Radiology*, *74*, 739–45.

Lewis, D. J., & Rozelle, D. (2016). Mindfulnesss-based interventions: Clinical psychology, Buddhadharma, or both? A wisdom perspective. In R. E. Purser, D.

Forbes & A. Burke (Eds.), *Handbook of mindfulness: Culture, context, and social engagement* (pp. 243–68). Cham: Springer.

Li, C. (1999). *The Tao encounters the West: Explorations in comparative philosophy.* Albany: State University of New York Press.

Li, C. (2006). The Confucian ideal of harmony. *Philosophy East & West, 56*(4), 583–603.

Li, L. (2010). Gentlemen and petty men. *Contemporary Chinese Thought, 41*(2), 54–65. doi:10.2753/CSP1097-1467410205.

Lindahl, L. (2015). Two theoretical approaches to mindfulness and compassion: Evaluating the merits and the weaknesses of the discovery model and the developmental model. Presentation at Mindfulness and Compassion: The Art and Science of Contemplative Practice Conference, San Francisco.

Liu, L. (2020). Examining the usefulness of mindfulness practices in managing school leader stress during COVID-19 pandemic. *Journal of School Administration Research and Development, 5*(1), 15–20.

Long, B. (2021). The universe's doorway: Long-term mindfulness as a way to leadership. In S. K. Dhiman (Ed.), *The Routledge companion to mindfulness at work* (pp. 170–88). Oxon: Routledge.

Loy, D. R. (2016). The challenge of mindful engagement. In R. E. Purser, D. Forbes & A. Burke (Eds.), *Handbook of mindfulness: Culture, context, and social engagement* (pp. 15–26). Cham: Springer.

Lyddy, C. J., & Good, D. J. (2017). Being while doing: An inductive model of mindfulness at work. *Frontiers in Psychology, 7*, 2060. doi:10.3389/fpsyg.2016.02060.

Magee, R. V. (2016). Community-engaged mindfulness and social justice: An inquiry and call to action. In R. E. Purser, D. Forbes & A. Burke (Eds.), *Handbook of mindfulness: Culture, context, and social engagement* (pp. 425–39). Cham: Springer.

Magrì, E. (2019). Empathy, respect, and vulnerability. *International Journal of Philosophical Studies, 27*(2), 327–46.

Mahfouz, J. (2018). Mindfulness training for school administrators: Effects on well-being and leadership. *Journal of Educational Administration, 56*(6), 602–19. doi:10.1108/JEA-12-2017-0171.

Maibom, H. L. (2009). Feeling for others: Empathy, sympathy, and morality. *Inquiry, 52*(5), 483–99.

Marques, J. (2021). Sleepwalking versus mindfulness: A conscious leadership choice. In S. K. Dhiman (Ed.), *The Routledge companion to mindfulness at work* (pp. 111–23). Oxon: Routledge.

Masood, H., & Karajovic, S. (2021). Workplace mindfulness: The role of human resource management in engendering a mindful workplace. In S. K. Dhiman (Ed.), *The Routledge companion to mindfulness at work* (pp. 266–79). Oxon: Routledge.

Mayer, C. H., & Oosthuizen, R. (2021). Love, creativity, and mindfulness in international leaders: Qualities for successful future world of work. In S. K. Dhiman (Ed.), *The Routledge companion to mindfulness at work* (pp. 507–22). Oxon: Routledge.

McCown, D. (2018). Co-creating the ethical space of mindfulness-based interventions. In S. Stanley, R. E. Purser & N. N. Singh (Eds.), *Handbook of ethical foundations of mindfulness* (pp. 143–66). Cham: Springer.

McGhee, P., & Grant, P. (2021). Spiritual mindfulness for management. In S. K. Dhiman (Ed.), *The Routledge companion to mindfulness at work* (pp. 219–33). Oxon: Routledge.

McLaughlin, T. H. (1992). Citizenship, diversity and education: A philosophical perspective. *Journal of Moral Education, 21*(3), 235–50.

Melwani, S., & Barsade, S. (2011). Held in contempt: The psychological, interpersonal, and performance consequences of contempt in a work context. *Journal of Personality and Social Psychology, 101*(3), 503–20.

Meredith, R. (2022). Mindfulness studies find little benefit to all pupils. *BBC News*, July 13. Retrieved from https://www.bbc.co.uk/news/uk-northern-ireland-62141626.amp

Meyers, S., Rowell, K., Wells, M. & Smith, B. C. (2019). Teacher empathy: A model of empathy for teaching for student success. *College Teaching, 67*(3), 160–8.

Miller, L. D. (2016). The ultimate Rx: Cutting through the delusion of self-cherishing. In R. E. Purser, D. Forbes & A. Burke (Eds.), *Handbook of mindfulness: Culture, context, and social engagement* (pp. 337–52). Cham: Springer.

Mischenko, P. P., & Jennings, P. A. (2019). Cultivating passion for practising and teaching mindfulness: A multiple-case study of Compassionate Schools Project teachers. In P. A. Jennings, A. A. DeMauro & P. P. Mischenko (Eds.), *The mindful school: Transforming school culture through mindfulness and compassion* (pp. 135–65). New York: Guilford Press.

Mitra, J. L., & Greenberg, M. T. (2016). The curriculum of right mindfulness: The relational self and the capacity for compassion. In R. E. Purser, D. Forbes & A. Burke (Eds.), *Handbook of mindfulness: Culture, context, and social engagement* (pp. 411–24). Cham: Springer.

Moloney, P. (2016). Mindfulness: The bottled water of the therapy industry. In R. E. Purser, D. Forbes & A. Burke (Eds.), *Handbook of mindfulness: Culture, context, and social engagement* (pp. 269–92). Cham: Springer.

Monteiro, L. M. (2016). Implicit ethics and mindfulness: Subtle assumptions that MBIS are values-neutral. *International Journal of Psychotherapy, 20*(1), 210–24.

Mortlock, J. T. (2021). More than meditation: How managers can effectively put the science of workplace mindfulness to work. In S. K. Dhiman (Ed.), *The Routledge companion to mindfulness at work* (pp. 251–65). Oxon: Routledge.

Mou, B. (2004). A reexamination of the structure and content of Confucius' version of the golden rule. *Philosophy East and West, 54*(2), 218–48.

Ng, E. (2016). The critique of mindfulness and the mindfulness of critique: Paying attention to the politics of ourselves with Foucault's analytic of governmentality. In R. E. Purser, D. Forbes & A. Burke (Eds.), *Handbook of mindfulness: Culture, context, and social engagement* (pp. 135–52). Cham: Springer.

Niu, W., & Sternberg, R. J. (2006). The philosophical roots of Western and Eastern conceptions of creativity. *Journal of Theoretical and Philosophical Psychology*, *26*(1–2), 18–38.

Noble, T., Wyatt, T., McGrath, H., Roffey, S., & Rowling, L. (2008). Literature review: Scoping study into approaches to student wellbeing. *Report to the Department of Education, Employment and Workplace Relations*. Retrieved from https://researchdirect.westernsyd ney.edu.au/islandora/object/uws:29490.

Nylan, M., & Wilson, T. (2010). *Lives of Confucius*. New York: Doubleday.

O'Donnell, A. (2015). Contemplative pedagogy and mindfulness: Developing creative attention in an age of distraction. *Journal of Philosophy of Education*, *49*(2), 187–202.

Organization for Economic Co-operation and Development [OECD] (2019). *TALIS 2018 results (Volume I): Teachers and school leaders as lifelong learners*. Château de la Muette, Paris: TALIS, OECD Publishing. doi:10.1787/1d0bc92a-en.

Orr, D. (2018). Ethics, mindfulness, and skilfulness. In S. Stanley, R. E. Purser & N. N. Singh (Eds.), *Handbook of ethical foundations of mindfulness* (pp. 121–40). Cham: Springer.

Payne, R. K. (2016). Mindfulness and the moral imperative for the self to improve the self. In R. E. Purser, D. Forbes & A. Burke (Eds.), *Handbook of mindfulness: Culture, context, and social engagement* (pp. 121–34). Cham: Springer.

Payne, R. K. (2018). Mindfulness and morality. In S. Stanley, R. E. Purser & N. N. Singh (Eds.), *Handbook of ethical foundations of mindfulness* (pp. 323–37). Cham: Springer.

Petranker, J. (2016). The mindful self in space and time. In R. E. Purser, D. Forbes & A. Burke (Eds.), *Handbook of mindfulness: Culture, context, and social engagement* (pp. 95–106). Cham: Springer.

Pickert, K. (2014, February 3). The mindful revolution. *Time Magazine*. Retrieved from https://time.com/1556/the-mindful-revolution/.

Piotrowski, S. A., Binder, M. J. & Schwind, J. K. (2017). Primary teachers' perceptions of mindfulness practices with young children. *LEARNing Landscapes*, *10*(2), 225–40.

Pipe, T. B., & Bortz, J. J. (2009). Mindful leadership as healing practice: Nurturing self to serve others. *International Journal for Human Caring*, *13*(2), 34–8.

Pirson, M. (2014). Mindfulness at work. In A. Ie., C. T. Ngnoumen & E. J. Langer (Eds.), *The Wiley Blackwell handbook of mindfulness* (pp. 458–70). West Sussex: John Wiley.

Pirson, M. A., Langer, E. & Zilcha, S. (2018). Enabling a socio-cognitive perspective of mindfulness: The development and validation of the Langer Mindfulness Scale. *Journal of Adult Development*, *25*, 168–85.

Pojman, L. P. (1990). *Ethics: Discovering right and wrong*. Belmont: Wadsworth Publishing.

Prinz, J. (2011). Against empathy. *Southern Journal of Philosophy*, *49*, 214–33.

Purser, R. (2015). Clearing the muddled path of traditional and contemporary mindfulness: A response to Monteiro, Musten, and Compson. *Mindfulness*, *6*, 23–45.

Purser, R. E. (2018). Critical perspectives on corporate mindfulness. *Journal of Management, Spirituality & Religion*, *15*(2), 105–8.

Purser, R. E., Forbes, D. & Burke, A. (2016). In R. E. Purser, D. Forbes & A. Burke (Eds.), *Handbook of mindfulness: Culture, context, and social engagement* (pp. v–xxv). Cham: Springer.

Purser, R. E., & Loy, D. (2013, July 1). Beyond McMindfulness. *Huffington Post*. Retrieved from https://www.huffpost.com/entry/beyond-mcmindfulness_b_3519289.

Purser, R. E., & Milillo, J. (2014). Mindfulness revisited: A Buddhist-based conceptualization. *Journal of Management Inquiry, 24*, 3–24.

Rant, M. B., & Mihelič, K. K. (2021). Being present is a present: Mindfulness as a strategy to manage interactions in work and non-work life. In S. K. Dhiman (Ed.), *The Routledge companion to mindfulness at work* (pp. 234–50). Oxon: Routledge.

Rechtschaffen, D. J. (2014). *The way of mindful education: Cultivating well-being in teachers and students*. New York: W. W. Norton.

Reina, C. S. (2021). A multidimensional conceptualization of mindfulness at work: Development and initial validation of the work mindfulness scale. In S. K. Dhiman (Ed.), *The Routledge companion to mindfulness at work* (pp. 54–80). Oxon: Routledge.

Repetti, R. (2016). Meditation matters: Replies to the anti-McMindfulness bandwagon! In R. E. Purser, D. Forbes & A. Burke (Eds.), *Handbook of mindfulness: Culture, context, and social engagement* (pp. 473–93). Cham: Springer.

Ritchie-Dunham, J. L. (2014). Mindful leadership. In A. Ie., C. T. Ngnoumen & E. J. Langer (Eds.), *The Wiley Blackwell handbook of mindfulness* (pp. 443–57). West Sussex: John Wiley.

Roberts, J. A., & David, M. E. (2017). Put down your phone and listen to me: How boss phubbing undermines the psychological conditions necessary for employee engagement. *Computers in Human Behaviour, 75*, 206–17.

Rodgers, C. R., & Raider-Roth, M. B. (2006). Presence in teaching. *Teachers and Teaching: Theory and Practice, 12*(3), 265–87.

Rowland, D. (2017). *Still moving: How to lead mindful change*. Chichester: John Wiley.

Salleh, H., & Tan, C. (2013). Novice teachers learning from others: Mentoring in Shanghai schools. *Australian Journal of Teacher Education, 38*(3), 152–65.

Salovey, P., & Mayer, J. D. (1990). Emotional intelligence. *Imagination, Cognition and Personality, 9*(3), 185–211.

Samuel, G. (2016). Mindfulness within the full range of Buddhist and Asian meditative practices. In R. E. Purser, D. Forbes & A. Burke (Eds.), *Handbook of mindfulness: Culture, context, and social engagement* (pp. 47–62). Cham: Springer.

Santucho, F. B., & Arce-Trigatti, A. (2021). Using mindfulness to teach Spanish grammar in rural Argentina. *Kappa Delta Pi Record, 57*(1), 23–9. doi:10.1080/00228 958.2021.1851583.

Schertz, M. (2007). Avoiding 'passive empathy' with Philosophy for Children. *Journal of Moral Education, 36*(2), 185–98.

Segal, E. A. (2011). Social empathy: A model built on empathy, contextual understanding, and social responsibility that promotes social justice. *Journal of Social Service Research*, *37*(3), 266–77.

Seigle, P., Wood, C. & Sankowski, L. (2019). Turn and listen: Strengthening compassion and leadership in the adult community in schools. In P. A. Jennings, A. A. DeMauro & P. P. Mischenko (Eds.), *The mindful school: Transforming school culture through mindfulness and compassion* (pp. 59–77). New York: Guilford Press.

Semple, R. J., Droutman, V. & Reid, B. A. (2017). Mindfulness goes to school: Things learned (so far) from research and real-world experiences. *Journal in Psychology in The Schools*, *54*(1), 29–52.

Senge, P., Cambron-McCabe, N., Lucas, T., Smith, B. & Dutton, J. (2012). *Schools that learn: A fifth discipline fieldbook for educators, parents, and everyone who cares about education*. New York: Crown Business.

Sethi, D. (2009). Mindful leadership. *Leader to Leader*, *51*, 7–11.

Shapiro, S., Rechtschaffen, D. & de Sousa, S. (2016). Mindfulness training for teachers. In K. Schonert-Reichl & R. Roeser (Eds.), *Handbook of mindfulness in education: Integrating theory and research into practice* (pp. 83–98). New York: Springer.

Shi, S. Z. (2010). 非常师生：孔子和他的弟子们 [*Feichang shisheng: Kongzi he tade dizimen, Extraordinary teacher and students: Confucius and his disciples.*]. Beijing: Shangwu yinshuguan.

Shun, K. L. (1993). Jen and li in the "Analects". *Philosophy East and West*, *43*(3), 457–79.

Silverthorne, S. (2010). Mindful leadership: When east meets west. *HBS Working Knowledge*. Retrieved from https://hbswk.hbs.edu/item/mindful-leaders hip-when-east-meets-west.

Slingerland, E. (2001). Virtue ethics, the "Analects," and the problem of commensurability. *Journal of Religious Ethics*, *29*(1), 97–125.

Slingerland, E. (trans.) (2003). *Confucius Analects: With selections from traditional commentaries*. Indianapolis: Hackett Publishing.

Smeyers, P., & Marshall, J. D. (1995). Epilogue. In P. Smeyers & J. D. Marshall (Eds.), *Philosophy and education: Accepting Wittgenstein's challenge* (pp. 221–4). Dordrecht: Kluwer Academic.

Soloway, G. B. (2016). Preparing teacher candidates for the present: Investigating the value of mindfulness-training in teacher education. In K. A. Schonert-Reichl & R. W. Roeser (Eds.), *Handbook of mindfulness in education: Integrating theory and research into practice* (pp. 191–205). New York: Springer. doi:10.1007/978-1-4939-3506-2.

Songhorian, S. (2019). The contribution of empathy to ethics. *International Journal of Philosophical Studies*, *27*(2), 244–64.

Spillane J. P. (2006). *Distributed leadership*. San Francisco: Jossey Bass.

Stanley, S., & Longden, C. (2016). Constructing the mindful subject: Reformulating experience through affective-discursive practice in mindfulness-based stress reduction. In R. E. Purser, D. Forbes & A. Burke (Eds.), *Handbook of mindfulness: Culture, context, and social engagement* (pp. 305–22). Cham: Springer.

Stanley, S., Purser, R. E. & Singh, N. N. (2018). Ethical foundations of mindfulness. In S. Stanley, R. E. Purser & N. N. Singh (Eds.), *Handbook of ethical foundations of mindfulness* (pp. 1–29). Cham: Springer.

Stingl, A. I., & Weiss, S. M. (2014). Mindfulness as/is care: Biopolitics, narrative empathy, and technoscientific practices. In In A. Ie., C. T. Ngnoumen & E. J. Langer (Eds.), *The Wiley Blackwell handbook of mindfulness* (pp. 608–29). West Sussex: John Wiley.

Stone-Johnson, C., & Weiner, J. M. (2020). Principal professionalism in the time of COVID-19. *Journal of Professional Capital and Community*, 5(3/4), 367–74.

Sullivan, M., & Arat, A. (2018). Postsecular charisma: Thich Nhat Hanh and the ethics of mindfulness. In S. Stanley, R. E. Purser & N. N. Singh (Eds.), *Handbook of ethical foundations of mindfulness* (pp. 339–54). Cham: Springer.

Sutcliffe, K. M., & Vogus, T. J. (2014). Organizing for mindfulness. In A. Ie., C. T. Ngnoumen & E. J. Langer (Eds.), *The Wiley Blackwell handbook of mindfulness* (pp. 407–23). West Sussex: John Wiley.

Tabancalı, E., & Öngel, G. (2020). Examining the relationship between school mindfulness and organizational trust. *International Education Studies*, 13(6), 14–25.

Tan, C. (2013). *Confucius*. London: Bloomsbury.

Tan, C. (2015a). Beyond rote-memorization: Confucius' concept of thinking. *Educational Philosophy and Theory*, 47(5), 428–39.

Tan, C. (2015b). Teacher-directed and learner-engaged: Exploring a Confucian conception of education. *Ethics and Education*, 10(3), 302–12.

Tan, C. (2016a). Beyond 'either-or' thinking: John Dewey and Confucius on the subject matter and the learner. *Pedagogy, Culture and Society*, 24(1), 55–74.

Tan, C. (2016b). Confucius and creativity. *Journal of Genius and Eminence*, 1(1), 84–9.

Tan, C. (2016c). Understanding creativity in East Asia: Insights from Confucius' concept of junzi. *International Journal of Design Creativity and Innovation*, 4(1), 51–61.

Tan, C. (2017a). A Confucian conception of critical thinking. *Journal of Philosophy of Education*, 51(1), 331–43.

Tan, C. (2017b). A Confucian perspective of self-cultivation in learning: Its implications for self-directed learning. *Journal of Adult & Continuing Education*, 23(2), 250–62.

Tan, C. (2018a). Mencius' extension of moral feelings: Implications for cosmopolitan education. *Ethics and Education*, 14(1), 70–83.

Tan, C. (2018b). To be more fully human: Freire and Confucius. *Oxford Review of Education*, 44(3), 370–82.

Tan, C. (2018c). Whither teacher-directed learning? Freirean and Confucian insights. *Educational Forum*, 82(4), 461–74.

Tan, C. (2019a). Challenging gendered social norms: Educational insights from Confucian classics. *Asian Philosophy*, 29(3), 264–76.

Tan, C. (2019b). Rethinking the concept of mindfulness: A neo-Confucian approach. *Journal of Philosophy of Education, 53*(2), 359–73.

Tan, C. (2020a). Beyond high-stakes exam: A neo-Confucian educational programme and its contemporary implications. *Educational Philosophy and Theory, 52*(2), 137–48.

Tan, C. (2020b). A Confucian interpretation of creativity. *Journal of Creative Behaviour, 54*(3), 636–45.

Tan, C. (2020c). A Confucian interpretation of women's empowerment. *Journal of Gender Studies, 30*(8), 927–37. doi:10.1080/09589236.2020.1852917.

Tan, C. (2020d). *Confucian philosophy for contemporary education*. London: Routledge.

Tan, C. (2020e). Digital Confucius? Exploring the implications of artificial intelligence in spiritual education. *Connection Science, 3*(23), 280–91.

Tan, C. (2020f). An ethical foundation for global citizenship education: A neo-Confucian perspective. *Journal of Beliefs & Values, 41*(4), 446–57.

Tan, C. (2021a). Confucius and Langerian mindfulness. *Educational Philosophy and Theory, 53*(9), 931–40. doi:10.1080/00131857.2020.1814740.

Tan, C. (2021b). Mindfulness and morality: Educational insights from Confucius. *Journal of Moral Education, 50*(3), 356–67. doi:10.1080/03057240.2020.1779045.

Tan, C. (2021c). *Mindful education: Insights from Confucian and Christian traditions*. Singapore: Springer.

Tan, C. (2022). Empathy for post-pandemic education. In Y. Baiza (Ed.), *Education in Troubled Times: A Global Pluralist Response* (pp. 110–26). Cambridge: Cambridge Scholars Publishing.

Tan, R. Y., & Molinari, C. (2017). Being mindful may not make you a team player: Does meditation help or hurt online group work? *Journal of Educators Online, 14*(2). doi:10.9743/jeo.2017.14.2.4.

Tan, C., & Ibrahim, A. (2017). Humanism, Islamic education and Confucian education. *Religious Education, 112*(4), 394–406.

Tan, C., & Tan, L. (2016). A shared vision of human excellence: Confucian spirituality and arts education. *Pastoral Care in Education, 34*(3), 156–66.

Taylor, C., Jennings, P. A., Harris, A., Schussler, D. L. & Roeser, R. W. (2019). Embodied teacher mindfulness in the classroom. In P. A. Jennings, A. A. DeMauro & P. P. Mischenko (Eds.), *The mindful school: Transforming school culture through mindfulness and compassion* (pp. 107–34). New York: Guilford Press.

Thich, N. H. (2011). *True love: A practice for awakening the heart*. Boston: Shambhala Publications.

Titmuss, C. (2016). Is there a corporate takeover of the mindfulness industry? An exploration of Western mindfulness in the public and private sector. In R. E. Purser, D. Forbes & A. Burke (Eds.), *Handbook of mindfulness: Culture, context, and social engagement* (pp. 181–94). Cham: Springer.

Todd, S. (2003). *Learning from the other: Levinas, psychoanalysis and ethical possibilities in education*. Albany: State University of New York Press.

Todd, S. (2004). Teaching with ignorance: Questions of social justice, empathy, and responsible community. *Interchange, 35*, 337–52.

Tomassini, M. (2016). Mindfulness in the working life: Beyond the 'corporate' view, in search for new spaces of awareness and equanimity. In R. E. Purser, D. Forbes & A. Burke (Eds.), *Handbook of mindfulness: Culture, context, and social engagement* (pp. 215–30). Cham: Springer.

Tong, R. (1997). Feminist perspectives on empathy as an epistemic skill and caring as a moral virtue. *Journal of Medical Humanities, 18*(3), 153–68.

Trube, B. (2017). Mindfulness practices in mentoring and teaching. *Childhood Education, 93*(2), 159–67. doi:10.1080/00094056.2017.1300495.

Tsang, K. K. Y., Shum, K. K., Chan, W. W. L., Li, S. X., Kwan, H. W., Su, M. R., ... Lam, S. (2021). Effectiveness and mechanisms of mindfulness training for school teachers in difficult times: A randomized controlled trial. *Mindfulness, 12*(11), 2820–31. doi:10.1007/s12671-021-01750-1.

Tschannen-Moran, M. (2014). *Trust matters: Leadership for successful schools*. San Francisco: Jossey-Bass.

Tu, W. M. (1968). The creative tension between jên and li. *Philosophy East and West, 18*(1/2), 29–39.

Tu, W. M. (1985). *Confucian thought: Selfhood as creative transformation*. Albany: State University of New York Press.

Van Dam, N. T., van Vugt, M. K., Vago, D. R., Schmalzl, L., Saron, C. D., Oledzki, A., ... Meyer, D. E. (2018). Mind the hype: A critical evaluation and prescriptive agenda for research on mindfulness and meditation. *Perspectives on Psychological Science, 13*(1), 36–61.

Walker, A. R. (2020). 'God is my doctor': Mindfulness meditation/prayer as a spiritual well-being coping strategy for Jamaican school principals to manage their work-related stress and anxiety. *Journal of Educational Administration, 58*(4), 467–80. doi:10.1108/JEA-06-2019-0097.

Wallis, G. (2016). Criticism matters: A response to Rick Repetti. In R. E. Purser, D. Forbes & A. Burke (Eds.), *Handbook of mindfulness: Culture, context, and social engagement* (pp. 495–504). Cham: Springer.

Walsh, Z. (2016). A meta-critique of mindfulness critiques: From McMindfulness to critical mindfulness. In R. E. Purser, D. Forbes & A. Burke (Eds.), *Handbook of mindfulness: Culture, context, and social engagement* (pp. 153–66). Cham: Springer.

Washburn-Moses, L. (2010). Rethinking mentoring: Comparing policy and practice in special and general education. *Education Policy Analysis Archives, 18*(32), 1–21.

Watts, L. S. (2016). Toward mindful assessment in higher education: A case study in contemplative commentary on student work to promote creative learning. In L. S. Watts & P. Blessinger (Eds.), *Creative learning in higher education: International perspectives and approaches* (pp. 98–122). New York: Routledge.

Weare, K. (2014). Evidence for mindfulness: Impacts on the wellbeing and performance of school staff. Retrieved from Mindfulness iIn Schools Project website: https://

mindfulnessinschools.org/wp-content/uploads/2014/10/Evidence-for-Mindfulness-Impact-on-school-staff.pdf.

Weick, K. E., & Roberts, K. H. (1993). Collective mind in organizations: Heedful interrelating on flight decks. *Administrative Science Quarterly, 38*, 357–81.

Weick K. E., & Sutcliffe, K. M. (2006). Mindfulness and the quality of organizational attention. *Organization Science, 17*, 514–24.

Weick K. E., & Sutcliffe, K. M. (2008). Information overload revisited. In G. P. Hodgkinson & W. H. Starbuck (Eds.), *The Oxford handbook of organizational decision making* (pp. 56–75). New York: Oxford University Press.

Weintraub, J., & Dust, S. B. (2021). Workplace mindfulness theory and research in review: A call for temporal investigations. In S. K. Dhiman (Ed.), *The Routledge companion to mindfulness at work* (pp. 24–38). Oxon: Routledge.

Wells, C. M. (2015). Conceptualizing mindful leadership in schools: How the practice of mindfulness informs the practice of leading. *Education Leadership Review of Doctoral Research, 2*(1), 1–23.

Wilkin, M. (1992). *Mentoring in schools.* London: Kogan Page.

Williams, M., & Penman, D. (2011). *Mindfulness: An eight-week plan for finding peace in a frantic world.* New York: Rodale.

Wilson, S. A. (1995). Conformity, individuality, and the nature of virtue: A classical Confucian contribution to contemporary ethical reflection. *Journal of Religious Ethics, 23*(2), 263–89.

Wongkom, S., Sanrattana, W. & Chusorn, P. (2019). The structural relationship model of indicator of mindful leadership for primary school principals. *International Journal of Higher Education, 8*(5), 135–42.

Yadav, M. K. (2021). Workplace mindfulness: individual-, group-, and orgnizational-level antecedents and consequences. In S. K. Dhiman (Ed.), *The Routledge companion to mindfulness at work* (pp. 81–107). Oxon: Routledge.

Yu, J. (1998). Virtue: Confucius and Aristotle. *Philosophy East and West, 48*(2), 323–47.

Yukl, G. (2006). *Leadership in organizations.* (6th ed.). Cranbury: Pearson Education.

Zhang, Y. M., & Tan, C. (2021). Transformational school leadership from a neo-Daoist Lens. *Philosophical Inquiry in Education, 28*(1), 26–42.

Zimmerman, S. J. O., & Musilli, S. (2016, April). *Heightening cultural awareness through reflective contemplative practices.* Paper presented at the annual meeting of the American Educational Research Association, Washington, DC.

Index

acts of doing 11
altruism 63, 150
Analects xvii, 33, 35–7, 40, 42, 47, 49, 53, 57–8, 65–7, 69, 71–2, 79, 81–3, 86–7, 89, 92, 97–9, 105–6, 108, 114, 123, 130–1, 135, 158, 163 n.22, 178 n.3, 178 n.7, 178 n.8, 180 n.24, 178 n.25, 182 n.38, 185 n.11, 185 n.12, 191 n.6, 201 n.23, 202 n.25, 209 n.15
analogy 44, 103, 108, 131, 184 n.50, 201 n.20
appropriateness 130, 135, 138, 148, 165 n.9, 207 n.11, 208 n.12
aristocrat 39–40, 48, 81, 113, 179 n.16, 179 n.17, 179 n.18, 183 n.41, 181 n.4, 198 n.1
autonomy xv, 28, 138, 145
auto-pilot xi, 4, 10, 65, 83, 130

barbarian 134
benevolence 20, 29, 40–1, 50, 63, 100, 140, 150, 187 n.18, 187 n.22, 195 n.28, 214 n.13
Bill George 11, 168 n.28, 171 n.52, 172 n.54
Book of History 37, 67, 180 n.25
Book of Odes 42, 111, 180 n.25
Book of Songs 37, 42, 198 n.1
breathing 6, 8, 18–20, 22, 25, 46, 59, 64, 72, 121, 153, 156, 189 n.31,
Buddhadharma 165 n.9, 182 n.35
Buddhism xvi, 3, 7, 17, 43, 46, 71–2, 158, 162 n.16, 165 n.9, 166 n.14, 181 n.35, 184 n.49

capitalism 28, 176 n.89
Catholicism 31. *See also* St Ignatius Loyola
China x, 34–7, 39–40, 45, 54–5, 59–61, 106, 113, 162 n.14, 177 n.1, 179 n.19, 180 n.25, 189 n.32, 200 n.15, 200 n.19, 215 n.23
Christianity 8, 17, 26, 194 n.23
classics 40, 42, 67, 87, 92, 94, 163 n.22, 172 n.53, 180 n.25, 181 n.34, 215 n.20
coaching 84, 94, 97, 106, 112–13, 115–17, 119–20, 122, 148, 201 n.22, 203 n.29. *See also* mentoring
community
    building 97, 106, 110, 112, 122, 148
    moral 110, 184 n.47
counsellor 68, 87, 133, 191 n.10, 192 n.12, 201 n.19, 202 n.24
customized teaching 39, 116

Daoism xvi, 3, 216 n.24
democracy 138, 184 n.49
dialogue 36, 38, 99, 113, 122, 146, 158, 165 n.13, 205 n.37, 212 n.34
doing one's best 104, 149
dualism
    Cartesian 70
    mind-body 48
Duke Ding 127
Duke Huan 134
Duke Ling 134
Duke of Zhou 81, 192 n.12
dynasty 35, 45, 81, 124, 136, 139, 162 n.12, 180 n.25, 192 n.12

East xvi, 7–8, 22, 43, 45–6, 50, 140–1, 151, 154, 158, 167 n.22, 168 n.32, 169 n.32, 169 n.33, 188 n.29, 216 n.24
Ellen Langer 4–5, 8, 11, 16, 43, 166 n.18, 166 n.19, 167 n.20, 167 n.21, 168 n.32, 169 n.32, 171 n.50, 172 n.60, 174 n.74, 183 n.40
emotional intelligence 11–12, 77, 96, 150, 171 n.49, 172 n.57, 172 n.60, 189 n.34
empathy
    affective xx
    cognitive 177 n.97
    concern 30, 103, 105, 118, 122, 150, 156, 177 n.99, 199 n.10

Confucian 120
interpersonal 122
moral 206 n.57
pedagogy 205 n.46
perspective-taking 29
social 122
ethical cultivation
 developmental model 94, 196 n.31
 discovery model, 196 n.31
eudamonia 31
excellence 51, 81, 88, 123–4, 126, 138–9, 147, 149, 155–8, 176 n.93, 183 n.44, 184 n.47, 206 n.2, 212 n.1

female 40, 81, 179 n.17. *See also* gender-neutrality
Former King 106
Foucault 3, 8
frame of heart-mind 48, 56–8, 60, 65, 68, 70, 74, 94, 101–2, 122

gender-neutrality 82, 180 n.24, 186 n.13, 186 n.17, 181 n.6
gong See reverence
Google xiv, 11, 161 n.9
Guanzhong 134, 209 n.18

harmonization 59, 108
harmony 84, 93, 106–7, 109, 120, 122, 131, 135, 148, 176 n.88, 200 n.16, 200 n.17, 200 n.18, 201 n.20, 214 n.7. *See also* harmonization
he See harmony
heart-mind 48–9, 55–58, 60–1, 65, 68, 70, 74, 94, 101–2, 110, 122, 124, 131, 148, 182 n.38, 182 n.39, 183 n.40, 187 n.19, 206 n.4
heaven 36–7, 54, 71–2, 123–4, 129, 178 n.9, 182 n.36, 189 n.30, 214 n.7
Hinduism 3, 216 n.24
human nature 93, 195 n.30
humanity 97–101, 104–7, 111, 113, 118–20, 122, 131–2, 135, 139, 148–51, 154, 156, 158, 187 n.22, 209 n.15, 209 n.18, 214 n.8

individualism 119, 138, 184 n.49

Ji Kangzi 84

Jon Kabat-Zinn 4–5, 8, 43, 165 n.9, 165 n.10, 166 n.16, 166 n.17, 167 n.22, 193 n.22

karma xiii, 71
King Wen 111, 126
King Wu 81, 126

leadership
 authentic 11, 155, 171 n.52
 caritas-focused 30–1, 77
 metta-based 93–4, 195 n.28
 resonant 11, 171 n.49, 171 n.51
 transformation 177 n.95
li See normative behaviours
Lunyu See Analects

mass education 50, 113
McMindfulness xv, 27–8, 49, 92–3, 96, 146, 148, 157, 162 n.10, 193 n.21, 194 n.22
mentoring: 25, 112–13, 116, 119–20, 148, 201 n.22,
mindful organizing xiv, 12–14, 30, 73, 146, 148, 173 n.67
Mindfulness in Schools Project 1, 8
mindfulness
 classroom 151–2
 collective 5, 9, 12–15, 30, 46, 119, 146, 148, 173 n.63
 movement 71, 92–3, 118, 162 n.11, 162 n.16, 175 n.84, 181 n.35, 189 n.31
 organizational xiv, 12–14, 30, 146
 as practice xv, 6, 16–21, 23–7, 49, 68–73, 92, 153–4, 168 n.30, 174 n.74, 175 n.86, 193 n.22, 194 n.22, 196 n.32
 state 6, 46–7, 60, 101, 168 n.28, 168 n.30
 trait 5–6, 12, 47–8, 73, 101, 167 n.26, 168 n.30
Mindfulness-Based Cognitive Therapy 8–9
Mindfulness-Based Stress Reduction 4, 8–9, 19, 164 n.6, 204 n.30, 216 n.24
mindlessness xvii, 4, 33, 41–3, 50, 55, 135, 167 n.20, 180 n.23, 181 n.31
Montessori 8
multi-tasking x, 1
music 37, 40, 42, 81, 107–8, 121, 132, 136, 181 n.34, 190 n.38, 200 n.14, 200 n.18
musician 104–5, 108, 118

nature of mind
  awakening view 9, 93–4
  enlightenment view 9, 93–4
neoliberalism 28, 92, 119, 162 n.10, 175 n.86, 176 n.88, 193 n.21, 210 n.24
non judgement 1, 6, 10, 12, 13, 16, 71, 136, 151, 154, 166 n.16, 166 n.17, 176 n.91, 181 n.35, 188 n.29, 193 n.22, 213 n.3
normative behaviours 40, 63–4, 68, 76, 81, 83, 87, 102–3, 110, 115, 128, 135, 139, 148, 151, 154, 199 n.12, 209 n.18

Organization for Economic Co-operation and Development 119

pandemic x, 1, 10, 22, 26, 122, 143
Plato 155–6

quiet sitting 7, 189 n.32

Ran Qiu 38
Ranyou 35, 91, 115, 118
rectification of names 131–3, 148,
religion 162 n.16, 181 n.35, 205 n.43
ren See humanity
reverence 54, 68, 101, 186 n.13, 186 n.17, 188 n.24
rite 34–5, 37, 40, 62–3, 179 n.15, 180 n.25, 186 n.15, 187 n.18, 187 n.21
ritual 31, 35, 40, 47, 55, 62–3, 67, 87, 173 n.62, 177 n.2, 179 n.15, 200 n.14,
role model 84–5, 91, 94, 96, 112, 122, 131, 133, 204 n.36, 214 n.9
rote-memorization 41, 112
ru See counsellor

sage-king 35, 38, 50, 62, 64, 81, 91, 106, 111, 124, 126, 133, 135–6, 178 n.9, 190 n.2
sati 3, 164 n.8, 188 n.29, 194 n.23
scholar (*shi*) 128
school principal xv, 23, 51, 93, 119, 121–2, 150
self-care 12, 22, 65, 213 n.5
self-cultivation 50, 56, 61, 70, 73, 76, 81–2, 84, 93–7, 140, 148, 184 n.45, 186 n.12, 202 n.26, 212 n.36
self-therapy 27–8, 76, 154
shi See scholar

shu See empathy
Shun 62, 82, 91
Sima Niu 116
Social Emotional Learning 95, 175 n.86
social justice 24, 133, 138, 141, 211 n.27, 211 n.29
Socrates 3, 8
spirituality 175 n.84, 178 n.88
Spring and Autumn period 35, 200 n.19, 203 n.28
St Ignatius Loyola 8
state of Lu 35, 81, 87, 108, 201, 202 n.25

T. W. Rhys Davids 3–4, 164 n.8, 166 n.17, 194 n.23
Teaching and Learning International Survey 119
Thich Nhat Hanh 165 n.10
thinking
  creative 117
  critical 127, 129–30, 137, 139–40, 187 n.19, 211 n.33, 212 n.33
  inferential 44, 117, 154
  independent 113, 117, 120
  systems 134, 148
tian See heaven

virtue ethics 48, 149, 183 n.42, 183 n.44, 184 n.44, 215 n.36
virtue
  executive 149–50, 214 n.11
  leading by 87–8, 90, 135, 155–6
  moral 29–32, 176 n.93, 176 n.94, 192 n.15, 214 n.13
  nonmoral 29, 176 n.93, 176 n.94, 214 n.13
  substantive 149–50, 214 n.11

ways of being 11, 172 n.53
wellbeing 27, 29, 71, 174 n.73
West 3, 7, 140–1, 154, 158, 162 n.16, 165 n.9, 166 n.14, 167 n.22, 169 n.32, 169 n.33, 169 n.34, 181 n.31, 182 n.39, 183 n.40, 188 n.25, 189 n.35, 215 n.23, 216 n.25
whole-heartedness 13, 45, 55–8, 61, 67, 70, 73–4, 76, 79, 86, 104, 121, 129, 147–8, 185 n.2

wisdom 89, 102, 129, 135, 143, 156, 180 n.25, 212 n.1, 216 n.24
women 40, 179 n.18, 179 n.19. *See also* female

xiaoren See petty person
xin See joy

Yan Hui 92, 111, 115, 187 n.18
Yao 82, 106
yi See appropriateness
yoga 7, 25

zhengming See rectification of names
zhong See doing one's best
Zhonggong 202 n.25
Zigong 102, 111, 158, 202 n.25
Zilu 39, 61–2, 72, 105, 111, 115–17, 178 n.9, 185 n.12, 186 n.12, 186 n.13, 202 n.25, 203 n.28
Zixia 91, 111, 203 n.27
Zizhang 100, 104, 113–14, 118, 202 nn.25, 26, 203 n.27

www.ingramcontent.com/pod-product-compliance
Lightning Source LLC
Chambersburg PA
CBHW062133300426
44115CB00012BA/1908